LPS2/90 £16.50
_.

The Enlightenment and Scottish Literature

Volume Two

The Rise of the Historical Novel

The Enlightenment and Scottish Literature

Volume Two

The Rise of the Historical Novel

JOHN MACQUEEN

1989

SCOTTISH ACADEMIC PRESS

EDINBURGH

Published by
Scottish Academic Press Ltd
33 Montgomery Street, Edinburgh EH7 5JX

First published 1989
SBN 0 7073 0500 4

© 1989 John MacQueen

British Library Cataloguing in Publication Data

MacQueen, John, *1929* –
  The enlightenment and Scottish literature.
  Vol. 2: The rise of the historical novel.
  I. Title. II. The rise of the historical novel
  820.9'9411

  ISBN 0-7073-0500-4

Typeset at Oxford University
Computing Service

Printed in Great Britain by
Macdonald Lindsay (Printers) Ltd., Edinburgh

CONTENTS

PREFACE

During the second and third decades of the nineteenth century the scope and power of the novel as a literary form was dramatically increased, primarily by the appearance of a number of works by Scottish authors. Walter Scott was the chief, but John Galt and James Hogg each made his own distinctive and distinguished contribution. The work of these men is remarkable in itself, but also made possible later achievement in the novel, as represented, for instance, by the works of Balzac, Tolstoy, Proust and Joyce. All three Scottish authors have frequently been associated with the English and European Romantic movement, but in fact their work represents the finest imaginative realisation of intellectual experience during the Scottish Enlightenment. This book thus completes the analysis begun in *Progress and Poetry*, published in 1982.

Versions of some parts have already appeared elsewhere, as "Scott and *Tales of My Landlord*" in *Scottish Studies* 15.2 (1971), pp.85-97; as "John Galt and the Analysis of Social History" in Alan Bell (ed), *Scott Bicentenary Essays* (Edinburgh and London, 1973), pp.332-42, and as "*Ringan Gilhaize* and Particular Providence" in Christopher A. Whatley (ed), *John Galt 1779-1979* (Edinburgh, 1979), pp.107-19. Parts have been delivered in lecture form in Eastern Michigan University, Ypsilanti, Guelph University, Ontario, and to the Postgraduate Seminar in the Department of English Literature, University of Edinburgh. I am grateful to the editors and publishers of the books and journal, and to the audience at the lectures for their comments and criticisms. I should also like to thank my wife for the many and varied ways in which she has aided me in the writing of this book. The late Mrs Anna Belfourd somehow produced typescript for the earlier stages, despite the chaotic condition of the manuscript which I gave her. I owe a general debt to my Edinburgh colleagues, who have helped me, sometimes in ways which they themselves can scarcely have recognised.

CHAPTER I

PROLEGOMENON

The achievement of eighteenth century Scottish poetry was considerable, and its influence extended well beyond the British Isles. Its great days, however, were over before the beginning of the nineteenth century, and in some ways the chief literary triumphs of the Enlightenment belong not to poetry but to the novel. The form had been in existence for more than a century when Walter Scott published *Waverley* (1814), but the originality of his treatment, and the consequent enlargement of the intellectual and imaginative bounds open to fiction, make him essentially the creator of a new genre.

This is not to lessen what had already been done — the accomplishment of *Clarissa*, for example, or *Tom Jones* requires no defence from anyone. The achievement of Scott, shared to a degree by his contemporaries, John Galt (1779-1839) and James Hogg (1770-1835), and to a much lesser extent by his predecessors, Henry Mackenzie (1745-1831) and John Moore (1729-1802), was to introduce into the fabric of their works the quality which, regardless of period, makes a particular stretch of time unique to itself; secondly, in terms of that quality, and without diminishing the individuality of separate characters, to dramatize what each author saw as the features common to human nature at all times; and thirdly, in doing so, to take into account the necessary failures, the imperfections of human knowledge and its transmission. All these were factors the importance of which had been established for Scott and his contemporaries by their predecessors in the Scottish Enlightenment, and which have already been discussed in *Progress and Poetry*.

In such terms, moreover, the Scots are to be contrasted with earlier English novelists, particularly with Henry Fielding (1707-1754), whose work characteristically is presented through the agency of the omniscient narrator, unlimited by the handicaps

1

peculiar to human knowledge of events, and who, as an author, is often in himself genuinely indifferent to matters of time, period, and precise place. Interactions and relationships are his main concern. "In that part of the western division of this kingdom which is commonly called Somersetshire, there lately lived (and perhaps still lives) a gentleman whose name was Allworthy." This opening sentence of the main narrative in *Tom Jones* (1749) stands in remarkable contrast to the opening of almost any Scottish novel written in the period under consideration, and serves to show something of the difference between the two cultures. Contrast, for instance, the first words of *The Antiquary* (1816): "It was early on a fine summer's day, near the end of the eighteenth century, when a young man, of genteel appearance, journeying towards the north-east of Scotland, provided himself with a ticket in one of those public carriages which travel between Edinburgh and the Queensferry, at which place, as the name implies, and as is well-known to all my northern readers, there is a passage-boat for crossing the Firth of Forth."

The ultimate object of both authors is human nature. Fielding however puts it in a setting virtually independent of time and precise locality, yet known to the narrator in every detail. Scott sets it among the mental and physical characteristics of an exact period and locality, and often (though not, as it happens, in *The Antiquary*) indicates how his narrator obtained such information as he has.

In *Tom Jones*, at least, Fielding laid himself open to a straightforward comparison with Scott. He directly introduced the '45 into the middle portion — Books VII-XII. The events which follow Jones's expulsion from Allworthy's house at the end of Book VI are carefully synchronized with the Jacobite invasion of England in which Scott makes Edward Waverley take a part.

The first direct indication of this occurs in VIII.XI., where Jones falls in with a party of soldiers at a village inn:—

> The serjeant had informed Mr Jones, that they were marching against the rebels, and expected to be commanded by the glorious Duke of Cumberland. By which the reader may perceive (a circumstance which we have not thought necessary to communicate before)

that this was the very time when the late rebellion was
at the highest; and indeed the banditti were now
marching into England, intending, as it was thought, to
fight the king's forces, and to attempt pushing forward
to the metropolis.

The initial effect on the reader may (and Fielding seems half to
expect that it will) be surprise that in a meticulously plotted
work no indication has hitherto been given that the date of
events possesses any special significance. This impression, however, is not entirely accurate. Fielding has already made it clear,
for instance, that Squire Western, with his toasts to kings who
are not named, and dislike of his sister's Hanoverian ways, is
some kind of Jacobite. Had he known the word, Western would
have described himself as a legitimist. In VI.IV. Mrs Western is
discovered "expounding the Gazette to Parson Supple", and was
never in a better humour because "Things look so well in the
North" — in Scotland, that is to say, before the Jacobite forces
had gained the upper hand. In VI.XIV., however, Western
declares, "Pox! the world is come to a fine pass indeed, if we are
all fools, except a parcel of roundheads and Hanover rats. Pox! I
hope the times are a coming that we shall make fools of them,
and every man shall enjoy his own. That's all, sister, and every
man shall enjoy his own. I hope to zee it, sister, before the
Hanover rats have eat up all our corn, and left us nothing but
turnips to feed upon." The reference to the Old Pretender ("The
king shall have his own again") and to the initial success of the
rising, is unmistakable, and indeed is well understood by Mrs
Western, though she effects not to know what her brother
means. At this point, it is clear that Prince Charles has established
himself in Scotland, and that Western expects a successful
invasion of England to follow.

The manner in which Fielding hints at the '45 in the course of
Book VI, does not, in other words, lack art. Books VII–XII bring
it closer to the forefront of the reader's attention. Partridge, for
instance, is portrayed throughout as a superstitious Jacobite, and
his first impression (VIII.IX.) is that Jones is on his way to join
the invaders. In XI.II. Sophia and Mrs Fitzpatrick are taken for
"some of the rebel ladies, who, they say, travel with the young
Chevalier; and have taken a roundabout way to escape the

duke's army". Sophia herself is mistaken for Madam Jenny Cameron, the supposed mistress of Prince Charles.

The countryside round the inn where the misidentification takes place only partly conceals its sympathy for the legitimist cause; it is this indeed which leads the landlord to his mistake:—

> When our politic landlord, who had not, we see, undeservedly the reputation of great wisdom among his neighbours, was engaged in debating this matter with himself (for he paid little attention to the opinion of his wife), news arrived that the rebels had given the duke the slip, and had got a day's march towards London; and soon after arrived a famous Jacobite squire, who, with great joy in his countenance, shook the landlord by the hand, saying, "All's our own, boy, ten thousand honest Frenchmen are landed in Suffolk. Old England for ever! ten thousand French, my brave lad! I am going to tap away directly."
>
> The news determined the opinion of the wise man, and he resolved to make his court to the young lady, when she arose; for he had now (he said) discovered that she was no other than Madam Jenny Cameron herself.

Fielding's irony shows his own party-stance, but also reveals his feeling for the general political importance of the situation. (He was himself a notable opponent of the Jacobites, as is shown by the articles which from 1745 to 1748, the period during which he was working on *Tom Jones*, he contributed to *The True Patriot* and *The Jacobite's Journal.*[1]) In addition, it may be suggested that he wrote the episode (VIII.X–XV) of the Man on the Hill, often rightly criticized as an artistic excrescence, to show something of the historical case for the Hanoverian succession, a background which would, he assumed, show the overwhelming balance in favour of the new regime. (Much of his argument, incidentally derives ultimately from George Buchanan's *De Jure Regni apud Scottos*, mentioned in volume 1.[2]) The improbably ancient Man on the Hill, born in 1657, and so in 1745 88 years old, had in 1685 taken part in Monmouth's rebellion against James VII and II, which is regarded by Fielding as a tragically unsuccessful prologue to the Glorious Revolution of 1688. The Man on the Hill is astonished (VIII.XIV.) to discover the Jacobites as a species still exist:—

"What you say," interrupted Jones, "is very true; and it has often struck me, as the most wonderful thing I ever read of in history, that so soon after this convincing experience which brought our whole nation to join so unanimously in expelling King James, for the preservation of our religion and liberties, there should be a party among us mad enough to desire the placing his family again on the throne." — "You are not in earnest!" answered the old man; "there can be no such party. As bad an opinion as I have of mankind, I cannot believe them infatuated to such a degree. There may be some hot-headed papists led by their priests to engage in this desperate cause, and think it a holy war; but that Protestants, that are members of the Church of England, should be such apostates, such *felos de se*, I cannot believe it; no, no, young man, unacquainted as I am with what has past in the world for these last thirty years, I cannot be so imposed upon as to credit so foolish a tale; but I see you have a mind to sport with my ignorance." "Can it be possible," replied Jones, "that you have lived so much out of the world as not to know that during that time there have been two rebellions in favour of the son of King James, one of which is now actually raging in the very heart of the kingdom?" At these words the old gentleman started up, and, in a most solemn tone of voice, conjured Jones by his Maker to tell him if what he said was really true; which the other as solemnly affirming, he walked several times about the room in a profound silence, then cried, then laughed, and at last fell down on his knees, and blessed God, in a loud thanksgiving prayer, for having delivered him from all society with human nature, which could be capable of such monstrous extravagances.

Fielding's treatment of the rising is biased, but, so far at least as Jacobites in southern England are concerned, not wholly lacking in sympathy. They are confined to the South-West and the West

Midlands, belong for the most part to the lower orders and the befuddled Tory squirearchy, and contribute a certain amount to the mock-heroic effect of the prose-epic, but in general they are treated with humorous tolerance. As against this, there is no attempt to portray, sympathetically or otherwise, anyone taking an active part in the rising — the Jacobite army, referred to simply as "the banditti", is as alien as if it had been composed of Sicilians or Calabrians — nor does either Tom or Sophie come into any kind of contact with active Jacobites. With the separate arrivals in London of the pair, the rebels disappear from the narrative; the last six books scarcely mention them, and there is no hint of the retreat from Derby or of Culloden. Fielding's peripheral interest, unlike Scott's, has no basis either in anthropology or the picturesque; for him they are a part merely of the comic machinery, to be discarded at will. Allowances must, of course, be made for him as an Englishman and as a politician, vitally involved with the events which he describes, but a comparison of *Tom Jones* with another account by a contemporary politician opposed to the Jacobites, that of Clerk of Penicuik,[3] will show the great difference of approach at this time between writers who had felt the initial effects of the Scottish Enlightenment and those who had not. The contrast between Walter Scott and Fielding approaches the absolute. If Tom Jones had met Edward Waverley in 1750, the two would have found little to discuss. Jones would have questioned the possibility of Waverley ever having had a historical existence, and Waverley have found Jones totally lacking in knowledge of history and anthropology.

The contrast is not one of Augustan and Romantic literary techniques; it involves the entire cast of mind of the two men. Fielding's imaginative range is limited to his own time, place and circumstance; he perceives brilliantly whatever happens within the charmed circle, but nothing outside it can affect him. As a portrait even of a southern Englishman in the seventeenth century, the Man on the Hill is a disaster of the historical imagination. The misdeeds of Blifil are suitably punished by exile to Yorkshire from London and the south; not even his proposed purchase of a seat in the next parliament can restore him to real existence. Jacobite rebels are mere bogies on the verge of things. The Man on the Hill expresses opinions on foreigners ("I had infinitely rather pass my life with the

Hottentots, than set my foot in Paris again. They are a nasty people, but their nastiness is mostly without; whereas in France, and some other nations that I won't name, it is all within, and makes them stink much more to my reason than that of Hottentots does to my nose." VIII.XV.) which on the general evidence of the novel seem to come close to those of his creator. The mind of Fielding is active and energetic, but by comparison with Scott's, or even Mackenzie's, it is unphilosophical, insensitive, provincial.

The particular concept of historical time developed in the Scottish Enlightenment entailed the idea of movement and change which was at least partially unpredictable, and of contrast between one era, or one population group, and another, even when the two were closely adjacent. The unpredictability implied the abolition of the omniscient narrator, while at the same time the element of contrast heightened rather than diminished the immediate sense of the present. The present, no less than the past, entered the novelist's work as a special creation of the movement of history.

The historical novel is thus uniquely the discovery of the Scottish Enlightenment during its latest phase, a point missed by Georg Lucacs in his influential study of the form.[4] Lucacs's account of Scott unfortunately combines occasional brilliant insights with a profound ignorance of Scottish literary and historical circumstances. He is nevertheless entirely accurate when he observes that "What is lacking in the so-called historical novel before Sir Walter Scott is precisely the specifically historical, that is, derivation of the individuality of characters from the historical peculiarity of their age". Nor does he confine his remarks to the "so-called historical novel", by which he means, for instance, the seventeenth-century romances of Mlle. de Scudery (1607-1701) and Gauthier de Costes de la Calprenede (1614-1663), together with eighteenth-century Gothic pieces like Horace Walpole's *Castle of Otranto* (1764); he includes "the great realistic social novel of the eighteenth century, which in its portrayal of contemporary morals and psychology accomplished a revolutionary breakthrough to reality for world literature", but which nevertheless was "not concerned to show its characters as belonging to any concrete era. The contemporary world is portrayed with unusual plasticity and truth-to-life, but is accepted naively as something given: whence and how it has developed have not yet become problems for the writer." Scott was the first to become fully aware of such problems.

ii

From a later point of view, it might seem inevitable that the historical novel should have become the main imaginative outlet for the experience of the Scottish Enlightenment, in particular where that experience drew directly upon seventeenth and eighteenth-century developments — an outlet which should, one might be tempted to think, have been discovered well before the beginning of the nineteenth century. Smollett, and in a different way Macpherson, had already established a prose fiction which from a distinctively Scottish point of view was capable of tackling a wide range of intellectual and emotional concerns. Burns had followed and surpassed Ramsay and Fergusson in the use of Scots to give significance to the life and ambitions of the poor man (and in a sense all Scots were poor) in the changing world of the improvers and economists. Hume, Robertson and Adam Smith had analyzed, and in their works exemplified, how important a part Scotland had played in political, social and economic history and theory. Scotland had remained what it always had been, the historical nation, but had developed new tools in philosophic and theoretical or conjectural history. Hume, Reid and Boswell, in their different ways, had advanced the study and literary treatment of group and individual psychology. The '45 had revealed that the Gaelic-speaking Highlands were still within striking distance of Edinburgh, and even London. Adam Ferguson, beginning from his experience of Highland and Lowland society, had discussed principles of development for human society as a whole. Yet *Waverley* was not published until 1814, well beyond the period to which the Enlightenment is usually confined.

Such lags are by no means infrequent in literary history. An instance has already been given in the first volume of the present study.[5] The first book of Newton's *Principia* was published in 1687, but it was not until the second decade of the following century that it effectively made its mark on imaginative literature. Such delays may result from the intrinsic difficulty of new ideas, or simply from the fact that ideas have not yet become fashionable. In particular, some other intellectual influence may have served as an effective hindrance to the introduction of concepts which now, with the advantage of hindsight, are seen to be more important.

This last appears to be the case with the development of the historical novel. From the point of view of the late twentieth century, the most intellectually influential figures in eighteenth-century Scotland were Hume, Smith, Reid and Ferguson, but to a contemporary it was by no means so obvious. In particular, the Irish presbyterian philosopher, Francis Hutcheson (1694-1746) professor of Moral Philosophy in the University of Glasgow from 1729 until his death, dominated intellectual life to a degree which it is now rather hard to comprehend. He found himself unable to accept the full rigidity of Calvinistic morality: even during his tenure of the Glasgow chair, he found himself in conflict with some members at least of his own presbytery.[6] He was a disciple of the third Earl of Shaftesbury (1671-1713), the "generous Ashley", commemorated by Thomson in a passage already[7] quoted:—

> the friend of man
> Who scanned his nature with a brother's eye,
> His weakness prompt to shade, to raise his aim,
> To touch the finer movements of the mind,
> And with the moral beauty charm the heart.
> ("Summer", 1551-1555)

Hutcheson's intellectual antecedents are indicated in the somewhat cumbrous full title of his first work (1725), *An Inquiry into the Original of our ideas of Beauty and Virtue, in two treatises in which the principles of the late Earl of Shaftesbury are explained and defended against the author of "The Fable of the Bees", and the "Ideas of Moral Good and Evil" are established according to the sentiments of the Antient Moralists, with an attempt to introduce a mathematical calculation on subjects of Morality*. The title refers to Shaftesbury by name; two very different philosophers receive less specific, but also less favourable, reference. One is Bernard de Mandeville (1670-1733), notorious author of *The Fable of the Bees, or Private Vices, Public Benefits* (1715); the other Samuel Clarke (1675-1729), regarded in his day as the first of English metaphysicians, whose Boyle lectures, delivered at Cambridge during 1704 and 1705, were eventually published together as *A Discourse concerning the Being and Attributes of God, the Obligations of Natural*

Religion, and the Truth and Certainty of the Christian Revelation, in answer to Mr Hobbes, Spinoza, the author of the "Oracles of Reason" and other deniers of Natural and Revealed Religion. The "Ideas of Moral Good and Evil" mentioned by Hutcheson in his title are those of Clarke, whose treatment of the moral law as proceeding from logical necessity (almost Kant's Categorical Imperative) offended many of his contemporaries.[8]

Hutcheson found it impossible to accept Clarke's rationalistic *a priori* arguments. His own system was founded chiefly on the idea of the benevolence characteristic of the Creator, and implanted in his creatures. He postulated a human moral sense, instinctively perceiving the virtue or vice inherent in an action or affection, and in its activity akin to the sense of beauty, which he also postulated. Standing somewhat apart from these was the public sense, or *sensus communis*, "a determination to be pleased with the happiness of others and to be uneasy at their misery". The instinctive moral faculty was to be distinguished however from the moral standard; the criterion of right action was its tendency to promote the general welfare of mankind. Hutcheson's famous phrase, "the greatest happiness of the greatest number" in turn gave rise to the otherwise unexpected "mathematical calculation on subjects of morality". Later in the century the concept was accepted as axiomatic by Jeremy Bentham (1748-1832) in the development of his Utilitarianism and philosophic radicalism.

Hutcheson's moral philosophy depends on two processes which differ almost to the degree of melodrama; on the one hand, the operation of the moral sense, which is instinctive; on the other, the intellectual calculation required to assess the relation between any single action and the general welfare. Obviously his position was in some ways non-intellectual; the disagreement with Clarke depends ultimately on the fact that one was primarily a rationalist, the other not. Hutcheson became influential, not least because he gave benevolence, a readily perceived off-shoot of the not-necessarily-rational human will, priority over abstract reason operating within a metaphysical system which involved absolute right and wrong. Clarke held, for instance, that it was as absurd to deny that I should do to my neighbour as he should do to me as to assert that, though two and three are equal to five, five is not equal to two and three. Hutcheson opposed such moral absolutism. Unfortunately, the step from his own system to sentimentality in moral matters was fatally easy, and was soon taken by others.

Hutcheson himself stood close to a central Enlightenment position. Long ago, A.N. Whitehead (1861-1947) pointed out[9] that the historical revolt which marked the beginnings of modern science was through and through an anti-intellectualist movement. "The world required centuries of contemplation of irreducible and stubborn facts. That was the sort of thing they had to do after the rationalistic orgy of the Middle Ages. It was a very sensible reaction; but it was not a protest on behalf of reason." This statement he later clarified and enlarged in a comment on the phrase "the unbridled rationalism of the thought of the later Middle Ages." "By this rationalism I mean the belief that the avenue to truth was predominantly through a metaphysical analysis of the nature of things, which would thereby determine how things acted and functioned. The historical revolt was the definite abandonment of this method in favour of the study of the empirical fact of antecedents and consequences. In religion, it meant the appeal to the origins of Christianity; and in science it meant the appeal to experiment and the inductive method of reasoning."

The Enlightenment, which grew out of the scientific revolution, maintained the same non-rational approach. In contrast, it should be noted, Calvinism, with its heavy dependence on Augustine, was the most metaphysical form of Protestantism. The intellectual distaste felt for it by men of the Enlightenment depends, at least partly, on this fact. One cause often adduced by contemporaries for the slowness of the Scottish peasantry to adapt themselves to improvements was the addiction to metaphysical speculation encouraged by the particular form of their religious observance. A major tension of eighteenth-century life in Scotland was that between the new philosophy and Calvinist metaphysics. The men of the Enlightenment, it seems likely, would have strenuously denied the substance of Whitehead's charge, but the fact remains that no system which gives predominance to observed facts and the inductive method can be purely rational.

This hostility to pure rationalism is clearly visible in the thought, not only of Hutcheson, but of the two most philosophic among his successors, Reid and Hume. Reid's analysis tends to be directed to the actual process of perception, and his complex system of postulates, largely based on the limitations, as he sees them, of perception, put formidable restraints on the effective use of man's purely intellectual resources. Reid, it will be remembered, was pre-eminently the Newtonian among eighteenth-century Scottish philosophers, and the non-rationalistic basis of his thought is consistent with this allegiance.

Whitehead tends to think of Hume as a rationalist rather than an adherent of scientific method. "Science repudiates philosophy", he remarks.[10] "In other words, it has never cared to justify its faith or to explain its meanings; and has remained blandly indifferent to its refutation by Hume." Yet Hume too claimed to be a Newtonian, and gave a central place in his philosophy to the paradox "Reason is, and ought only to be, the slave of the passions",[11] a saying perilously close to another, dear to the hearts of non-rationalists and sentimentalists, Pascal's "The heart has reasons reason knows not of".[12]

The Scottish Enlightenment, in other words, consistently underplayed the importance of systems based on pure reason, and tended to emphasize the limitations of intellect and the importance of the non-rational passions and emotions in its account of the human mind. The process came early to a head in Hutcheson, in whom, as has been mentioned, it was paradoxically combined with a utilitarian moral standard capable of mathematical expression. The same combination is to be found, time and again, in what may be called the diagrammatic method adopted in the imaginative literature of the period for the analytical display of instinctive passions. Two instances drawn from *The Man of Feeling*, a novel which has already more than once been mentioned, and which will be further discussed below, may serve to illustrate.

In chapter XXVI, Harley succours Miss Atkins, a starving London prostitute of respectable origins, who accosts him in the street one night. He gives her food and sends her home in a chair, promising help when he visits her the next morning. He keeps the appointment, and hears the story of her seduction and abandonment by Mr Winbrooke, the son of a squire, neighbour to her father in the country. As she finishes her tale, her father, a retired army captain, bursts into the room, determined to avenge her loss of honour on Harley, whom he assumes to be her seducer. When the error is revaled, Harley persuades him to take back his daughter, and finds temporary accommodation for them both in his own lodgings.

In chapter XXXIV, he meets old Edwards, whom he had known and loved in his own childhood, returning home with his personal integrity intact, but in military disgrace, from the army service in India which he had undertaken to save his son from the press-gang, and his son's family from consequent destitution. In the course of their journey together, they meet an elderly school-mistress with two of her charges, a boy and a girl, who turn out to be Edwards's grandchildren, orphaned by the death from broken hearts of their parents when the small farm, left them by old Edwards when he was pressed, went bankrupt. Harley sets them up on a small farm in his own estate.

The concatenation of events in these scenes, however improbable in itself, forms an almost Euclidean structure, illustrating the relationships and transformations possible between a variety of human passions and affections, and at the same time enabling Harley (and vicariously the benevolent reader) to extract from it the maximum available illumination and profit. The transform-ations — despair to hope, anger to forgiveness — are plotted in terms more advanced than anything in Hutcheson's calculus; the method used almost approaches that found in Hume's *Treatise*. This does not of course in turn transform *The Man of Feeling* into great literature; it remains sentimental melodrama — melod-rama, however, which is governed by philosophic principles in a way not usual for sentimental novels of later periods.

iii

The emphasis on passion and instinct, as opposed to reason, led, it is clear, to the emergence of sentimentality as a governing factor in the literature of the time. Literary sentimentality of course existed elsewhere before it migrated to Scotland. Lauren-ce Sterne's *A Sentimental Journey* (1768) is a well-known late example. The emphasis changed, however, with the movement north of the border. The background in ideas just described, combined with such factors as resentment, on the one hand, at the loss of Scottish independence in 1707; on the other, at the paucity of early Scottish records as contrasted with the abun-dance preserved in Ireland, and in Irish Gaelic, led directly to Macpherson's *Ossian*, which, as has been noted[13], appeared in the years around 1760. In Ossian, sentimentality is combined with the Gothic (the eighteenth century comprehended the Gothic as including the Celtic), and takes on a heroic form; the lonely bard who has outlived all his contemporaries, and whose sole attendant is the devoted Malvina, retells, against a background of mountains, mists and the spirits of the dead concealed in clouds, the story of ancient, improbably noble and improbably great achievements; the note of lamentation and regret is dominant. Macpherson also began his Ossianic work with a volume of fragments,[14] the very form of which indicated the sense of loss which dominates the epics as a whole, and at the same time indicates the imperfection inherent in all forms of human tradition. He is making a point virtually identical with that of Reid in his analysis of the imperfections of human sense-perception.

Macpherson lived until 1796, but *Temora*, the last of his epics, was published in 1763. In terms of the novel, Mackenzie is the major figure of the period which separates *Temora* from *Waverley*. *The Man of Feeling* (1771) was followed in 1773 by *The Man of the World*, and in 1777 by *Julia de Roubigné*. The title of the first settled for all time Mackenzie's position in the folk-lore of the novel; he is not the most widely read, but is probably the best-known of all novelists to whom the term sentimental is disparagingly applied. He lived long. Scott was personally acquainted with him, and often refers, half admiringly, half condescendingly, to his work, the immediate success of which was almost as great as that of Ossian.

Mackenzie was of direct Highland descent, and was born in the very year of the '45. Some features of Macpherson's work are paralleled in his own; *The Man of Feeling*, for instance, is presented as a collection of apparently disjointed fragments, the form of which corresponds to the limitations of human memory and perception. His form of sentimentality, however, is different; it contains no element of the Gothic, but demonstrates to its own satisfaction that a romantic attachment to a vanishing older order (usually on the surface English) may be of some relevance for unwilling participants in the profitable, but apparently heartless, activities which constitute the new world of the assumed present and its improvers.

The sentimental novel, at least in its eighteenth-century Scottish form, had a necessary connection with changes in society, some analysis of which, at however superficial a level, was necessary for the development of the story. The effect of such changes on the character and passions of the individual human being also had to be taken into account, as had the dominant features of the older society, now in process of replacement. All these were seen, again at however superficial a level, in terms of the sociology, the economics, the psychology, the concept of history, developed in the Enlightenment. In a real sense, the sentimental novel marks a stage in the transformation of the mainstream eighteenth-century novel to the new form which came to dominate the nineteenth, a transformation best exemplified by the contrast of Fielding with Scott.

Mackenzie lays considerable emphasis on the contrast between Harley, the Man of Feeling, and the society in which he lives. Harley is himself the last representative of an ancient family, which, like society as a whole, has seen better days. He is afflicted with an extreme sensitivity, which Mackenzie, rather curiously, seems to regard as characteristic of the old order. Most of his neighbours belong to the new:—

> Some part of his [Harley's] external appearance was modelled from the company of those gentlemen, whom the antiquity of a family, now possessed of bare 250 l. a year, entitled its representative to approach; these indeed were not many; great part of the property in his neighbourhood being in the hands of merchants, who had got rich by their lawful calling abroad, and the sons of stewards, who had got rich by their lawful calling at home: persons so perfectly versed in the ceremonial of thousands, tens of thousands, and hundreds of thousands (whose degrees of precedency are plainly demonstrable from the first page of the Compleat Accomptant, or Young Man's best Pocket Companion) that a bow at church from them to such a man as Harley, — would have made the parson look back into his sermon for some precept of Christian humility."
>
> (Chapter XI)

Such prospects in the new world as Harley has, depend on a distant relative, a rich old lady, whom he cultivates with a singular lack of adroitness, and who leaves him accordingly nothing, and, secondly, on his obtaining the lease of some crown lands, which adjoin his little estate. To obtain these last, he sets out for London, home of the new Mammon, where he fails in everything, except the redemption of Miss Atkins. The visit however gives him the opportunity of meeting a wide range of characters who typify the new order. Eventually he returns to the country, meeting in the coach Ben Silton, and on the road old Edwards and the survivors of his family. Soon afterwards he dies, owning no more than his little estate, the love of the Edwardses and that of Miss Walton, with whom he comes to an understanding just before his death. Miss Atkins and her father, Ben Silton, old Edwards and Miss Walton have been, in effect, the only honest people of his acquaintance.

Even from this brief summary, it is clear that the book is less genuinely a collection of fragments than the preliminary narrative and the system of chapter numbering would have led one to expect. Plot exists, but in its simplicity is more closely related to the discursive moral essay, as practised by Steele and Addison in *The Spectator*, than to the novel of Fielding, Richardson and Smollett. Mackenzie eventually gave up fiction for essays of this kind, which appeared in *The Mirror* (1779-1780) and *The Lounger* (1785-1787).[15] The diagrammatic method, already discussed, particularly suits such a novel.

Mackenzie shared with James Thomson the literary habit of having Scottish circumstances primarily in mind while working apparently within an English setting. Two incidents from *The Man of Feeling* will illustrate. In chapter XIV, Harley hears the life-story of a beggar who makes his living by fortune-telling;—

> I was brought to my idleness by degrees; first I could not work, and it went against my stomach to work ever after. I was seized with a jail-fever at the time of the assizes being in the county where I lived; for I was always curious to get acquainted with the felons, because they are commonly fellows of much mirth and little thought, qualities I had ever an esteem for. In the height of this fever, Mr. Harley, the house where I lay took fire, and burnt to the ground: I was carried out in that condition, and lay all the rest of my illness in a barn. I got the better of my disease however, but I was so weak that I spit blood whenever I attempted to

work. I had no relation living that I knew of, and I never kept a friend above a week, when I was able to joke; I seldom remained above six months in a parish, so that I might have died before I had found a settlement in any; thus I was forced to beg my bread, and a sorry trade I found it, Mr. Harley —— I changed my plan, and, instead of telling my own misfortunes, began to prophesy happiness to others. This I found by much the better way: folks will always listen when the tale is their own; and of many who say they do not believe in fortune-telling, I have known few on whom it had not a very sensible effect.

It is a rather unconvincing part of the Enlightenment that even the beggar makes no pretence to faith in his own powers; with this, one may contrast the more romantic spae-wives and fortune-tellers in Scott and Galt. More convincing is the account of the economic forces and ideas which brought a decent labourer on to the road as a beggar — forces which suggested to Burns, for instance, prospects which at once frightened and exhilarated him:—[16]

> 'Mair spier na, nor fear na,'
>   Auld age ne'er mind a feg;
> The last o't, the warst o't,
>   Is only but to beg.

> To lye in kilns and barns at e'en,
> When banes are craz'd, and bluid is thin,
>   Is, doubtless, great distress;
> Yet then *content* could make us blest;
> Ev'n then, sometimes we'd snatch a taste
>   Of truest happiness.
>   ("Epistle to Davie, a Brother Poet", 25-34)

To some extent, this is written in the devil-may-care fashion which Burns carried to the limits in *Love and Liberty*. In the "Epistle to Davie" it is more restrained, conveying as it does a full realization of the troubles of old age in poverty to qualify the exhilaration which is also present. Rather unexpectedly, the fear of beggary is most powerfully expressed in "To a Mouse, On turning her up in her Nest", a poem which generally has been

read more for its direct sentimentality than for the more oblique
social relevance. In the mouse, Burns (like Henryson three
centuries earlier) sees the emblem of the poor tenant farmer,
helpless in face of crushing economic forces and callous landlords. To a greater extent than Henryson, he identified himself
with his symbol:—[17]

> Thy wee bit *housie*, too, in ruin!
> It's silly wa's the win's are strewin!
> An' naething, now, to big a new ane,
>   O' foggage green!
> An' bleak *December's winds* ensuin,
>   Baith snell an' keen!
>
> Thou saw the fields laid bare an' wast,
> An' weary *Winter* comin fast,
> An' cozie here, beneath the blast,
>   Thou thought to dwell.
> Till crash! the cruel *coulter* past
>   Out thro' thy cell.
>
> That wee-bit heap o' leaves an' stibble,
> Has cost thee monie a weary nibble!
> Now thou's turn'd out, for a' thy trouble,
>   But house or hald,
> To thole the Winter's *sleety dribble*,
>   An' *cranreuch* cauld!
>
> But Mousie, thou art no thy-lane,
> In proving *foresight* may be vain:
> The best laid schemes o' *Mice* an' *Men*
>   Gang aft agley,
> An' lea'e us nought but grief an' pain.
>   For promis'd joy.
>
> Still, thou art blest, compar'd wi' *me*!
> The *present* only toucheth thee:
> But Och! I *backward* cast my e'e
>   On prospects drear!
> An' *forward*, tho' I canna *see*,
>   I *guess* an' *fear*!
>   (19–48)

Burns is closer than any other major writer to the situation which he describes, but it is easy enough to find further parallels, for instance in Scott's treatment of the gypsies in *Guy Mannering*, and in the recurrent references to roving bands of beggars as well as individual mendicants in the works of Galt.

In the episode of old Edwards, which begins in Chapter XXXIV, Mackenzie treats a similar theme in much greater detail. Edwards is the tenant of a farm which '"had been possessed by my father, grandfather, and great-grandfather, which last was a younger brother of that very man's ancestor who is now lord of the manor"' (p.87). (The emphasis on kinship, the kindly tenant, fits the Scottish tradition very closely.) Edwards' tribulations begin at the hands of the lord of the manor, and one has only to substitute the word 'laird' for 'squire' to see how closely Mackenzie's description fits Scottish circumstances. The squire hitherto has clearly operated the older system of short leases to small tenants, but is now anxious to consolidate and enclose his estate:—

> "My last lease was out soon after you left that part of the country; and the squire, who had lately got a London-attorney for his steward, would not renew it, because, he said, he did not chuse to have any farm under 300l. a year value on his estate; but offered to give me the preference on the same terms with another, if I chose to take the one he had marked out, of which mine was a part."

Edwards' acceptance of the proposal reduced him to comparative poverty, and he was forced to leave South-hill.

Henry Hamilton in *An Economic History of Scotland in the Eighteenth Century*[18] has described the same process less emotionally than Mackenzie:—

> The substitution of compact holdings for scattered strips of land, the physical enclosure of fields and the amalgamation of holdings, could not have been effected without disturbance to the existing social order — The creation of larger farms necessarily involved some displacement of small tenants, but at the same time it created a demand for wage labour; while the replace-

ment of the township by the isolated farm house with cottar dwellings disrupted the social organization resting on co-operation in the main farming operations. — All this could be carried out in Scotland by the heritor himself, without the process of law required in England.

(p.81)

One may also compare the story of James Somerville, father of the Alexander Somerville, who wrote the classic *The Autobiography of a Working Man* (London, 1848) Christopher Smout has summarised his career thus:—[19]

Somerville began as a small independent farmer in the Ochils, lost his holding in the landlord's programme of amalgamations, and went to Alloa to try to support himself as a carter. When his only horse died there he had been too poor to buy another, and took work as a docker at Lymekilns in Fife: he abandoned this when his brother who worked at the same job died in a horrible accident under the limedust in a ship's hold. He ended as an agricultural labourer, ploughman and quarryman, sometimes in very straitened circumstances, on the improved farms of the Berwickshire Merse.

(p.315)

As is revealed by the autobiographical letter to Dr Moore[20] the story of William Burnes, father of Robert Burns, followed a very similar pattern.

In Mackenzie's second novel, *The Man of the World*, the benevolent nabob, Mr Rawlinson, reverses such procedures on the estate which he has inherited. A similar course is followed by Henry Bolton, the hero of the latter part of the novel, who addresses his tenants thus, on succeeding Mr Rawlinson:—

"I have given orders to my steward to renew such of your leases as are near expiring at the rent which you have heretofore paid. If there is any article of encouragement or convenience wanting to any of you, let

him apply to myself, and I will immediately inquire
into it. No man is above the business of doing good.

It is customary, I believe, on such occasions, for the
tenant to pay a certain fine or premium to the landlord.
I too, my friends, will expect one; you and your
families shall pay it me, — be industrious, be virtuous,
and be happy."

(ii., pp.101-2)

The fine Bolton refers to is the grassum or gersum, "a fine
paid in consideration of a lease for a term of years" (*DOST*). The
effects seem to have been more resented and to have lasted
longer, in Scotland than in England. Already in the fifteenth
century the iniquities of the system had become a by-word:—

> The thrid Wolf ar men of heritage,
> As Lordis that hes land be Goddis lane,
> And settis to the Mailleris ane Village,
> And for ane tyme Gressome payit and tane;
> Syne vexis him, or half his term be gane,
> With pykit querrellis for to mak him fane
> To flit, or pay his Gressome new againe.
> ("The Wolf and the Lamb", *Morall Fabillis*,
> 1742-48).

Henryson's attitude corresponds across the gap of three centuries
to that of Mackenzie. His men of heritage behave very much as
did William Burnes's landlords and their overseers.

Mackenzie inevitably, and perhaps unconsciously, projects
Scottish conditions and preconceptions on to what is presented as
an English landscape. At the same time, he certainly intended to
make a genuine study of characters and circumstances which
were not Scottish. *Julia de Roubigné* confirms this by its study of
relationships within French society. The English viewpoint is
established at the beginning of *The Man of Feeling*, partly by the
presentation of the curate, by whose agency something at least of
the memoir of Harley comes to be preserved, partly by the echo
of Montesquieu which opens the actual memoir:—

> There is some rust about every man at the beginn-
> ing; though in some nations (among the French, for

instance) the ideas of the inhabitants from climate, or what other cause you will, are so vivacious, so eternally on the wing, that they must, even in small societies, have a frequent collision; the rust therefore will wear off sooner: but in Britain, it often goes with a man to his grave; nay, he dares not even pen a *hic jacet* to speak out for him after his death.

(p.7)

Equally, the opening of *The Man of the World* possesses obvious English rural characteristics:—

"Alackaday!" says Jack, "There have been many changes among us since you left this; here has died the old gauger Wilson, as good a cricket-player as ever handled a bat; Rooke at the Salutation is gone too; and his wife has left the parish, and settled in London, where, I am told, she keeps a gin-shop, in some street they call Southwark."

(i., p.7)

This approach is only apparently contradicted by a remark from the Introduction to *Julia de Roubigné*:— "I confess myself particularly delighted with an intercourse, which removes the barrier of national distinction, and gives to the inhabitants of the world the appearance of one common family." It is clear that Mackenzie found as much to interest him in the differences between members of the human family as in the similarities. In the first paragraph of the first letter, for instance, he establishes that Julia was marked out from most young women in the British Isles by her convent education, the effects of which are clearly to be seen in the later developments of her character. Her husband, Louis de Montauban, is the son of a French father and a Spanish mother, and has lived most of his life in Spain. To a great extent, the development of the plot turns on what Mackenzie regarded as Montauban's Spanish characteristics operating in a French rural setting. The setting is essential for the development both of plot and character. Mackenzie is aware that it was unusual for French aristocrats to live in their country seats, and is careful to explain the reasons for this unusual conduct on the part both of de Roubigné and of de Montauban. He does not give a very profound analysis of European national character-istics, but it is obvious that he intended to give some.

The novels of his older contemporary, Dr John Moore (1729–1802), the friend of Burns, are later than Mackenzie's, but their full titles — *Zeluco: Various Views of Human Nature, taken from Life and Manners, Foreign and Domestic* (1786); *Edward: Various Views of Human Nature, taken from Life and Manners, chiefly in England* (1796); *Mordaunt: Sketches of Life, Character and Manners in Various Countries, including the Memoirs of a French Lady of Quality* (1800) — show how far the work of the two novelists overlapped. Within the limits of the epistolary novel, Moore was able to attempt a serious, unsensational treatment of the French Revolution. It is a pity that he lacked Mackenzie's structural ability, or that Mackenzie lacked his wit, vigour, and the range of experience and observation gained by a humane and widely travelled physician.

The importance, politically, socially and economically, of England and France explains the prominence of the two nations in the novels of Mackenzie and Moore. They represent society in its most developed form, which neither novelist found more than moderately acceptable. They share elements of the common European discontent expressed with differing emphasis by Rous-seau in *La Nouvelle Héloïse* (1761) and *Du Contrat Social* (1762) and by Macpherson in the Ossianic poems. Mackenzie in particular tends to counterpoint the vices of European civiliz-ation against the virtues of less materially advanced communities. In *The Man of Feeling* Edwards is press-ganged into military service in India, where as a consequence of rescuing an Indian from the brutality of his fellow-soldiers, he in turn receives help from the Indian. '"You are an Englishman", said he, "But the Great Spirit has given you an Indian heart; may he bear up the weight of your old age, and blunt the arrow that brings it rest."' (p.94)

In a more extended episode of *The Man of the World*, obviously derived from Lismahago's narrative in *Humphry Clinker*, young Annesley, who has been corrupted by Sindall, is reduced to theft, and sentenced to transportation. Eventually he escapes, and by the endurance of torture proves his fitness to become a member of the Cherokee tribe. The hard life of the

Cherokee comes to seem much superior to that of European civilization as he has experienced it:—

> In this society I lived till about a year and a half ago; and it may seem extraordinary to declare, yet it is certainly true, that during the life of the old man who had adopted me, even had there been no legal restraint on my return to my native country, scarce any inducement could have tempted me to leave the nation to which he belonged, except perhaps the desire of revisiting a parent, and a sister, whom I had left in England, sunk beneath that ignominy which the son and the brother had drawn on his guiltless connections. When we consider the perfect freedom subsisting in this rude and simple state of society, where rule is only acknowledged for the purpose of immediate utility to those who obey, and ceases whenever that purpose of subordination is accomplished; where greatness cannot use oppression, nor wealth excite envy; where the desires are native to the heart, and the languor of satiety is unknown; there, if there is no refined sensation of delight, there is also no ideal source of calamity; we shall the less wonder at the inhabitants feeling no regret for the want of those delicate pleasures of which a more polished people is possessed. Certain it is, that I am far from being a single instance, of one who had even attained maturity in Europe, and yet found his mind so accommodated, by the habit of a few years, to Indian manners, as to leave that country with regret.
>
> (ii., pp.182-3)

This opinion is only confirmed when eventually he leaves the Cherokees to return to England.

In *Julia de Roubigné* European ideals are brought into sharp contact with the institution of slavery in Martinique, where Julia's lover, Savillon, goes in search of fortune. Savillon's relationship with the black slave Yambu contributes nothing to the plot of the book. Slavery however, as it exists in Martinique becomes symptomatic of the narrow confines of French society, to which Julia herself, Savillon and de Montauban are as much slaves as is Yambu himself. "Man was born free, and he is everywhere in chains." The immediate good sense and good feeling of this passage at the literal level do not prevent it from having, in terms of the entire work, a more extended meaning:—

> I have been often tempted to doubt whether there is not an error in the whole plan of negro servitude, and whether whites, or creoles born in the West Indies, or perhaps cattle, after the manner of European husbandry, would not do the business better and cheaper than the slaves do. The money which the latter cost at first, the sickness (often owing to despondency of mind) to which they are liable after their arrival, and the proportion that die in consequence of it, make the machine, if it may be called so, of a plantation extremely expensive in its operation. In the list of slaves belonging to a wealthy planter, it would astonish you to see the number unfit for service, pining under disease, a burden on their master. I am talking only as a merchant; but as a man — good heavens! when I think of the many thousands of my fellow-creatures groaning under servitude and misery! Great God! hast thou peopled those regions of thy world for the purpose of casting out their inhabitants to chains and torture? No; thou gavest them a land teeming with good things, and lightest up thy sun to bring forth spontaneous plenty; but the refinements of man, ever at war with thy works, have changed this scene of profusion and luxuriance into a theatre of rapine, of slavery, and of murder!
>
> (ii., pp.38-9)

This preoccupation with racial differences, contrasted social systems, and contrasts within a single social system, links Mackenzie to his predecessors, Smollett, Adam Ferguson and Macpherson, and to his successors, Scott and Galt. (Scott in *The Bride of Lammermoor*, for instance, certainly had *Julia de Roubigné* in mind.) The matrix of their intellectual and imaginative life was the complexity of Lowland, Highland and English elements in the society which they had known as children and young men, a complexity which corresponded strikingly with their

C

adult experience of a wider world, and which could easily provide an instrument for the interpretation of history. Mackenzie was the least radical and least original of the authors mentioned, but his kinship with them cannot be mistaken.

In narrative method, he sometimes anticipates the later Scottish novel. *The Man of Feeling* first appeared anonymously. Mackenzie seems to have shared with Scott a certain need to distance himself from his own literary work, and as a consequence the further need to create some kind of auctorial *persona* intermediate between the work and himself. The contemporary impulse towards realism, as the word has been defined by Ian Watt,[21] led to the creation of what might almost be termed a pre-history of the individual novel, a pre-history involving not merely the person of the narrator, but also the sources from which he drew his material. Henry Mackenzie does not appear in *The Man of Feeling*; the book is presented as the work of an editor, who obtained from the Curate part of the memoir of Harley, the Man of Feeling, which had been composed by The Ghost, who 'was known by the slouch in his gait, and the length of his stride' (p.4), and who had visited Harley in his last illness. In *The Man of the World*, the same editor is introduced by Jack Ryland to Mrs. Wistanly, who has in her possession a box of letters and papers dealing with the affairs of the Annesley and Sindall families. The letters which make up *Julia de Roubigné* he obtains from a young Frenchman, the son of an old friend, who in turn obtained them from a little boy, who was attempting to sell them to a grocer for use as wrapping paper. This device of setting the book in an imaginary world larger than itself had already been used in a similar way by Marivaux (1688-1763) in *La Vie de Marianne* (1731-42), and was to become one of Scott's favourite narrative devices. Galt on occasions tries something of the same kind, but the most elaborate example is probably the double structure of Hogg's *Memoirs and Confessions of a Justified Sinner* (1824).

Hogg uses the technique to create a perpetual ambiguity. The reader is forced to ask himself whether the narrative before him is one of historical fact, or rumour magnified by the passage of a century, or whether the basis is psychological abnormality and hallucination. The effect, in other words, is not primarily realistic. Elsewhere however the technique gives rise to realism of a very particular kind, based on the continuity between present and past, with the emphasis tending to fall on the latter. The editor is the only, or the chief contemporary of the reader to appear in the book; all others belong to a past which may be moderately distant, and which may differ significantly from the present of the narrator. The first part of *La Vie de Marianne* for instance, appeared in 1731; Marianne herself, we are told, had written her autobiography forty years earlier, and the events which she describes begin a half-century earlier still — somewhere, that is to say, about 1640. Marivaux does not always keep his chronology in mind, but at least his references often make it clear that the events described belong to the seventeenth rather than the eighteenth century. The contrast contributes to the total effect, and the continuity of past and present is essential to the realism of the novel. *La Vie de Marianne*, in other words, is at least tending towards the historical novel. The distance between Harley and the editor of The Ghost's memoir is not so great. Miss Walton is still a young woman when the Curate mentions that the papers are in his possession, but Harley himself had died before the Curate came to the parish. The chronology of *The Man of the World* is more complicated. In his fairly distant youth, the editor had known parson Annesley, his wife, and his two young children, whose calamitous story forms Part I of the novel. Some years later, when Part II begins, Lucy Sindall and Miss Walton visit Harley's grave. The relationship of *The Man of the World* with *The Man of Feeling* is thus established. Afterwards Lucy is rescued from Sindall's incestuous passion by her uncle, parson Annesley's son, who has just returned to England more than twenty years after his sentence of transportation. When the editor completes his narrative Lucy and Bolton have been happily married for some little while. The time scale of the novel extends over more than forty years and three generations. The action of *Julia de Roubigné* is set in a past which is not particularized to anything like the same degree.

Mackenzie did not use his distancing technique, as he might have, to illustrate the social and economic changes which furnish the excuse for much of his sentimentality. The harsh nature of the new world appears rather in the experiences of Savillon, counterbalanced though they are by the human qualities displayed by the victims. The specifically Scottish contrast of old and new is never more than subliminally present, but the germ of the historical novel as developed by Scott and Galt is to be found in Mackenzie.

NOTES

In this chapter and elsewhere Scott is quoted from the Dryburgh edition, ed. A. Lang (London, 1892-4). For Fielding, the edition used is Saintsbury's (London, 1893); for *The Man of Feeling*, Brian Vicker's edition (Oxford, 1965). W.L. Renwick edited John Moore's *Mordaunt* (Oxford, 1965). Unless noted below, other quotations are from first or early editions of the relevant works. The reader may profitably consult Basil Willey, *The Eighteenth Century Background* (London, 1940); Ian Watt, *The Rise of the Novel* (London, 1957); David Craig, *Scottish Literature and the Scottish People 1680-1830* (London, 1961); Francis Russell Hart, *The Scottish Novel* (London, 1978); Ian Campbell, *Kailyard* (Edinburgh, 1981).

The most useful bibliographical guide to current work is *The Year's Work in Scottish Literary and Linguistic Studies*, published annually by *Scottish Literary Journal* for ASLS. Reference should also be made to LASH, the list of articles on Scottish history, which appears annually in *Scottish Historical Review*.

1. *The True Patriot* was a weekly journal which appeared from 5th November, 1745 to 10th June, 1746. *The Jacobite Journal* ran from December 1747 to November 1748.

2. Pp.3, 38, n.8, 51. See the translation by D.H. MacNeill, *The Art and Science of Government among the Scots* (Glasgow, 1964).

3. J.M.Gray (ed), *Memoirs of the Life of Sir John Clerk of Penicuik, Baronet* (SHS, Edinburgh, 1892). See also *Progress and Poetry*, pp.97-8.

4. Hannah and Stanley Mitchell (trs.), *The Historical Novel* (London, 1962: Peregrine reprint, 1969). The quotations will be found on pp. 15 and 16.

5. Pp. 42ff., 55ff.

6. *Encyclopedia Britannica* s.v. "Hutcheson".

7. *Progress and Poetry*, p. 62.

8. Berkeley's *Alciphron, or the Minute Philosopher* (1732) impinges on the same areas of philosophic debate.

9. *Science and the Modern World* (Cambridge, 1925), pp.20, 49.

10. *op. cit.*, p.20.

11. *Treatise of Human Nature* II,iii,3.; L.A. Selby-Bigge (ed), *Hume's Treatise* (Oxford, 1888 and reprints), p.415.

12. *Pensées*, iv, 277.

13. *Progress and Poetry*, pp. 88ff.

14. *Fragments of Ancient Poetry* (1760).

15. See especially Horst W. Drescher, *Themen und Formen des Periodischen Essays im Späten 18.Jahrhundert* (Frankfurt am Main, 1971).

16. James Kinsley (ed), *The Poems and Songs of Robert Burns* (3 vols., Oxford, 1968), I. p.66.

17. *op. cit.*, I.pp.127-8.
18. Oxford, 1963.
19. *A History of the Scottish People 1560-1830* (London, 1969), p.315. Alexander
     Somerville lived from 1811 to 1885; he was James Somerville's eleventh
     son, a sawyer by original trade, who had an unhappy experience of
     military life, in the course of which he underwent a flogging, and
     subsequently wrote on Reform and Chartism. Eventually he emigrated to
     Canada, where he died in poverty. The *Autobiography* was published in
     1848.
20. Letter 125; J. De Lancey Ferguson (ed.), *The Letters of Robert Burns* (2 vols.,
     Oxford, 1931), I, pp.104-116.
21. *The Rise of the Novel*, pp. 9-35.

CHAPTER II

WALTER SCOTT

The influence exerted by Hutcheson through his books and lectures, and also by way of his distinguished pupils (one of whom was Adam Smith, the author of *The Theory of Moral Sentiments* as well as *The Wealth of Nations*[1]) affected most educated Scots of the eighteenth century. His ideas were gradually refined and developed, most notably by David Hume, whose *A Treatise on Human Nature* was essentially an investigation into the constitution and operation of the human mind, based on the assumption, only partly Hutchesonian, that "Reason is, and ought only to be, the slave of the passions."

Hume's contribution lies, not in the apparent paradox, but in the Newtonian exposition of mental forces, the interactions of which resolve the paradox. One is the universal tendency to associate ideas by means of such factors as Resemblance, Contiguity in Time and Place, Cause and Effect. "These are therefore the principles of union or cohesion among our simple ideas, which in the imagination supply the place of that inseparable annexion, by which they are united in our memory. Here is a kind of ATTRACTION, which in the mental world will be found to have as extraordinary effects as in the natural, and to shew itself in as various forms." (*Treatise* I.iv). David Hartley (1705-1757) was as much responsible as Hume for the spread of the doctrine; his influence may, indeed, have been even more general because, unlike Hume, he was himself a convinced Christian[2].

For Hume, another important mental property was sympathy.

> No quality of human nature is more remarkable, both in itself and in its consequences, than the propensity we have to sympathize with others, and to receive by communication their inclinations and sentiments, however different from, or even contrary to, our own. . . .

To this principle we ought to ascribe the great uni-
formity we may observe in the humours and turn of
thinking of those of the same nation, and it is much
more probable, that this resemblance arises from sympathy, than from any influence of the soil and climate,
which, tho' they continue invariably the same, are not
able to preserve the character of a nation the same for a
century together. . . . 'Tis obvious that nature has
preserv'd a great resemblance among all human creatures, and that we never remark any passion or
principle in others, of which, in some degree or other,
we may not find a parallel in ourselves. The case is the
same with the fabric of the mind, as with that of the
body. However the parts may differ in shape and size,
their structure and composition are in general the same.

(*Treatise* II i.ii)

These last three sentences are, of course, the philosophical
justification for the existence of the historical novel. Hume
allows that differences of mental habit exist among nations and
between historical epochs, even in the same nation. These
however are differences of degree only, bridgeable by the
sympathy which is capable of uniting all humankind and of
comprehending all forms of human behaviour. The remarks
crystallize a general perception without which the literary form
would neither have appeared nor survived.

Any account of the human mind which sets the primacy on
reason is bound to be static — under all circumstances the
reasonable retains its identity — and hostile to non-rational
instinct. The virtue of Hume's psychology is first, its dynamism,
its concern with transitions of idea and passion, and secondly, its
incorporation of the non-rational in human thought, feeling and
action. A psychology of this kind necessarily has a place for such
factors as heredity, upbringing, environment, and the traumatic
or beneficial effect of single events on the individual. Everything
derives from the mind itself and the general mental climate
within which it operates. In the passage just quoted,
Montesquieu's "influence of the soil and climate" are treated
with some disrespect; they are not excluded, but Hume clearly
regards them as subordinate to the effect on a man's mind of his
own mental processes and experiences. The insistence on necess-

ity, finally, gives his psychology a force and direction much like that found in the structure of any well-written novel.

Novels might be, and indeed have been, written on some of the problems investigated by Hume. One thinks, for instance, of his man of good family but narrow circumstances:— "Nothing is more usual than for men, of good families but narrow circumstances, to leave their friends and country, and rather seek their livelihood by mean and mechanical employments among strangers, than among those who are acquainted with their birth and education" (II.i.ii). The French novels, which Hume was fond of reading, may sometimes have furnished him with such examples, but this particular one might as easily be paralleled from later Scottish fiction as from the history of Scottish families in the eighteenth century. One thinks, for instance, of Mr Crystal Croftangry, the assumed author of Scott's *The Chronicles of the Canongate*, who dissipated such small fortune as he had, and afterwards could not endure to return to his native place, but settled in the liberty of the Edinburgh Canongate, which had been the scene of his greatest misery as a bankrupt.

Again, "According to the hypothesis of liberty. . . a man is as pure and untainted, after having committed the most horrid crimes as at the first moment of his birth, nor is his character any way concern'd in his actions; since they are not deriv'd from it, and the wickedness of the one can never be us'd as a proof of the depravity of the other. 'Tis only upon the principles of necessity, that a person acquires any merit or demerit from his actions, however the common opinion may incline to the contrary" (II.iii.2.). Hume's version of the "hypothesis of liberty" closely resembles the tenets of the more extreme Calvinist antinomians — a point in which, no doubt, he found some satisfaction — and in effect the passage anticipates the conflict in James Hogg's *The Private Memoirs and Confessions of a Justified Sinner* (1824), a conflict which is also present, less centrally and less acutely, in the character of Balfour of Burleigh in Scott's *Old Mortality* (1816), as in that of Claude Walkinshaw in Galt's *The Entail* (1823) and of Ringan Gilhaize in the novel of the same name (1823).

The hypothesis thus contains in itself the possibility of tragic development, as illustrated by Hogg's novel and by *The Entail*, but in general Hume's psychology is better suited to the more intellectual forms of comedy than to tragedy. His own judgement of the latter genre was notoriously uncertain, as may be illustrated by his overestimation of Home's *Douglas*, and by what he has to say of Shakespeare. Tragedy as a literary kind was almost totally alien to the limited optimism which underlies much thought of the Enlightenment period, an optimism also to be found with differing degrees of certainty in Scott, Galt and Hogg. One might say that intellectual comedy became the dominant, although never the sole, characteristic of the historical novel of the late Scottish Enlightenment, a point illustrated by much of the material brought forward in this and subsequent chapters.

Such comedy is to be found even in Mackenzie. No-one, I think, has done justice to the comic force (to be compared, say, with that of Goldsmith in *She Stoops to Conquer* (1767)) especially of the London scenes, in *The Man of Feeling*. There is considerable verve, for instance in the account of the various confidence tricksters who take advantage of Harley's vaunted knowledge of physiognomy; one instance is his encounter (Chapter XXV) with the "fresh-looking elderly gentleman" in the Park, who is in fact a member of the card-sharping gang by whom Harley finds himself fleeced. It is part of Mackenzie's wit that, contrary to the expectations which have thus been roused, the simplicity of the Man of Feeling is not deceived when he meets a fellow victim of the new world in the person of Miss Atkins.

Hume's interest in the subtleties and difficulties of psychological analysis corresponds to the interest expressed by Scott in "curious anomalous facts in the history of mind"[3]. But there is more to it than that. Hume's Newtonianism made him feel that he should test his theories by experiments such as those suggested in *Treatise*, II.ii.2.. Scott similarly felt that his fictional investigations should maintain some verifying contact with historic fact. In *The Heart of Midlothian*, one remarkable aspect of the Presbyterian character is presented through fiction, but validated by the experience in real life of the historical Helen Walker. *The Bride of Lammermoor* is based on events in the annals of the Dalrymple family. *The Highland Widow* and *The Two Drovers* are likewise based on historical occurrences, and the list might easily be extended. This does not indicate any lack of invention, which in Scott was always abundant. His concern was manners — not the chronicling of external peculiarities of speech and behaviour, but a study of human understanding, passions and morals as these had been shaped and directed into action by circumstances, particular beliefs, family, companions or surroundings. The success of such an enterprise might be judged by the extent to which the completed tale illuminated events in the historical period under consideration, without losing its relevance for contemporary characters and happenings.

For Scott, as for Hume, character is dynamic and substantially non-rational; it is most fully expressed in action, which often contains a quality of the unexpected. Often by this very quality, the action leads the reader back to the motives which produced it, motives implicitly accepted or condemned in terms of universally recognized concepts — love, benevolence, compassion, justice — which might however be strangely mutated by factors peculiar to individual, sect, district or nation. The character of Jeanie Deans is most perfectly expressed by her solitary journey on foot from Edinburgh to London to obtain a royal pardon for her sister, a journey which she undertakes without resources, rather than make the false declaration which would more easily, more certainly and even, apparently, more humanely, have brought about the same result, and which everyone, even her own father, hopes that she will make. Jeanie, as an individual, has been so conditioned by heredity and upbringing that no other possibility is really open to her.

Her action is remarkable, but in itself neither praise-worthy nor blame-worthy:— "'Tis evident, that when we praise any actions, we regard only the motives that produced them, and consider the actions as signs or indications of certain principles in the mind and temper. The external performance has no merit. We must look within to find the moral quality" (Hume, *Treatise*, III.ii.1.).

It is Jeanie's motives, not her actions, that make her unique and admirable; her father, for instance, though even more a Cameronian than herself, could not have made the journey, and Effie's life demonstrates that environment and heredity alone can not produce a Jeanie. The biography of Helen Walker, however, shows the possibility of such a development, which becomes imaginatively credible in terms of the way in which Jeanie's character has been shaped by her life-history, as revealed in chapter VIII -X of the novel.

Her father was the true-blue Presbyterian, Davie Deans, who "stude beside blessed Alexander Peden, when I heard him call the death and testimony of our happy martyrs but draps of blude and scarts of ink in respect of fitting discharge of our duty". Her mind was filled with the glory of Covenanting steadfastness, "the persecuted remnant . . . warstling wi' hunger, and cauld, and fear of death, and danger of fire and sword, upon wet brae-sides, peat-haggs, and flow-mosses". Her father adhered to his tradition, and rejected the Scottish courts; "I haud a' your gleg-tongued advocates that sell their knowledge for pieces of silver — and your worldy-wise judges, that will gie three days of hearing in presence to a debate about the peeling of an ingan, and no ae half-hour to the gospel testimony — as legalists and formalists, countenancing, by sentences, and quirks, and cunning terms of law, the late begun courses of national defections — union, toleration, patronages, and Yerastian prelatic oaths".

On the death of her mother, when Jeanie was scarcely more than a baby, Davie "so schooled and trained the young minion, as he called her, that from the time she could talk, upwards, she was daily employed in some task or other suitable to her age and capacity; a circumstance which, added to her father's daily instructions and lectures, tended to give her mind, even when a child, a grave, serious, firm and reflecting cast. An uncommonly strong and healthy temperament, free from all nervous affections and every other irregularity, which, attacking the body in its more noble functions, so often influences the mind, tended greatly to establish this fortitude, simplicity, and decision of character". Her sense of responsibility and compassion was fostered by the help she gave to the physical weaknesses of the young Reuben Butler, the grandson of a neighbour, and by her care for her half-sister Effie, some fifteen years younger than herself.

Yet, at the same time, she had learned that it might sometimes be better to bridle her compassion. "'Do ye mind,' she said, 'Effie, when you were in the fever before we left Woodend, and how angry your mother, that's now in a better place, was wi' me for gieing ye milk and water to drink, because ye grat for it? Ye were a bairn then, and ye are a woman now, and should ken better than to ask what canna but hurt you — But come weal or wo, I canna refuse ye onything that ye ask me wi' the tear in your ee.'" Yet she does refuse. The power of Davie Deans's influence is most clearly shown by the fact that, even in the Tolbooth under sentence of death, Effie cannot ask her sister to swear falsely on her behalf. "'No, Jeanie,' replied her sister, after an effort, 'I am better minded now. At my best, I was never half sae gude as ye were, and what for suld you begin to mak yoursel waur to save me, now that I am no worth saving? God knows, that in my sober mind, I wadna wuss ony living creature to do a wrang thing to save my life. I might have fled frae this tolbooth on that awfu' night wi' ane wad hae carried me through the warld, and befriended me, and fended for me. But I said to them, let life gang when gude fame is gane before it.'"

Scott's philosophical position differs from that of Hume, but it is not difficult to see how sympathy, together with the concurrence of association of ideas and association of impression in one object, Effie, make it inevitable that Jeanie's nature should choose the more arduous and more heroic way of rescuing her sister. Jeanie is a rational being, but at this stage reason scarcely comes into play. Although the seat of royal power is now almost unimaginably distant ("far ayont the saut sea", says poor Effie), the status, still comparatively recent, of Edinburgh as a capital city makes it instinctive in Jeanie to think of appealing in person to royalty on her sister's behalf. It is only after this central decision has been made, and only in order to carry it out, that reason leads her to ask the Laird of Dumbiedykes for "a small sum to pay my expenses" and Reuben Butler for a letter to the descendant of his grandfather's patron, the Duke of Argyle — "gie me the paper for MacCallummore, and bid God speed me on my way".

In lowland Scotland, the dominant external factors in moral decision-making were religion and politics; much depended on whether a person was an extreme or a moderate Presbyterian, an Episcopalian, or a Catholic; whether his or her sympathies were Hanoverian or Jacobite. Broadly speaking, the moderate Presbyterians inclined to the House of Hanover, while Episcopalians and Catholics were Jacobite, and extreme Presbyterians took an almost equally unfavourable view of both forms of political allegiance. More ultimately important, perhaps, was the inclination of the moderate, and eventually even the extreme, Presbyterians towards an innovative, "improving" form of society; of the remainder towards something more conservative and hierarchical. Religious and political affiliations were related to ties of kinship, but these were often fragile. Scott's study of Jeanie Deans shows all these things, not merely by externals, but inwardly, and so with a double vividness. Jeanie is an individual, unique, but not isolated from her society, whether that is regarded as Edinburgh, Scotland or Great Britain. The influences which affect her have affected everyone else — the Scottish legal system which condemned Effie and tried unsuccessfully to reprieve Captain Porteous; the English alternative which hanged Meg Murdockson on Harabee and lynched her daughter; the mob; the political system which set Queen Caroline and the Duke of Argyle at odds, but united them in admiration of an uncouth girl from Scotland; the possibility of improving the moral, as well as the agricultural, system of the country as a whole. Davie Deans eventually played a part in agricultural improvement, but Jeanie, the true Heart of Midlothian in the title, is the instinctive source of moral betterment and the healing of old divisions in her society.

ii

I do not wish to suggest that Scott was exclusively concerned with psychological and other forms of naturalism, although to a limited degree this was so, particularly in his treatment of the central characters in his narratives. Henry Morton in *Old Mortality* is one of several possible masculine counterparts to Jeanie Deans. The charge of colourlessness often urged against these figures results largely from the fact that they are presented in a calmly realistic way, which differs strikingly from the simpler, often more immediately vivid and comic, presentation of others, whose apparent importance in the narrative is less. Such characters generally, but not invariably, belong to the lower orders of society. Scott makes an interesting comment on this, which will be discussed below; here it is enough to say that his method with so-called minor characters often comes close to that of Ben Jonson in his comedy of humours, still in Scott's day sometimes to be seen on the stage, and available, of course, in every gentleman's library. Scott's success as a novelist derives from the combination of naturalism in his main characters, realism in his settings, and the possibility of allegorical and other more abstract effects implicit in comedy of humours.

In *Progress and Poetry* I attempted to show that there was no absolute break separating earlier Scottish literature from that of the Enlightenment[4]. This earlier literature, as exemplified, for instance, by Sir David Lindsay's *Ane Satyre of the Thrie Estaitis*, often shares features with comedy of humours; in particular, the abstract pattern of its personification-allegory is often combined with a realistic and satirical portrayal of contemporary society. Scott was well acquainted with this literature. He and his friends edited, or financed editions of, many texts, quotations from which are to be found in the body of his novels, or were used therein to head individual chapters. He was also, of course, widely read in English literature, echoes and quotations of which often occur in his work. His prose, in short, has a rich verbal texture, something which any attempt at analysis must take into account. *The Antiquary* (1816) is one of the most richly textured among his novels, high in Scott's own esteem, and always much appreciated by the common reader. It has fared less well with the critics, partly at least because variety of the kind that characterizes such stylistic richness does not always fit the assumption that the novel as a form is inevitably naturalistic. As the point is of importance for the general thesis of this book, it may be worth while to discuss it here at some length.

"The Problem of Coherence in *The Antiquary*", Robin Mayhead's title for an interesting study[5], is significant. He does not himself fully accept the idea, put forward by others whom he quotes, that in the book "heterogeneous elements are yoked by violence together", and that it contains "discordant juxtapositions" and "purposes mistook"; heterogeneity nevertheless is the foundation on which he builds his interpretation, which regretfully I do not find completely satisfying. He is right to emphasize that abstract patterns play a part in the novel, but to make, as he does, the unifying theme The Vanity of Human Wishes is to miss some essential features — not least, how it is possible for David Daiches, another good critic whom he quotes, to feel that in *The Antiquary* "the prevailing atmosphere is comic"[6].

In two separate sentences (pp.141-2 and 145), Dr Mayhead hints at one aspect of what is otherwise missing. The first sets the kind of tradition in which Scott felt himself to be writing, a tradition which belongs to the eighteenth century and to earlier writers with whom the eighteenth century felt a particular kinship. "More to the point, though, is to think of writers Scott knew especially well: Swift, Dryden, Ben Jonson, and, once again, the Samuel Johnson of *The Vanity of Human Wishes*". To this I personally would add the Scottish writers of the period from the sixteenth to the eighteenth centuries already mentioned here or in *Progress and Poetry*.

The second illustrates one literary technique by which Scott is linked to the predecessors listed above, and at the same time introduces Edie Ochiltree, one of the principal characters of the novel:— "To complain that he is too conveniently on hand to help out, is to expect a realistic convention alien to this novel, for Edie is almost an allegorical embodiment of dependability where so many others lack it, and Scott presses this point home." Dependability is, I think, only one, relatively minor, aspect of Edie, but the suggestion of personification-allegory as part of Scott's stock-in-trade serves to link him still further with his predecessors, all of whom made extensive use of just this technique, often, but not invariably, for purposes of satire. One recalls King Humanitie and his attendants in *Ane Satyre of the Thrie Estaitis* and Peter, Martin and Jack in *A Tale of a Tub*. In *The Hind and the Panther*, Dryden combines personification-allegory with the beast-fable, as does Ben Jonson in *Volpone*. Undiluted personification-allegory reappears in *The Alchemist*, with Subtle, Face, Lovewit and Sir Epicure Mammon, and it dominates the verse of Samuel Johnson in *The Vanity of Human Wishes*:—

> With distant voice neglected Virtue calls,
> Less heard and less, the faint remonstrance falls;
> Tir'd with contempt, she quits the slipp'ry reign,
> And Pride and Prudence take her place in vain.
> In crowd at once, where none the pass defend,
> The harmless Freedom, and the private Friend.
> The guardians yield, by force superior ply'd;
> To Int'rest, Prudence; and to Flatt'ry, Pride.
> Now Beauty falls, betray'd, despis'd, distress'd,
> And hissing Infamy proclaims the rest.
>   (331-340)

(Johnson's use here of the heroic couplet is as diagrammatic as any scene in *The Man of Feeling*, but more powerful, because the sequence of events is more concentrated in presentation, and more accurately observed. Note the ironic precision of "harmless" and the emotional power of the carefully positioned "distress'd". Ten lines are more than equivalent to half the episode of Miss Atkins. The names in Mackenzie's fiction are individual, but Johnson uses either abstracts or, occasionally, common nouns — "Friend", for instance, in "the private Friend", used like Ami in the *Roman de la Rose* - which are little more than abstractions.No one, however, can deny the power of Johnson's brief narrative. Allegory cannot, perhaps, have the absolute narrative effectiveness of complete naturalism; nevertheless, in the hands of a Johnson, or a Pope, or indeed a David Lindsay, the power is considerable — a point not to be forgotten when one is discussing Scott.)

Ben Jonson, even more than Samuel Johnson, is particularly important for *The Antiquary*. *The Alchemist*, for instance, is quoted at the end of chapter 23 (II.viii), when Oldbuck turns on Dousterswivel after the discovery of the second treasure at St Ruth:—

> "Why, Mr. Dousterswivel, do you pretend to have had any hand in our good success? — you forget you refused us all aid of your science, man. And you are here without your weapons that should have fought the battle, which you pretend to have gained in our behalf. You have used neither charm, lamen, sigil, talisman, spell, crystal, pentacle, magic mirror, nor geomantic figure. Where be your periapts and your abracadabras, man? your May-fern, your vervain,
>
>> Your toad, your crow, your dragon, and your panther,
>> Your sun, your moon, your firmament, your adrop,
>> Your Lato, Azoch, Zernich, Chibrit, Heautarit,
>> With all your broths, your menstrues, your materials,
>> Would burst a man to name? —
>
> Ah! rare Ben Jonson! long peace to thy ashes for a scourge of the quacks of thy day! — who expected to see them revive in our own?"[7]

Dr Mayhead remarks (p.144):— "It is not surprising that *The Antiquary* should be Scott's most Ben Jonsonian work as well as his most Samuel Johnsonian, for the extremes of character and situation he here depicts lead to a use of 'Humour' characters, of representative types (and consider the naming of so many of them), which again we can find elsewhere in Scott, but not on such a scale".

Such features are not derivative only of *The Alchemist*: for example, it has not, I think, previously been noted that Lovel, the appropriately named forlorn lover and lost heir, whose restoration to his father and resumption of his proper place in society (together with his marriage) brings the work to a conclusion, is consciously modelled on Lovel the hero of Ben Jonson's least publicly successful play *The New Inn*, from which Scott quotes eight lines as the motto to chapter 2. In *The Antiquary*, the name is assumed, presumably from the play, as Mr Oldbuck is quick to recognize. "Lovel? yes, Lovel or Belville are just the names which youngsters are apt to assume on such occasions — on my life, I am sorry for the lad." Lovel, it will be remembered, in Jonson's play is a melancholy gentleman, who secludes himself in the New Inn at Barnet, when he despairs of winning Frances, the young Lady Frampul, whose name (*frampold* in OED) means "sour-tempered, cross, disagreeable, peevish", adjectives appropriate with only the slightest modulation to the behaviour, not only of Jonson's character, but of Isabella Wardour at the beginning of *The Antiquary*, at least so far as *her* Lovel is concerned. One recollects Edie's words in chapter 12:— "Dinna ye sneer awa the lad Lovel, as ye did a while sinsyne on the walk beneath the Brierybank, when I saw ye baith, and heard ye too, though ye saw nae me". *The New Inn* ends with the reconciliation of Frances and Lovel, a reconciliation which also involves the restoration of her father, mother and sister, the long-lost Lord and Lady Frampul and Laetitia, all of whom had played a disguised part in the action at the New Inn. In *The Antiquary*, the situation is reversed; it is Lovel who is revealed as the rightful son and heir of Lord Glenallan, and who marries the frampold Isabella.

Scott's conscious literary debt extended well beyond the authors mentioned by Dr Mayhead (and equally beyond what I shall add. Neither of us, for instance, tackles the field of antiquarian and alchemical literature, about which Scott is precise and accurate). To limit oneself to Scottish literature, in chapter 6 Scott, or rather the Antiquary, mentions a work, the relevance of which extends beyond its immediate context, "the history of Sister Margaret" — *The History*, that is to say, *of the Proceedings in the Case of Margaret, Commonly Called Peg, Only Sister to John Bull Esq.*, a continuation (1761), by the Adam Ferguson already often mentioned as a pioneer sociologist, of John Arbuthnot's *The History of John Bull* (1712), briefly discussed in *Progress and Poetry*[8]. Arbuthnot's work in turn is related to *A Tale of a Tub*, which had appeared a decade earlier, and indeed, as the publication was anonymous, was itself often attributed to Swift. Scott was well aware of the true authorship, but included *The History of John Bull* in his edition of Swift, published two years before *The Antiquary*[9]. His comments are interesting:— "It is not only a satire original in its outline, but the exquisite simplicity, brevity and solemnity of the narrative is altogether inimitable. . . . With the disadvantage of northern birth and education, he (Arbuthnot) wrote a pure English style, although it may be remarked that he sometimes calls in the aid of national idiom, where he conceives it will add force to his picture. Lewis Baboon is for example termed 'a false loon', and the whole character, conduct and language of Sister Peg is traced with a Scottish pencil".

John Bull and *Sister Margaret* exploit personification-allegory and the animal fable for historical, political and satiric purposes. In such a context, the comments of the most recent editors of *John Bull*[10] may help to establish the critical attitude most appropriate for consideration of *The Antiquary*:—

> We need not regard "allegory" ("a speaking otherwise") as simply a trope in which a second meaning is to be read beneath and concurrent with the narrative surface. In good allegory much is happening, and our effort of interpretation must be itself an "unfolding of the subject" on several levels at once, not the quickly exhausted game of one to one equations. Arbuthnot collaborated with history, the inexhaustible story-teller, in creating his pamphlets; we as his readers must collaborate with the story and with history: but there is a unique pleasure to be derived, in Ellen Layburn's words, from 'the indirection which compels the search of the imagination and its consequent leap into the significance of . . . allegorical satire'.

Scott twice refers to a much earlier Scottish personification-allegory (in this case a dream-allegory), with strong political and historical overtones. In chapter 3 the Antiquary is described as possessing a copy of *The Complaynt of Scotland* (c. 1550)[11]:—"For that mutilated copy of the Complaynt of Scotland, I sat out the drinking of two dozen bottles of strong ale with the late learned proprietor, who, in gratitude, bequeathed it to me by his last will". The book is less directly introduced in chapter 22 (II.vii), where the Antiquary quotes an important marginal note from it to confute Sir Arthur's superstitious belief in planetary influences:— "Simple suffumigation? simple nonsensification — planetary hour? planetary fiddlestick — *sapiens dominabitur astris*". The very condensed Latin is difficult to translate; the meaning may perhaps be paraphrased as "The philosopher will exercise a dominance over his own life superior to that exercised by the planets".

Formally *The Complaynt of Scotland* is a prose equivalent of earlier verse dream-allegories (*The Kingis Quair* and *The Palice of Honour* are Scottish examples which come to mind), and as Scott's friend, John Leyden (1775-1811), remarked in his edition, published in 1801:— "the work is naturally divided in three parts, of which the first may be properly denominated, the Complaint of the author; the second, the Monologue of the author; and the third, the Dream of the author, or the Complaynt of Scotland. In the first, the author, deeply afflicted by the miseries of his country, begins to speculate concerning their causes. In the second, which has little connexion either with the first or the third, a variety of rural scenes and occupations are depicted, which are ingeniously diversified with a sea fight and a dissertation on natural philosophy. This division is terminated by the author falling into a profound sleep, during the unsuccessful experiment of shutting his eyes, and looking through his eye-lids; and, in the third part, he relates his dream or vision. The subject of the third part is the same with that of the first — the miseries of Scotland; but the description is more particular, and the machinery is allegorical"(p.74).

Sapiens dominabitur astris is a marginal comment on the conclusion of the dissertation on natural philosophy delivered by a shepherd as part of the Monologue of the author, the second part of the *Complaynt*. It refers to the words "Al thir thingis befor rehersit, of the circlis of the speir, & of the hauynis and planetis, is said, to gar zou considir that man kynd is subiect to the planetis and to ther influens. ther for ve suld prepair and prouid to resist ther euil constellations. for quhou be it that thai ar the instramentis of god, zit nochtheless he of his gudnes resistis there euyl influens, fra tyme that ve be cum obedient tyl his command"[12]. Leyden thought that this part had little connexion with the remainder of *The Complaynt*, but with the better understanding of dream-allegory now available, it is possible to see that the Monologue of the author presents two images — the ship, and the life of the shepherds — of the uncorrupted world, which stands in Boethian contrast to the Complaynt of the author and the Complaynt of Scotland, the first and third parts of the work as a whole. The ship, which becomes involved in a naval battle, is also an image of the precarious state of the uncorrupted world. *Sapiens dominabitur astris* comes significantly at the climax of the demonstration of order in the world of the five elements. Part 3, the dream-vision proper, treats circumstances in Scotland after the shameful defeat by the English at Pinkie (1547), in terms of Alain Chartier's *Quadrilogue invectif* (1422), composed after the shameful French defeat by the English at Agincourt (1415), and in the form of a dialogue (or, as Chartier would have said, a quadrilogue) between Dame Scotia and her three sons "callit the thre estaitis of Scotland " — the Temporality (nobility and gentry), Spirituality (bishops and mitred abbots), and Commonalty (merchants and burgesses), who, with the post-Reformation exception of the mitred abbots, made up the Scottish Parliament before the Union of 1707.

The Three Estates make a similar allegorical appearance in *The Antiquary*, indirectly by way of *The Complaynt of Scotland*, more directly by way of a series of later literary reminiscences which stems from Swift. In *A Tale of a Tub*, the brothers Peter, Martin and Jack (St Peter, Martin Luther and John Calvin) represent the three chief traditions of western Christianity since the Reformation. Each inherits from his father a coat, representing the doctrine and discipline of his particular church. Swift's successful development of this clothing metaphor led to its adoption and adaptation by others. Thus in Allan Ramsay's *A Tale of Three Bonnets*[13], first published anonymously in 1722, Bristle, Joukum and Bawsy are three brothers, each left a bonnet by their father, Duniwhistle, on his death-bed, with instructions to keep them for ever:—

Here's three Permission Bonnets for ye,
Which your *Grand Gutchers* wore before ye;
And if ye'd hae nae Man betray ye,
Let naithing ever wile them frae ye,
But keep the Bonnets on your Heads,
And Hands from signing foolish Deeds,
And ye shall never want sic Things
Shall gar ye be made of by Kings:
But if you ever with them part,
Fou sair ye'll for your Folly smart.
                              (Canto 1, 21-30)

Joukum however is seduced by Rosie to hand over his own and Bawsy's bonnet, an action which renders Bristle as well as Bawsy subject to Rosie and Joukum. Bristle saves something of his independence with his bonnet, which he is now forced to keep locked away. Ramsay's most recent editors, A.M. Kinghorn and A. Law remark[14]:— "Rosie is England, Joukum and Bawsy weak and easily swayed Scotsmen, Bristle an independent Scotsman, and the theme is the Union of Parliaments and its sequel".

An even more precise interpretation is, I think, possible. Bristle, Joukum and Bawsy represent party alignments in the final session of the Three Estates; their bonnets, primarily the symbol of their freedom to make independent decisions (Permission Bonnets), become, secondly, the votes cast for or against the 1707 Act of Union. The Articles were passed with votes generally 2:1 in favour; the actual numbers were of the order 100:50. The bonnets of Joukum and Bawsy represent the affirmative majority; that of Bristle the dissident minority. The fact that Bristle retains his bonnet, though he keeps it hidden, is a hint at Jacobite separatism, based on the *status quo* of the reign of James VII.

In Ramsay, the three bonnets are partly identified with the Three Estates. Scott produced an individual variation. By the 1790's, still more the second decade of the nineteenth century, the Three Estates were long superannuated, and in *The Antiquary* they are represented by the three wigs, which survive all changes of fashion to adorn the parish in lonely glory. Sir Arthur Wardour represents Temporality — he is a baronet. The minister, the Rev. Mr Blattergowl, is Spirituality, and the

Antiquary himself, with his German printer ancestor and father who has been provost of Fairport, is Merchants and Burgesses. The three play little direct part in the action, but form a kind of chorus; observers, sometimes victims, but scarcely ever actors. This is most obviously true in the account (chapters 17-19: II.ii.iv) of the picnic among the ruins of St Ruth Priory, formally introduced as it is by the wigs:—

> The reverend gentleman was equipped in a buzz wig, upon the top of which was an equilateral cocked hat. This was the paragon of the three remaining wigs of the parish, which differed, as Monkbarns used to remark, like the three degrees of comparison — Sir Arthur's ramilies being the positive, his own bob-wig the comparative, and the overwhelming grizzle of the worthy clergyman figuring as the superlative."

The first interest of each wig — some aspect of the past — is pursued with a self-centred concentration which, for the speaker at least, excludes everything else:

> The orators, like three racers, each pressed forward to the goal, without much regarding how each crossed and jostled his competitors. Mr Oldbuck harangued, the Baronet declaimed, Mr Blattergowl prosed and laid down the law, while the Latin forms of feudal grants [the Antiquary] were mingled with the jargon of blazonry [Sir Arthur] and the yet more barbarous phraseology of the Teind Court of Scotland [Mr Blattergowl].

If the three wigs represent the Three Estates, it is also notable that the three chief families of the novel, the Glenallans, the Wardours and the Oldbucks, stand to each other in the same relation as Swift's three brothers, Peter, Martin and Jack. The Glenallans are Catholic, Sir Arthur Wardour is a staunch Episcopalian — 'a true though unworthy son of the Episcopal Church', as he calls himself — and Oldbuck a Presbyterian of somewhat Laodicean tendencies, well illustrated by his attitude to the minister, Mr Blattergowl:

> No divine was more attentive in visiting the sick and

afflicted, in catechising the youth, in instructing the ignorant, and in reproving the erring. And hence, notwithstanding impatience of his prolixity and prejudices, personal and professional, and notwithstanding, moreover, a certain habitual contempt for his understanding, especially on affairs of genius and taste, on which Blattergowl was apt to be diffuse, from his hope of one day fighting his way to a chair of rhetoric or belles-lettres — notwithstanding, I say, all the prejudices excited against him by these circumstances, our friend the Antiquary looked with great regard and respect on the said Blattergowl, though I own he could seldom, even by his sense of decency and the remonstrances of his womankind, be *hounded out*, as he called it, to hear him preach.

(This must surely be the longest, most obliquely constructed, and most legalistically qualified sentence in Scott's entire *opus*!)

The division is re-emphasised when Edie seeks alms at the Catholic Glenallan House:

"Are ye a triple man, friend, that ye press forward sae bauldly? — I'm thinking no, for there's nae Catholics wear that badge."

"Na, na, I am no a Roman", said Edie.

"Then shank yoursell awa to the double folk, or single folk, that's the Episcopals or Presbyterians yonder — it's a shame to see a heretic hae sic a long white beard, that would do credit to a hermit."

Dr Mayhead's second comment, that on Edie Ochiltree, is now, I hope, beginning to come into some kind of focus. The presentation of Edie is as much allegorical as that of the three wigs, or the three families. He corresponds to the Poor Man, or to John the Commonweal in Lindsay's *Ane Satyre*, and personifies natural man, human nature, fallen from an absolute good, of which nevertheless it retains manifold traces; human nature, let us say, viewed, not by a Calvinist, but by a moderate and tolerant Scottish Episcopalian, such as Scott himself was. Necessarily, he lacks material resources. "Father Adam" and "old Adam" are the terms significantly applied to him by Lieutenant

Taffril in the duel scene (chapter 20: II.v.), where Edie certainly is the voice of natural feeling, as opposed to the socially conditioned posturing of the duellists:—

> "Are ye come amongst the most lovely works of God to break His laws? Have ye left the works of man, the houses and the cities that are but clay and dust, like these that built them; and are ye come here among the peaceful hills, and by the quiet waters, that will last whiles aught earthly will endure, to destroy each other's lives, that will have but an unco short time, by the course of nature, to make up a lang account at the close o't? O sirs! hae ye brothers, sisters, fathers, that hae tended ye, and mothers that hae travailed for ye, friends that hae ca'd ye like a piece o' their ain heart? And is this the way ye tak to make them childless and brotherless and friendless? Ohon! it's an ill feight whar he that wins has the warst o't. Think on't, bairns. I'm a puir man — but I'm an auld man too — and what my poverty takes awa frae the weight o' my counsel, grey hairs and a truthfu' heart should add it twenty times. Gang hame, gang hame, like guid lads".

Time and again Edie plays a similar part — often mingled with a little devilry, in token of his fallen nature — in encounters with Dousterswivel, with Elspeth Mucklebackit and Lord Glenallan, with Isabella Wardour and her father, even when he interrupts the Antiquary's ecstatic vision of the battle of Mons Graupius fought on the Kaim of Kinprunes:— "Praetorian here, Praetorian there, I mind the bigging o't"(chapter 4).

The form of *The Antiquary* is to some extent governed by the fact that it was originally published in three volumes, and it is significant that the first two volumes each concludes (in chapters 15 and 19) with the figure of Edie.

So far, almost everything I have said suggests that history, politics and religion form in some sense the allegorical subject-matter, and govern the detailed development of *The Antiquary*, a suggestion borne out, at least in part, by the original Advertisement, in which Scott briefly discussed the aims which in his first three novels he had set himself:—

"The present Work completes a series of fictitious narratives, intended to illustrate the manners of Scotland at three different periods. WAVERLEY embraced the age of our fathers, GUY MANNERING that of our own youth, and the ANTIQUARY refers to the last ten years of the eighteenth century. I have, in the last two narratives, especially, sought my principal personages in the class of society who are the last to feel the influence of that general polish which assimilates to each other the manners of different nations".

The three books mentioned established the literary form of the historical novel, yet none is historical in the sense of belonging to a past remote from the author (as, for instance, is Flaubert's *Salammbo*, set in ancient Carthage). Initially at least, Scott kept well within the span of domestic tradition — his time-scale scarcely differs from that of the main-stream eighteenth-century novel. *Waverley* is sub-titled "'Tis Sixty Years Since". Defoe's *A Journal of the Plague Year* (1722) deals with events fifty-seven years earlier; the central historical incident in Fielding's *Amelia* (1751) is the seige of Gibralter (1727-8), during which Booth, Amelia's husband, was twice wounded. In his later novels, it is true, Scott sometimes very considerably overstepped these limits — often to the detriment of his fiction.

As the repetition of the word shows, Scott classified his work as comedy of manners, but with a difference, as witness the reference to the social position of his principal personages. By those he intends Dandy Dinmont, Meg Merrilees and Dominie Sampson in *Guy Mannering*, Edie Ochiltree and the Mucklebackits in *The Antiquary* — the people who represent humanity in a state closest to the natural, and who are immediately responsible for the major turns in the action. The part played by Edie in particular has already been discussed, but receives additional emphasis from the plot. After the duel with Macintyre, Lovel necessarily leaves Fairport. From the safe distance of Edinburgh, where he resumes his own name, he entrusts his business to Edie, whose naturally subterranean way of life make him an appropriate instrument for the task.

Scott also makes a distinction between the method used in his first, and in his two subsequent, novels, indicating — properly, I believe — that *Waverley* is prentice work, in which he had not yet fully developed the art visible in *Guy Mannering* and *The Antiquary*. Scott's knowledge of Highland life and character, central though it appears to *Waverley*, was pretty well confined to the external picturesque, a quality which still ensures the popularity of the book, as it earlier had that of *The Lady of the Lake* (1810); his genius as novelist and poet included much which neither work gave any real chance of development.

The gradual assimilation of Scottish manners to some kind of European norm may be illustrated by the fact that in *Waverley* the class which stands outside the norm includes not only the Baron of Bradwardine and his circle, but, at least in intention, the entire Gaelic-speaking world as it existed before Culloden and the Clearances; that in *Guy Mannering* it has become restricted to smugglers, gypsies and remote hill-farmers; in *The Antiquary* still further to beggars and fisher-folk. But this is not all. Although the general assimilation is readily visible, it remains at most superficial. In *The Antiquary*, which deals with the most recent, and therefore, it might be expected, the most normative series of events, the present existence of the three great families is still almost totally shaped, and indeed perverted, by a remote past which is Scottish rather than European. In psychological terms, the actions of the Glenallans (and Cheynes, as represented by the Mucklebackit grandmother, Elspeth) are governed by the outcome of Harlaw (1411), a battle fought four centuries earlier between Lowlands and Highlands:—

> "Did not somebody say that Joscelind, Countess of Glenallan, was departed from life?"
>
> "They said the truth, whaever said it," answered old Edie; "she was buried yestre'en by torchlight at St Ruth's, and I, like a fule, gat a gliff wi' seeing the lights and the riders."
>
> "It was their fashion since the days of the Great Earl that was killed at Harlaw — They did it to show scorn that they should die and be buried like other mortals. The wives o' the house of Glenallan wailed nae wail for the husband, nor the sister for the brother."
>
> (chapter 26: II.xi.)

Elspeth Mucklebackit's relation to the Countess is governed by her descent from the Ronald Cheyne whose advice led the Great Earl to his death in a preliminary skirmish at Harlaw:—

Were I Glenallan's Earl this tide,
  And ye were Ronald Cheyne,
The spur should be in my horse's side,
  And the bridle upon his mane.

If they hae twenty thousand blades,
  And we twice ten times ten,
Yet they hae but their tartan plaids,
  And we are mail-clad men.
                                    (chapter 40: III.xi.)

Conversely, she is also "the daughter of that Reginald Cheyne, who died to save his master, Lord Glenallan, on the field of Sherriffmuir" in 1715, during the first Jacobite rising. Harlaw and Sherriffmuir alike are tragi-comically refought in the duel (chapter 20: II.v.) between Lovel, the lost heir of Glenallan, and the Antiquary's Gaelic-speaking nephew, Hector M'Intyre, which indirectly leads to the restoration of the Glenallan line.

Sir Arthur Wardour's ancestral fixation is with his bastard predecessor, Malcolm Misticot:—

> "They ca'd them the Norman Wardours, though they cam frae the south to this country — So this Sir Richard, that they ca'd Red-hand, drew up wi the auld Knockwinnock o' that day, for then they were Knock-winnocks o' that Ilk, and wad fain marry his only daughter, that was to have the castle and the land. Laith, laith was the lass — (Sybil Knockwinnock they ca'd her that tauld me the tale) — laith, laith was she to gae into the match, for she had fa'en a wee ower thick wi' a cousin o' her ain that her father had some ill-will to; and sae it was, that after she had been married to Sir Richard jimp four months — for marry him she maun it's like — ye'll no hinder her gieing them a present o' a bonny knave bairn."
> (chapter 24: II.x. — the speaker, of course is Edie)

It is this Misticot who, in terms of Norman law, usurped the barony, built Misticot's Tower, and was buried with all his worldly goods in St Ruth's. "But the prophecy gat abroad in the country, that whenever Misticot's grave was fund out, the estate of Knockwinnock should be lost and won". The Wardour fixation has two causes. One is the normal gentlemanly distaste for bastardy. The second is perhaps the more important. In terms of the Celtic law, which preceded that of the Normans, Misticot was the legal heir to the estate of Knockwinnock, and his usurpation — "down came this Malcolm, the love-begot, frae Glen-isla, wi' a string o' lang-legged Highlanders at his heels, that's aye ready for onybody's mischief, and he threeps the castle and lands are his ain as his mother's eldest son, and turns a' the Wardours out to the hill" — his usurpation is merely the assertion of his proper rights. From one point of view, that is to say, the Wardours are the usurpers, and a sense of guilt is necessarily mingled with their pride of ancestry. The hereditary mixture of guilt with distaste motivates Sir Arthur's initial hostility to Lovel, at least partly shared by his daughter, a hostility inflamed during the unfortunate dinner given by the Antiquary, which determines the Wardours' choice of home-ward route along the sands, their near-destruction, and eventual rescue by Lovel.

The duel between Lovel and Macintyre, a rival suitor for the hand of Miss Wardour, parodies the single combat between brothers which led to the restoration of the Wardours to Knockwinnock. Here however the supposedly illegitimate is the victor, and eventually, during the rumoured French invasion, the combatants are completely reconciled. Lovel, the modern Mis-ticot, is also the instrument whereby the treasure is recovered, the lands of Knockwinnock are lost and won, and general harmony is not so much restored as created after centuries of dissension.

The Antiquary's fixation, finally, is with his great ancestor "Aldobrand Oldenbuck, my great-great-great-grandfather — it's a shame to the English language that we have not a less clumsy way of expressing a relationship, of which we have occasion to think and speak so frequently" (chapter 9). Aldobrand's motto, *Kunst macht Gunst*, "That is, skill, or prudence, in availing ourselves of our natural talents and advantages, will compel favour and patronage, even where it is withheld from prejudice or ignorance" (chapter 11), mysteri-ously revealed to Lovel by his dream in the Green Room, and illustrated by the story of how Aldobrand won the hand of his master's daughter, is adopted by him to his own advantage, and eventually leads to his restoration and marriage with Isabella Wardour.

Three further points are important. The characterization of Lord Glenallan, as well as Sir Arthur and the Antiquary, may serve almost as text-book illustrations of such later theories of comedy as Bergson's. (It is this, primarily, which led to David Daiches' comment quoted above.) The presentation of Sir Arthur, it might be objected, is melodramatic to a degree, that of Lord Glenallan almost exclusively so, but in Bergsonian terms melodrama is a form of the comic rather than a corruption of the tragic:—

> Yes, indeed, these whimsical wild enthusiasts, these madmen who are yet so strangely reasonable, excite us to laughter by playing on the same chords within ourselves, by setting in motion the same inner mechanism, as does the victim of a practical joke or the passer-by who slips down in the street. They, too, are runners who fall and simple souls who are being hoaxed — runners after the ideal who stumble over realities, child-like dreamers for whom life delights to lie in wait. But, above all, they are past-masters in absent-mindedness, with the superiority over their fellows that their absent-mindedness is systematic and organized around one central idea, and that their mishaps are also quite coherent, thanks to the inexorable logic which reality applies to the correction of dreams, so that they kindle in those around them, by a series of cumulative effects, a hilarity capable of unlimited expansion.[15]

Dousterswivel is a more broadly drawn specimen of the same species — one whose vice has "the same relation to character that the rigidity of a fixed idea has to intellect. . . . The vice capable of making us comic is . . . that which is brought from without, like a ready-made frame into which we are to step. It lends us its own rigidity instead of borrowing from us our flexibility. We do not render it more complicated; on the contrary, it simplifies us".[16] Bergson's exemplars are found primarily in the works of Cervantes, Moliere and La Bruyere, but Lindsay, Jonson, Swift or Arbuthnot would have served him almost as well. In *The Antiquary*, the figures of Bergsonian comedy are all to be judged in terms of Edie Ochiltree, who is seen, for the most part, in direct contact and contrast with them.

The cure for the various obsessions is to be found, however, not with Edie, but with Lovel. Even in the brief summaries given above, he is clearly both medicine and physician. In the case of Dousterswivel, Lovel is present (with Edie) when he practises on Sir Arthur's superstition at midnight in St Ruth's (chapter 21:II.vi.); he is the agent of the successful ruse *Search No. II* (chapter 24: II.ix.), and although an act of God is the immediate agency by which the absconding magician is captured, yet "he would have found twigs limed for him at Edinburgh" (chapter 42: III.xiii.). Lovel's eponymous status as despised, but persistent and eventually successful lover, expands, like that of Vanbeest Brown, the true heir of Ellangowan in *Guy Mannering*, to become that of general saviour. He restores the parish to itself as, in terms of the allegory, he restores Scotland.

Scott has one curious capacity, which may be described, though not quite in the sense intended by Keats, as negative capability. The plot of *The Antiquary* depends on one absence and two non-events. Lovel disappears in chapter 22 (II.vii.) and reappears, as *deus ex machina* in the person of Major Neville, only in chapter 45 (III,xvi.). His absence contributes of course to narrative suspense, but a more important effect is to make the reader aware that the text in front of him constitutes no more than the foreground of the action; that it belongs to, and depends on, a larger field of affairs, which in general is invisible. When Edie talks (chapter 12) to Isabella about her meeting with Lovel at the Brierybank, a meeting not otherwise mentioned or described, he contributes in a smaller way to the same effect. The ability to show with minimum fuss that an external world exists as much for the people inside the novel as for those outside is one of Scott's strengths as a novelist, and in particular as a historical novelist.

The two non-events contribute to the same effect. First is the *Caledoniad*, the epic poem which Lovel did not write, despite all Mr Oldbuck's pleas:—

> "It should be something at once solid and attractive
> — none of your romances or anomalous novelties — I
> would have you take high ground at once. Let me see
> — What think you of a real epic — the grand old-

fashioned historical poem which moved through twelve or twenty-four books. We'll have it so — I'll supply you with a subject — The battle between the Caledonians and Romans — The Caledoniad; or, Invasion Repelled. Let that be the title — it will suit the present taste, and you may throw in a touch of the times."

(chapter 14)

The *Caledoniad* ends the third and final volume, as Edie ended the first two:—

He (the Antiquary) regularly enquires whether Lord Geraldin has commenced the Caledoniad, and shakes his head at the answers he receives. *En attendant*, however, he has completed his notes, which, we believe, will be at the service of anyone who chooses to make them public, without risk or expense to THE ANTIQUARY.

Scott certainly intends a side-ways glance at his own "romances or anomalous novelties", the verse-tales which he had now more or less abandoned, and especially, I suspect, to *Marmion* (1808) and the much more recent *The Lord of the Isles* (1815), in both of which he had himself thrown in "a touch of the times", as will be illustrated below. This, and the reference to the unpublished notes for the unwritten epic are half-humorous examples of the negative capability already mentioned.

The second non-event, the French landing at Fairport, is a false alarm, raised by the bonfire which consumed Dousterswivel's abandoned mining gear in Glenwithershins, but which at the same time united all divisions and in literal and allegorical terms, restored Lovel to his own. In the novel Scott virtually turned inside-out the technique he had developed in the verse-romances. There he used the distant past to illuminate his own present; here, his own present, or very recent past, re-enacts the drama of the distant past, but in such a way as to cure old ailments, so long familiar as to be no longer recognized, by action in the present. Boece's monarchs and Ossian's heroes are forgotten. The battle of Mons Graupius is brought to a new and successful issue; invasion is repelled. The warring Pictish factions of Sir Arthur and Mr Oldbuck are reconciled. Harlaw is refought and leads, not to enmity, but to friendship and close alliance. Lovel, the lost heir, emerges from the ancient Catholic aristocracy, and marries the daughter of the Episcopalian baronet, to whom he has restored good name and fortune. The Three Estates play their part, and human nature in the person of Edie is vindicated. The more superstitious and criminal aspects of the past, exemplified by Dousterswivel, are overthrown, and progress in the form of public carriages, mail-coaches, post-offices, New Inns, and piped water is set free to flourish. The fairy-tale effect of the ending is not to be condemned; rather it is an essential part of the festal allegorical comedy which Scott attempts in *The Antiquary*. There was no need, finally, for Lovel to write his *Caledoniad*: a *Caledoniad* had already been brought to a successful conclusion in *The Antiquary*.

iii

The technique developed by Scott in *The Antiquary* is a variant, or rather a development, of the distinctively Scottish mock-heroic, seen, for instance, in *Tam o' Shanter*. Burns found in peasant life and belief, and in the linguistic range open to Scots, comic equivalents of epic subject-matter and style. The prototype, in so far as one exists, for Scott's prose narrative is probably Fielding's "comic epic in prose", but whereas Fielding (and Burns too, at a rather greater remove) based the heroic features of their work almost entirely on Greek and Latin originals, Scott, as has been demonstrated, made use of a wider range of literary reference. Unconsciously he was using mock-heroic to move towards what is usually considered a twentieth century innovation, exemplified by Joyce's *Ulysses* and Eliot's *The Waste Land*, the use, that is to say, of historical parallels and echoes to impose an order, which is itself a critical assessment, on the events of modern life. The comment which Eliot made in a review of *Ulysses*[17] has a relevance more extended than perhaps its author realized or would have approved:—

> In using the myth, in manipulating a continuous parallel between contemporaneity and antiquity, Mr Joyce (read 'Mr Scott') is pursuing a method which others must pursue after him. It is simply a way of controlling and ordering, of giving a shape and a

significance to the immense panorama of futility and anarchy which is contemporary history.

Even the futility and anarchy of the second sentence bears some relation to the fictitious present of *The Antiquary*, though Scott's criticisms of the world in which his characters live are gentler than those either of Joyce or of Eliot. Elsewhere he is less forbearing. The Waste Land, which for the twentieth century is London or Dublin, finds a closer parallel in the Spaw, with its supposed healing waters, which gives its name to *St. Ronan's Well*, generally considered unique among Scott's novels, because even more than *The Antiquary*, it deals with events substantially contemporary with its date of publication (1824), and certainly well within the bounds of the nineteenth century. The events described are assumed to have taken place during the final years of the Peninsular War (1807-1814). In chapter 23 (II.10.) Clara proposes to buy herself "Campbell's new work", *Gertrude of Wyoming*, that is to say, by Thomas Campbell (1777-1844), a narrative poem which has some relevance in plot to Clara's own situation, and which was published in 1809.

Scott describes his book as "a little drama of modern life", and it is central to the thesis of this study that modern life lies just as open to the techniques of the historical novel as does the life of the past, that *St Ronan's Well*, *The Member* or *Ulysses* is as fully a historical novel as *Old Mortality* or *The Heart of Midlothian*. What matters is not the assumed period of the action, but the perspective in terms of which it unfolds, involving, as it must, some kind of complementarity, or of creative tension, between the limited present of the novel and the more extended vistas of the past, even in some cases, discussed below, of the future.

In *St Ronan's Well*, the primary opposition is between the Fox Hotel, which is the centre of social life at the Well, the elegant new resort which has grown up in the vicinity of the health-giving spring, the virtues of which were discovered by Dr. Quackleben and Lady Penelope Penfeather, and the Aultoun of St. Ronan's with its ruined castle and old-fashioned Cleikum Inn. The Aultoun still has its middens and cess-pools in the public street, and lacks a post-office, the Well has a post-office-*cum*-circulating library-*cum*-pharmacy, situated on the Parade, midway between the Hotel and the Well itself. Commercial travellers form the hotel's passing trade, and together with the

E

resident guests — the spinster Lady Penelope, the unhappily married Lady Binks, Mr Winterblossom, Captain McTurk and the others — form the Napoleonic equivalent of the rootless and sterile society of post-Great-War Europe found in *The Waste Land*:—

> Summer surprised us, coming over the Starnbergersee
> With a shower of rain; we stopped in the colonnade,
> And went on in sunlight, into the Hofgarten,
> And drank coffee, and talked for an hour.
> Bin gar keine Russin, stamm' aus Litauen, echt deutsch.
> And when we were children, staying at the archduke's,
> My cousin's, he took me out on a sled,
> And I was frightened. He said, Marie,
> Marie, hold on tight. And down we went.
> In the mountains, there you feel free.
> I read, much of the night, and go south in winter.

Polite but malicious gossip, snobbery, intrigue, card-playing, the careful cultivation of a fictitious honour, duelling, all the sterile amusements of the hotel, are eventually but inevitably productive of destruction. The book ends with the demolition of the Spaw on the instructions of the proprietor, young Mowbray, with the result (chapter 39:III.xvi.) that:—

> The little watering-place has returned to its primitive obscurity; and lions and lionesses, with their several jackalls, blue surtouts, and bluer stockings, fiddlers and dancers, painters and amateurs, authors and critics, dispersed like pigeons by the demolition of the dovecot, have sought other scenes of amusement and rehearsal, and have deserted St Ronan's Well.

The central figure in all this desolation is Bulmer, the supposed Lord Etherington, whose visit in happier days before the Hotel was opened had already wasted three lives — those of Clara Mowbray, Hannah Irwin and Frank Tyrrel. The effect is summarised by Clara's words in chapter 9:—

> "Grief," replied Clara, "is the sickness of the mind, and its sister is the sickness of the body — they are

twin-sisters, Tyrrel, and are seldom long separate. Sometimes the body's disease comes first, and dims our eyes and palsies our hands, before the fire of our mind and of our intellect is quenched. But mark me — soon after her comes her cruel sister with her urn, and sprinkles cold dew on our hopes and on our loves, our memory, our recollections, and our feelings, and shews us that they cannot survive the decay of our bodily powers."

The contrast between Clara and her treacherous former companion, Anne Heggie or Hannah Irwin, who dies miserably in child-bed, is only apparent; both are victims, not so much of Bulmer, as of the society which produced him and the Spaw as well, the destructive effects of which extend far beyond rural Scotland. At its widest extent, for instance, it is linked to the evils, as Scott saw them of colonialism. "Already the great technical superiority of Western civilization was creating the assumption of a general cultural and moral superiority which could be used as justification of expanding Empire. In particular those forms of Christianity which preached salvation by faith rather than by works . . . could claim to rescue from eternal damnation the heathen who in his blindness bowed down to wood and stone, without considering either his interests or his utterly different cultural tradition." Humphrey House, whom I quote[18], is writing about Dickens, but his words apply also to Scott, and indeed, as has been shown, to his predecessors. In *St Ronan's Well*, Scott uses Mr Touchwood and Captain MacTurk to illustrate. Touchwood professes to regard Indian civilization as superior to his own, particularly in its innocence of the custom of duelling. The Captain disagrees:—

"I'll be tamned, then!" said Captain MacTurk. "Was I not in Tippoo's prison at Bangalore? and, when the joyful day of our liberation came, did we not solemnize it with fourteen little affairs, whereof we had been laying the foundation in our house of captivity, as Holy Writ has it, and never went farther to settle them than the glacis of the fort? By my soul, you would have thought there was a smart skirmish, the firing was so close; and did not I, Captain MacTurk, fight three of them myself, without moving my foot from the place I set it on?"

"And pray, sir, what might be the result of this Christian mode of giving thanks for your deliverance?" demanded Mr Touchwood.

"A small list of casualties, after all," said the Captain; "one killed on the spot, one died of his wounds — two wounded severely — three ditto slightly, and little Duncan Macphail reported missing. We were out of practice, after such long confinement. So you see how we manage matters in India, my dear friend."

"You are to understand," replied Touchwood, "that I spoke only of the heathen natives, who, heathen as they are, live in the light of their own moral reason, and among whom ye shall therefore see better examples of practical morality than among such as yourselves; who, though calling yourselves Christians, have no more knowledge of the true acceptation and meaning of your religion, than if you had left your Christianity at the Cape of Good Hope, as they say of you, and forgot to take it up when you came back again."

"Py Got! and I can tell you, sir," said the Captain, elevating at once his voice and his nostrils, and snuffing the air with a truculent and indignant visage, "that I will not permit you or any man to throw any such scandal on my character. I thank Cot, I can bring good witness that I am as good a Christian as another, for a poor sinner, as the best of us are; and I am ready to justify my religion with my sword — Cotamn! — Compare my own self with a parcel of black heathen bodies and natives, that were never in the inner side of a kirk whilst they lived, but go about worshipping stocks and stones, and swinging themselves upon bamboos, like peasts, as they are!"

Scott sees another image of this society in the bitterness of the old woman, who is herself a charge on the parish and who unwillingly receives another, Hannah Irwin, into the miserable hovel which the Poor-law allows her:—

"Have ye no had pennyworths for your charity?"
she said, in spiteful scorn. "Ye buy the very life o' us
wi' your shillings and sixpences, your groats and your
boddles — ye hae gar'd the puir wretch speak till she
swarfs, and now ye stand as if ye never saw a woman in
a dwam before. Let me till her wi' the dram — mony
words mickle drought, ye ken — Stand out o' my gate,
my leddy, if sae be ye are a leddy; there is little use of
the like of you when there is death in the pot."

(chapter 32: III.v.).

Unusually, Scott later added to this passage a note in which he
denounced, again with Dickensian intensity, both Poor-law and
the society which produced it. "To such a point have we been
brought by an artificial system of society, that we must either
deny altogether the right of the poor to their just proportion of
the fruits of the earth, or afford them some means of subsistence
out of them by the institution of positive law." This was written
before the English Malthusian new Poor Law of 1834, but I do
not imagine that the reform would have made Scott change his
opinion. The new, as much as the old, required "legal and
compulsory assessment for the proclaimed parish pauper . . . The
alms are extorted from an unwilling hand, and a heart which
desires the annihilation, rather then the relief, of the distressed
object." Earlier in the same note he remarks, "The system of
compulsory charity by poor's rates, of which the absolute
necessity can hardly be questioned, has connected with it on both
sides some of the most odious and malevolent feelings that can
agitate humanity."

As the last quotation shows, Scott was not, and could not be, a
reformer of the Dickensian kind, but, like Dickens, he embodied
and condemned in his fiction the evils which he saw in
contemporary society. The strongest expression of his views he
puts, with no more than a modicum of caricature, in the mouth
of an actual reformer, the same Benthamite Nabob, Mr Touchwood, in conversation with Meg Dods and the banker and man
of business, Mr Bindloose. Scott would probably have agreed
with much of it, although it should not be forgotten that he
presents Touchwood's attempt to organise a kind of personal
Welfare State in the vicinity of the Well as contributing to the
final catastrophe. Touchwood's benevolence is as sterile in

ultimate effect as any plot laid by Etherington or young Mowbray:—

"That is a supposition, sir," replied the lawyer, "which it would ill become me to put — But at any rate, if you knew this country formerly, ye cannot but be marvellously pleased with the change we have been making since the American war, — hill-sides bearing clover instead of heather, — rents doubled, trebled, quadrupled, the auld reekie dungeons pulled down, and gentlemen living in as good houses as you will see anywhere in England."

"Much good may it do to them, for a pack of fools!" replied Mr Touchwood hastily.

"You do not seem much delighted with our improvements, sir," said the banker, astonished to hear a dissentient voice where he conceived all men unanimous.

"Pleased!" answered the stranger — "Yes, as much pleased as I am with the devil, who, I believe, set many of them agoing. Ye have got an idea that everything must be changed — Unstable as water, ye shall not excel — I tell ye, there have been more changes in this poor nook of yours within the last forty years, than in the great empires of the East for the space of four thousand, for what I know."

"And why not," replied Bindloose, "if they be changes for the better?"

"But they are *not* for the better," replied Mr Touchwood, eagerly, "I left your peasantry as poor as rats indeed, but honest and industrious, enduring their lot in this world with firmness, and looking forward to the next with hope — Now they are mere eye-servants — looking at their watches, forsooth, every ten minutes, lest they should work for their master half a second after loosing-time — And then, instead of studying the Bible on the work days, to kittle the clergyman with doubtful points of controversy on the Sabbath, they glean all their theology from Tom Paine and Voltaire."

"Weel I wot the gentleman speaks truth," said Mrs Dods. "I fand a bundle of their bawbee blasphemies in

my ain kitchen — But I trow I made a clean house of
the packman loon that brought them! — No content
wi' turning the tawpies' heads wi' ballants, and driving
them daft wi' ribands, to cheat them out of their
precious souls, and gie them the deevil's ware, that I
suld say sae, in exchange for the siller that suld support
their puir father that's aff wark and bedridden!"

"Father! madam," said the stranger; "they think no
more of their father than Regan or Goneril."

"In gude truth, ye have skeel of our sect, sir," replied
the dame; "they are gomerils, every one of them — I
tell them sae every hour of the day, but catch them
profiting by the doctrine."

"And then the brutes are turned mercenary,
madam," said Mr Touchwood. "I remember when a
Scottishman would have scorned to touch a shilling
that he had not earned, and yet was as ready to help a
stranger as an Arab of the desert. And now I did but
drop my cane the other day as I was riding — a fellow
who was working at the hedge made three steps to lift
it — I thanked him and my friend threw his hat on his
head, and 'damned my thanks, if that were all' — Saint
Giles could not have excelled him."

"Weel, weel," said the banker, "that may be a' as
you say, sir, and nae doubt wealth makes wit waver,
but the country's wealthy, that cannot be denied, and
wealth, sir, ye ken —"

"I know wealth makes itself wings," answered the
cynical stranger, "but I am not quite sure we have it
even now. You make a great show, indeed, with
building and cultivation; but stock is not capital, any
more than the fat of a corpulent man is health or
strength."

"Surely, Mr Touchwood," said Bindloose, who felt
his own account in the modern improvements, "a set of
landlords, living like lairds in good earnest, and tenants
with better housekeeping than the lairds used to have,
and facing Whitsunday and Martinmas as I would face
my breakfast — if these are not signs of wealth, I do
not know where to seek for them."

"They are signs of folly, sir," replied Touchwood,

"folly that is poor, and renders itself poorer by desiring to be thought rich; and how they come by the means they are so ostentatious of, you, who are a banker, perhaps can tell me better than I can guess."

"There is maybe an accommodation bill discounted now and then, Mr Touchwood; but men must have accommodation, or the world would stand still — accommodation is the grease that makes the wheels go."

"Ay, makes them go down hill to the devil," answered Touchwood. "I left you bothered about one Air bank, but the whole country is an Air bank now, I think — And who is to pay the piper? — But it is all one — I will see little more of it — it is a perfect Babel, and would turn the head of a man who has spent his life with people who love sitting better than running, silence better than speaking, who never eat but when they are hungry, never drink but when thirsty, never laugh without a jest, and never speak but when they have something to say. But here, it is all run, ride and drive — froth, foam and flippancy — no steadiness — no character."

"I'll lay the burden of my life," said Dame Dods, looking towards her friend Bindloose, "that the gentleman has been at the new Spaw-waal yonder."

"Spaw do you call it, madam? — If you mean the new establishment that has been spawned down yonder at St Ronan's, it is the very fountain-head of folly and coxcombry — a Babel for noise and a Vanity-fair for nonsense — no well in your swamps tenanted by such a conceited colony of clamorous frogs."

(Chapter 15: II.ii.)

A gloss should perhaps be added that an accommodation bill is "a bill not representing an actual commercial transaction, but for the purpose of raising money on credit" (OED), and that the Ayr Bank failed, with disastrous consequences for the community in the west of Scotland, in 1772. Mr Touchwood does not himself precisely exemplify the gospel of silence which he preaches, and himself becomes an improver in the Aultoun, when the opportunity offers. The society of the Well, nevertheless, is the very type of all that he finds wrong with the society to which he has returned, and with which he has close links. He is in fact a near relative both of the Mowbrays, whose surname he refused to adopt, despite the insistence of his socially ambitious father, who therefore disinherited him, and of the more aristocratic Etheringtons, whose way of life he conspicuously refuses to accept, despite his great personal fortune.

Touchwood's contempt for the Spaw is necessarily shared by the reader who, like him, is forced to a preference for the ruinous Aultoun, all the features of which point to the more vital, if sometimes more barbarous, past. It must be granted that here too indications of degeneracy are to be seen everywhere. The Cleikum Inn had been the mansion of the Mowbray family in the first stages of their decline, when the castle of their ancestors, the ruins of which dominate the entire landscape, had been destroyed by Cromwell. The passing of an older generation, and the establishment of the new hotel, ensures that, even as an inn, it is an anachronism. The proprietor, Meg Dods, like Lady Penelope, is an obstinate spinster. The elegant external form, the remains of which distinguish the kirk, shows that it was built before the Reformation, but inside there is a clay floor and "an assemblage of wretched pews". The minister, a descendant of Donald Cargill (1619-1681) the celebrated Covenanting martyr of the seventeenth century, is a dreamy, self-forgetful scholar, who has lost any trace of ancestral fire. Despite Mr Touchwood, Saunders Jaup, a feuar of some importance, maintains the traditional jaw-hole, an uncovered common sewer, in the public street which fronts his house. Many of the other houses have fallen into ruin.

It is here, nevertheless, that everyone, whose character has any kind of life-enhancing quality, chooses to make his or her abode, or make contact with the society of the neighbourhood. Meg Dods, Frank Tyrrel, Mr Cargill make their homes here while Mr Bindloose, the humane sheriff-clerk of the county, "when summoned by official duty to that district of the shire . . . always advertised that his 'Prieves,' or 'Comptis,' or whatever other business was in hand, were to proceed on such a day and hour 'within the house of Margaret Dods, vintner in St Ronan's'" (Chapter 1). It is also the Aultoun which gives final sanctuary to Hannah Irwin and Clara Mowbray. After the destruction of the Spaw, the only house of entertainment permitted by Mowbray on his estate "is that in the Aultoun, where Mrs Dods reigns with undisputed sway, her temper by no means improved either by time, or her arbitrary disposition by the total absence of competition." (Chapter 39: III.xii)

Even the qualities which the Aultoun has succeeded in preserving are eventually all but lost as a consequence of the unhappy war with the Spaw. A sense of unprofitable conflict between ancient and modern dominates the narrative. Both should have been reconciled by the centre-piece of the book (19 chapters precede and follow it), the performance of *A Midsummer Night's Dream* in chapter 20 (II.7.). Grace and delicacy of language rather than power of characterization or plot makes this play pre-eminently life-giving and life-enhancing, but this is precisely what the company in its performance, part *tableau vivant*, part mime, ignores. The poetry, which belongs to the past, is lost; only the dumb-show of the present remains.

Plot however is also of some importance; the quarrel over Helena between Demetrius and Lysander, which almost leads them to mortal combat in the wood, provides a comic correspondence to the abortive duel in the glade at the Buckstane which is supposed to take place between Tyrrel and Sir Bingo Binks, and is counterpointed against the actual encounters between Bulmer and Tyrrel and between Bulmer and Mowbray — both fought in the immediate vicinity, the latter with fatal results for Bulmer. The wood, indeed, which also gives its name to Shaws-Castle, is to the novel more or less what the wood near Athens is to the play. It is here that Frank and Clara first meet; here that they lay their plans in company with Hannah and Bulmer. The four correspond to the two pairs of Athenian lovers, and the original relationship of Hannah with Clara, as described in chapter 32 (III.5) is more or less equivalent to that of Helena and Hermia, as described in III.2.:—

> We, Hermia, like two artificial gods,
> Have with our needles created both one flower,
> Both on one sampler, sitting on one cushion,
> Both warbling of one song, both in one key,
> As if our hands, our sides, voices, and minds,
> Had been incorporate. So we grew together,
> Like to a double cherry, seeming parted,
> But yet a union in partition.
> (203–210)

It is through the wood, finally, that Clara wanders on her last journey to the Aultoun.

Shakespeare's wood, however, is a place of enchantment and natural magic. The inevitable sequel to the scenes there is the marriage celebration at the court of Duke Theseus, and the happy aftermath promised by Oberon:—

> To the best bride-bed will we,
> Which by us shall blessed be;
> And the issue there create
> Ever shall be fortunate.
> So shall all the couples three
> Ever true in loving be;
> And the blots of Nature's hand
> Shall not in their issue stand,
>   (V.ii.33-40)

Particularly in Scott's original version, the event, stemming from the seduction of both girls by the half-brothers, is very different, involving the death of three among the lovers, and leaving the fourth as a celibate member of a Moravian missionary brotherhood.

The outcome is hastened by a material object, the Indian shawl worn by Clara in her presentation of Helena, the influence of which parallels that of the handkerchief which in *Othello* the Moor gives to Desdemona. By purchasing it for his sister, Mowbray outmanoeuvres and humiliates Lady Penelope, who had intended it for the adornment of her own person as Hermia. The humiliation is heightened by the comments of Mrs Blower during the performance:—

> "Oh, that puir Lady Penelope!" said honest Mrs Blower, who when her scruples against the exhibition were once got over, began to look upon it with particular interest, — "I am really sorry for her puir face, for she gars it work like the sails of John Blower's vessel in a stiff breeze. — Oh, Doctor Cacklehen, dinna ye think she wad need, if it were possible, to rin ower her face wi' a gusing iron, just to take the wrunkles out o't?"
>
> "Hush, hush! my good dear Mrs Blower," said the

Doctor; "Lady Penelope is a woman of quality, and my patient, and such people always act charmingly — you must understand there is no hissing at a private theatre — Hem!"

"Ye may say what you like, Doctor, but there is nae fule like an auld fule — To be sure, if she was as young and beautiful as Miss Mowbray — hegh me, and I didna use to think her sae bonny neither — but dress — dress makes an unco difference — That shawl o' hers — I dare say the like o't was ne'er seen in braid Scotland — It will be real Indian, I'se warrant."

After the performance, Clara, who knows nothing of her brother's machinations, is generous enough to make a gift of the shawl to Lady Penelope, disguised by which the latter receives the moral reproaches aimed by Mr Cargill, as he thinks, at Clara. Lady Penelope thus gains her first insight into the girl's past. Mowbray himself later aims a petulant remark at Lady Penelope, who responds in a way that effectively determines the later course of the novel:—

"My sister is not yet of quality sufficient, to entitle her to rob her friends of their shawls."

Lady Penelope coloured to the eyes, and bitter was the retort that arose to her tongue; but she suppressed it, and nodding to Miss Mowbray in the most friendly way in the world, she only said, "So you have told your brother of the little transaction we have had this morning? — *Tu me lo pagherai* I give you fair warning, take care none of your secrets come into my keeping — that's all."

(Chapter 22: II.ix.)

Hitherto, relations between the two women have been as open to reconciliation as those of Helena and Hermia — Helena's betrayal of Hermia's secret to Demetrius does not, after all, lead to any kind of permanent breach. Everything is now changed, as Scott points out in a Humean analysis of the growth of passion:— "If Lady Penelope had given way to her first movements of resentment, the probable issue would have been some such half-comic, half-serious skirmish, as her ladyship and

Mr Mowbray had often amused the company withal. But revenge which is suppressed and deferred, is always most to be dreaded; and to the effects of the deliberate resentment which Lady Penelope cherished upon this trifling occasion, must be traced the events which our history has to record." The shawl, it will be seen, successively precipitates the remarks of Mrs Blower, which as Scott signals, are meant to be overheard, the encounter with Mr. Cargill, which gives Lady Penelope the first hint of the information about Clara which she requires and subsequently uses, and finally Mowbray's outburst, which turns her mind towards the petty and malicious revenge, obtained by way of the tea-table gossip of chapter 34 (III.vii.). The tragic outcome is entirely disproportionate to the effective cause, a mere material object, the shawl.

The comment on its colour by Mr Touchwood is thematically revealing:—

"And a very bonny colour it is," said the dame; "something like a mouse's back only a thought redder — I wonder what they ca' that colour."

"The colour is much admired, madam," said Touchwood, who was now on a favourite topic; "the Mussulmans say the colour is betwixt that of an elephant and the breast of the *faughta*".

"In troth, I am as wise as I was," said Mrs Blower.

"The *faughta*, madam, so called by the Moors, (for the Hindhus call it *hollah*,) is a sort of pigeon, held sacred among the Moslems of India, because they think it dyed its breast in the blood of Ali."

(Chapter 20: II.vii)

The colour of the shawl, in other words, resembles that of blood. Ali is 'Ali ben Abu Talib (c.600-661), son-in-law of the Prophet, and fourth in order of the Caliphs, who was assassinated while attempting to uphold his claim against his eventual successor in the caliphate, the Omayyad Mu'awiya. 'Ali's ill-fated struggle and eventual death parallels that of Bulmer with Tyrrel for the earldom of Etherington.

The performance of *A Midsummer Night's Dream* at Shaws Castle includes only three scenes, none of which are directly concerned with the series of weddings which concludes the Shakespearean entertainment. The first "displayed Hermia, Helena, and their lovers, in attitudes corresponding to the scene of confusion occasioned by the error of Puck." As has been shown, this comes closest to the main action of the novel, where Bulmer and Tyrrel both come to pursue Clara, while Hannah is neglected. The second, the quarrel between Oberon and Titania, fairy king and fairy queen, corresponds to the enmity between Bulmer and Clara, Sir Bingo and Lady Binks, husbands and wives in sterile and unnatural marriages, which, like the fairies' quarrel, blight everything around them. The third, the antimask, as it is styled by Scott, presenting the behaviour of Bottom during his transformation, reflects, I think, on the absurd social peccadilloes which govern life at the Spaw, and, in particular, on the behaviour of the Man of Peace, Captain MacTurk, and of the First Physician and Man of Science, Dr Quackleben, particularly in his disinterested courtship of honest Mrs Blower, the wealthy widow of a Leith skipper. (Mrs Blower, it should be noted, has been turned against the drama by the episode of the sailor's wife in *Macbeth* I.iii.4 ff., and as a consequence refuses to allow the Doctor to play the part of Wall in *A Midsummer Night's Dream*. She has found her own parallel in Shakespeare, and in many ways is the most natural character to be found at the Well.)

According to the preliminary narrative, Mowbray is to play Theseus, Lady Binks Hippolyta, MacTurk Egeus, and Winterblossom Philostrate. None of these characters appears in the detailed account of the performance; save when Mowbray in the character of Theseus brings the proceedings to a conclusion, the names appear as if by oversight. They are important, however, in a different way. Shakespeare's most immediate "source" for *A Midsummer Night's Dream* was, as Scott must have realized, Chaucer's *Knight's Tale*, which begins with the return of Theseus and Hippolyta to Athens after their wedding, and deals primarily with the unnatural rivalry of the Theban cousins, Palamon and Arcite, for the hand of Emily, Hippolyta's younger sister. The disguised Arcite passes under the name of Philostrate at the court of Theseus, and fights two terrible duels with his cousin, when the latter escapes from the prison to which Theseus had originally condemned both. Arcite dies as the result of a fall from his horse at the moment of his triumph over Palamon, and Theseus can be comforted only by his old father Egeus. The parallel with the situation involving Bulmer and Tyrrel cannot be missed.

Scott knew the story, not only from Chaucer, but also from *The Two Noble Kinsmen*, a play in which Shakespeare, towards the end of his life, probably collaborated with John Fletcher (1579-1625). The cousins brought to blows by their love for the same woman obviously appealed to Shakespeare's sense of parody, and gave him the idea of the rivalry, almost leading to mortal combat, between Demetrius and Lysander.

A Midsummer Night's Dream, however, has little of the sense of the unnatural which pervades both Scott's novel and Chaucer's tale. This has classical origins, ultimately deriving from the Theban cycle of legends dealing with the family of Laius and Oedipus, and in particular from the epic *Thebaid* of the silver Latin poet, Statius (c. 45-96), the reputation of which stood in the middle ages much higher than it does at present. *The Knight's Tale* begins with the appeal made to Theseus on his victorious return from Scythia by the widows of the kings who had led the assault on Thebes, now best remembered not from Statius, but from Aeschylus' much earlier tragedy, *The Seven against Thebes* (467 B.C.). Creon, proclaimed king of Thebes after the repulse of the assault, had refused burial to the bodies of the principal attackers. The assault and the deaths resulted from a curse laid by the blind Oedipus on his sons, Eteocles and Polynices. After his death, they agreed to rule alternately, but when Eteocles had completed his own period of rule, he refused to hand the kingdom over to his brother. Polynices in turn raised the army which marched on Thebes. Each killed the other in single combat. The siege failed, and Creon, now king, refused burial rites to the fallen leaders of the invasion. Theseus led another, more successful invasion, which put an end to this denial of human and divine law.

Palamon and Arcite were close kinsmen of the Theban royal line, and gave the impression that they had inherited some element of their urge towards self-destruction. The point is still more emphasized, as one would expect, in *The Two Noble Kinsmen*. Even without the help of the Theban legend, Fletcher shared with Shakespeare a Jacobean zest for parricide, incest and other unpleasant personal failings, as witness many of his other plays, *The Bloody Brothers* (c.1616), for instance, and more particularly *A King and No King* (1611) in which he collaborated with Francis Beaumont.

This last is of special importance; a quotation from it is prefixed to chapter 12 of *St Ronan's Well*, and Scott obviously drew something of Captain MacTurk from Bessus and the pedantic Two Swordmen, around whom Fletcher created his subplot. More importantly, the play turns on the apparently unnatural love of Arbaces, king of Iberia, for his supposed sister Panthea, a dilemma only resolved when it is revealed that Arbaces is not in fact the son of the late king and queen, but of Gobrias, the Lord-Protector, and is thus entitled to marry Panthea, although with the disclosure he also loses his claim to the throne, a point over which the play does not linger. His ambiguous position, which gives the play its title, corresponds to a degree with that of Bulmer in relation to his title, contested by Tyrrel. The rival claims of Eteocles and Polynices to the Theban throne is an even closer parallel. Scott's novel contains an element of statutory incest in Tyrrel's love for Clara, who is married to his half-brother.

The link between *St Ronan's Well* and the Theban cycle is made explicit on two occasions, once near the beginning, and once towards the end of the novel. Chapter 1 is taken up with a description of the village and some of its inhabitants. The dominant feature is the castle, which forms the acropolis, the Cadmea, of the place:—

> It must, indeed, have been a place of formidable defence, for, on the side opposite to the town, its walls rose straight up from the verge of a tremendous and rocky precipice, whose base was washed by St Ronan's burn, as the brook was entitled. On the southern side, where the declivity was less precipitous, the ground had been carefully levelled into successive terraces, which ascended to the summit of the hill, and were, or rather had been, connected by staircases of stone, rudely ornamented. In peaceful periods these terraces had been occupied by the gardens of the Castle, and in times of siege they added to its security, for each commanded the one immediately below it, so that they could be separately and successfully defended, and all were exposed to the fire from the place itself — a

massive square tower of the largest size, surrounded, as usual, by lower buildings, and a high embattled wall . . . Seated on the threshold of this ancient pile, where 'the proud porter' had in former days 'rear'd himself,' a stranger had a complete and commanding view of the decayed village, the houses of which, to a fanciful imagination, might seem as if they had been suddenly arrested in hurrying down the precipitous hill, and fixed as if by magic in the whimsical arrangement which they now presented. It was like a sudden pause in one of Amphion's country-dances, when the huts which were to form the future Thebes were jigging it to his lute.

Amphion, the musician, and his brother Zethus, the herdsman, twin sons of Antiope and Zeus, were in mythology the builders of the city (as opposed to the acropolis, the Cadmea founded by Cadmus) of Thebes. Amphion in particular caused the outer walls to rise by the magical power of his music. Together they killed their predecessor in the kingship, Lycus, and his wife, Dirce, who had held Antiope captive, and Dirce was transformed into the famous Theban spring which after wards bore her name, and which perhaps forms a mythological precedent for the Spaw itself. The description is important, not only for the reference to Amphion, but also for the emphasis on the castle as a place which, like Thebes, had often been besieged, and the oblique gesture, in the words used to describe the porter, towards the ballad of "King Estmere" (Child 60), in which two brothers, Adler Younge and King Estmere, combine resources to obtain the daughter of King Adland as a bride for Estmere.

The second reference occurs in chapter 31 (III.iv.). Lady Penelope is talking to her friends in the postmaster-bookseller's establishment, when Bulmer enters the shop:—

> He entered unobserved, just as Lady Penelope had finished reading some verses, and was commenting on them with all the alacrity of a *femme savante*, in possession of something which no one is to hear repeated oftener than once.
> "Copy — no indeed!" these were the snatches which reached Lord Etherington's ear, from the group of

F

which her ladyship formed the centre — "honour bright — I must not betray poor Chatterly — besides his lordship is my friend, and a person of rank, you know — so one would not — You have not got the book, Mr Pott? — you have not got Statius? — you never have anything one longs to see."

"Very sorry, my lady — quite out of copies at present — I expect some in my next monthly parcel."

"Good lack, Mr Pott, that is your never-failing answer," said Lady Penelope; "I believe if I were to ask you for the last new edition of the Alkoran, you would tell me it was coming down in your next monthly parcel."

"Can't say, my lady, really," answered Mr Pott; "have not seen the work advertised yet; but I have no doubt, if it is likely to take, there will be copies in my next monthly parcel."

"Mr Pott's supplies are always in the *paullo post futurum* tense," said Mr Chatterly, who was just entering the shop.

"Ah! Mr Chatterly, are you there?" said Lady Penelope; "I lay my death at your door — I cannot find this Thebaid, where Polynices and his brother —"

"Hush, my lady! — hush, for Heaven's sake!" said the poetical divine, and looked towards Lord Etherington. Lady Penelope took the hint, and was silent.

The poet and clergyman, Mr Chatterly has, it would seem, composed and circulated anonymously a set of verses on the relationship between Tyrrel and Bulmer, verses which refer to Statius' account of the parallel strife between Eteocles and Polynices; these have sent Lady Penelope off to the bookshop to order a copy of the Latin, which unsurprisingly the local bookshop does not have.

As has been noted, the climax of the *Thebaid* is the battle between the brothers Eteocles and Polynices, which occupies Book XI. The opening lines of Book I, summarizing the course which the poem is to run, inevitably refer to this, putting it in the context of the ancestral passion for mutual strife characteristic of the Thebans, who, like the Mowbrays, sprang directly from the local soil, and shared in its harshness. The first inhabitant of the site of the future city was a dragon, killed by Cadmus, the Phoenician refugee, whose wanderings had been supernaturally directed to the spot. Still following divine instructions, he sowed the dragon's teeth, from which sprang a race of warriors, all save five of whom killed each other in the battle which followed. The five survivors, the Spartoi or sowed men, became the ancestors of the main Theban race, to which they bequeathed their own dragon-like propensities for strife. Amphion, one of their descendants, caused, as has already been noted, the walls of the city to rise from the mountainous soil which had given birth to the people. Such is the history briefly summarized by Statius in the allusive style of later Latin epic poetry:—

> *Fraternas acies alternaque regna profanis*
> *decertata odiis sontesque evolvere Thebas,*
> *Pierius menti calor incidit. unde iubetis*
> *ire, deae? gentisne canam primordia dirae,*
> *Sidonios raptus et inexorabile pactum*
> *legis Agenoreae scrutantemque aequora Cadmum?*
> *longa retro series, trepidum si Martis operti*
> *agricolam infandis condentem proelia sulcis*
> *expediam penitusque sequar, quo carmine muris*
> *iusserit Amphion Tyrios accedere montes.*
>
> (I.1-10.)

The strife of brethren, and the battle of the alternate reign fought out with impious hatred, and all the guilty tale of Thebes — to recount this, my spirit is touched by Pierian fire. Whence, O goddesses, do ye bid me begin? — Shall I sing the origins of the dreadful race, the Sidonian rape and the inexorable terms of Agenor's law, and Cadmus searching o'er the main? Far backward runs the story, should I tell of the anxious husbandman of hidden war, sowing battles in the unhallowed soil, and, searching to the uttermost, relate with what song Amphion bade the Tyrian mountains move to form a city's walls.

For the reader of *St Ronan's Well* these lines are immediately relevant, not only to Bulmer and Tyrrel, but also to the house of Mowbray, on whose Thebes-like ancestral land the tragic action is played out. The Etheringtons themselves belong to the "dreadful race" of the Mowbrays, their paternal grandfather having married a Scotswoman, whose mother's maiden name had been Mowbray, and who was a distant connection of the main St Ronan's line. In accordance with the more repressed sensibilities of a later age, Tyrrel is not permitted to kill his brother; Mowbray is the surrogate who fires the shot. Scott too differs from Statius in making Tyrrel less prepared than his brother to bring matters to a bloody conclusion, which nevertheless is only prevented by the intervention of Mowbray. Tyrrel is driven almost insane by the death of Clara:—

> "Mercy!" answered Tyrrel; "but why, then, is it denied to me? — I know — I know — My life is spared till I revenge her."
>
> He started from his seat, and hurried eagerly down stairs. But, as he was about to dash from the door of the inn, he was stopped by Touchwood, who had just alighted from a carriage, with an air of stern anxiety imprinted on his features, very different from their usual expression. "Whither would ye? Whither would ye?" he said, laying hold of Tyrrel, and stopping him by force.
>
> "For revenge — for revenge!" said Tyrrel. "Give way, I charge you, on your peril!"
>
> "Vengeance belongs to God," replied the old man, "and his bolt has fallen. — This way — this way," he continued, dragging Tyrrel into the house. "Know," he said, so soon as he had led or forced him into a chamber, "that Mowbray of St Ronan's has met Bulmer within this half hour, and has killed him on the spot."
>
> "Killed? — whom?" answered the bewildered Tyrrel.
>
> "Valentine Bulmer, the titular Earl of Etherington."
>
> "You bring tidings of death to the house of death," answered Tyrrel; "and there is nothing in this world left that I should live for."
>
> (Chapter 38: III.xi.)

The two explicitly Theban passages quoted are linked by an

intermediate series of references to unnatural fraternal relationships, especially frequent in the correspondence between Bulmer
and his friend, "Captain Jekyl, of the — regiment of Guards".
The first letter, given in chapter 19 (II.6.), is, as Jekyl realises, the
most directly revealing. One passage, the account of the duel,
shows Bulmer's basic hypocrisy, and also how fixed he is in his
murderous purposes:—

> "I saw no chance for it, however, but to put myself
> into a towering passion, which, thank Heaven, I can
> always do on short notice. I charged him with having
> imposed formerly on my youth, and made himself
> judge of my rights; and I accompanied my defiance
> with the strongest terms of irony and contempt, as well
> as with demand of instant satisfaction. I had my
> travelling pistols with me, (*et pour cause*) and, to my
> surprise, my gentleman was equally provided. For fair
> play's sake, I made him take one of my pistols — right
> Kuchenritters — a brace of balls in each, but that
> circumstance I forgot. I would fain have argued the
> matter a little longer; but I thought at the time, and
> think still, that the best arguments which he and I can
> exchange, must come from the point of the sword, or
> the muzzle of the pistol. — We fired nearly together,
> and I think both dropped — I am sure I did, but
> recovered in a minute, with a damaged arm and a
> scratch on the temple — it was the last which stunned
> me — so much for double-loaded pistols."

The reference to "a brace of balls" and "double-loaded pistols"
lie beyond my simple ballistic competence; much clearer is the
parallel between this passage and the exchanges between the
Theban brothers, more particularly the last words which Statius
gives to Polynices before their encounter:—

> *O mihi nunc primum longo post tempore, frater,*
> *congredere: hae leges, haec foedera sola supersunt.*
> (*Thebaid* XI.394—395.)

> "O once again after many a day my brother, engage!
> no law, no compact but this remains."

The laws and compacts which he thus abrogates are those of human society. Even "once again" has a special relevance to the situation in the novel, when one recollects the earlier engagement which followed Bulmer's attempt at the abduction of Clara. Again he is writing to Jekyl:—

> I jumped out of the carriage, pitched fraternity to the devil, and betwixt desperation and something very like shame, began to cut away with a couteau de chasse, which I had provided in case of necessity. — All was in vain — I was hustled down under the wheel of the carriage, and, the horses taking fright, it went over my body.
>
> Here ends my narrative; for I neither heard nor saw more until I found myself stretched on a sick-bed many miles from the scene of the action, and Solmes engaged in attending on me.
>
> (Chapter 26: II.xiii.)

The analysis might be continued in much greater detail, but sufficient evidence has now, I think, been presented to show that in the relationship between Scott's novel of modern life and ancient tragic legend we have indeed a parallel with the later work of Joyce and Eliot. The abortive performance of *A Midsummer Night's Dream*, centrally placed as it is, dismisses any possibility of alternative developments.

iv

It is the Latin epic of Statius rather than the Greek drama of Aeschylus which underlies the action of *St Ronan's Well*. But *St Ronan's Well*, unlike *The Antiquary*, is not in any sense an attempt at the mock heroic; the link with antiquity is to be found in subject-matter rather than style. The novel, in fact, is among the latest representatives of the characteristically Scottish Latin humanism, which in *Progress and Poetry* I defined in terms of Douglas, Boece, Buchanan, the *Delitiae Poetarum Scotorum*, Pitcairne, and Ruddiman, together with Ramsay and Fergusson who, though vernacular writers, stand only a little apart from the others.[19] The tradition is strongly evidenced in the novels produced by Scott during the early eighteen-twenties — *Redgauntler*, for instance, which appeared in 1824, is suffused both with Latinity and with historical reminiscences of the last days of the Roman republic. Much of the Latin quoted is, of course, to be explained by the presence in the narrative of Edinburgh lawyers and their clients; the close relationship of Scots law to Roman is too well-known to require comment. Nor is the legal presence in the novel random; Scott implies some kind of parallel between the long agonies of the Jacobite legitimists and the protracted intricacies of the other great cause, that of Peebles versus Plainstanes, which has trailed through the courts almost since the 'Forty-five itself. The appearance of Peter Peebles as plaintiff concludes volume I, as the departure of that other, more celebrated, plaintiff, the *ci-devant* Prince Charles, concludes both the second and third volume.

This implicit comment is given a new perspective by the fact that the plots and manoeuvres in which Darsie Latimer and Alan Fairford find themselves involved are in turn set against a background of the unsuccessful Roman revolutionary move-ments of the first century BC, the wars of Marius and Sulla, of Caesar and Pompey, and in particular, the Catilinarian conspi-racy of 63-62 BC and the later (44-42 BC) attempt, ultimately equally unsuccessful, of Brutus and Cassius to restore the Roman republic by murder and civil war. The effect is primarily achieved by echoes of the Latin writers of the period, in particular, Horace and Sallust. Horace had fought on the side of Brutus at Philippi, but afterwards, by way of his friendship with Maecenas, had become a sincere panegyrist of the new order. Like Scott, he wished to reconcile new with old, and his vivid sense of past tragedy in relation to present reality often seems to anticipate Scott:—

> *quis non Latino sanguine pinguior*
> *campus sepulcris impia proelia*
> *testatur auditumque Medis*
> *Hesperiae sonitum ruinae?*

> *qui gurges aut quae flumina lugubris*
> *ignara belli? quod mare Dauniae*
> *non decoloravere caedes?*
> *quae caret ora cruore nostro?*

'What field, made richer by Latin blood, does not bear the witness of its graves to impious battles and the

sound of Western ruin heard as far to the east as Persia?
What lake or what rivers are unacquainted with the
bitterness of civil war? What sea has the slaughter of
Italians not discoloured? What coast is unstained by our
gore?'

Sallust wrote a vivid account (*Bellum Catilinae*) of the
Catilinarian conspiracy, concerning which Cicero, the chief
opponent of Catiline, had also composed some of his most
effective speeches. These works were, and for more than a
century continued to be, the literary staple of Scottish grammar
schools, in one of which Scott, like Darsie Latimer and Alan
Fairford, had himself been educated.

The opening of *Redgauntlet* — "*Cur me exanimas querelis tuis?*
— In plain English, Why do you deafen me with your
croaking?" — is a misquotation (deliberately misrendered) of the
first line of Horace *Odes*, II.17., *Cur me querelis exanimas tuis?*.
Despite the initial apparent irritation, the ode develops into a
deeply affectionate address to Maecenas, who was subject to
periods of melancholy. Fraenkel comments[20], "The poem begins
on a note of gentle reproach, in which there can be heard,
perhaps, a slight impatience. . . . But this note fades out at once;
the voice becomes deep and urgent, anxious to conjure away the
friend's dark thoughts: *nec dis amicum est nec mihi te prius obire,
Maecenas*" ("It pleases neither the gods nor me that you should
die first, Maecenas") "— and then, throwing in the full weight
of his devotion, *mearum grande decus columenque rerum*" ("the great
ornament and pillar of my fortunes"). The affection between
Horace and Maecenas is obviously reflected by the friendship of
Latimer and Fairford, although it is Fairford — so far as the
novel and Latimer are concerned the equivalent of Maecenas —
who is to echo by his abrupt action in leaving Edinburgh
Horace's later declaration in the same poem:—

> *ibimus, ibimus,*
> *utcumque praecedes, supremum*
> *carpere iter comites parati.*

"We shall go, we shall go, wherever you lead, com-
rades prepared to take the final road together."

There is a further parallel. Fairford and his father are un-
doubted Hanoverians, but Latimer, at least by ancestry and
kinship, is a Jacobite, a position from which in effect he is rescued
by Fairford. Horace correspondingly had supported Brutus, but
his whole career had been changed by means of his friendship
with Maecenas, one of Octavian's (later Augustus) most influential supporters. The most charming and self-deprecatory reference
to Horace's revolutionary past is to be found in *Odes* II.7., *O
saepe mecum tempus in ultimum*, addressed to Pompeius, once his
brother-officer in Brutus' army:—

> *tecum Philippos et celerem fugam
> sensi relicta non bene parmula*

> "With you I experienced Philippi and swift flight
> after I had ignobly abandoned my poor little shield"

Scott applies these lines (again in a misquotation, which
however is in this case perhaps deliberate), not to Latimer, but to
Alan's father, who had fought, or rather failed to fight, at Falkirk
against the retreating Jacobite army. Latimer describes the
situation (Letter III) when he writes to Alan:—

> All his impressions concerning the Highlanders are
> taken from the recollections of the Forty-five, when he
> retreated from the West-Port with his brother volun-
> teers, each to the fortalice of his own separate dwelling,
> so soon as they heard the Adventurer was arrived with
> his clans as near them as Kirkliston. The flight of
> Falkirk — *parma non bene selecta* — in which I think
> your sire had his share with the undaunted western
> regiment, does not seem to have improved his taste for
> the company of the Highlanders.

Again, the parallel between the Scottish eighteenth century
and the last years of the Roman republic is close to the surface.

The most striking reference to Sallust occurs when Alan
Fairford is attempting to find Redgauntlet, the Laird of the
Solway Lakes, and crosses the Solway Firth in Nanty Ewart's
brig. Ewart is surprised to see him hurl overboard *Merry
Thoughts for Merry Men; or Mother Midnight's Miscellany for the*

Small Hours, the bawdy, supposed hymn-book given to him by the austere Sabbatarian, Thomas Trumbull, and instead take out the copy of Sallust which is his more usual travelling companion. Ewart assumes that as he is carrying a letter to an obdurate Jacobite, he must himself be no less dissolute and hypocritical than the generality of Redgauntlet's fellow-conspirators (himself included):—

> As he opened the book, Nanty Ewart, who had been looking over his shoulder, made his own opinion heard.
>
> "I think now, brother, if you are so much scandalized at a little piece of sculduddery, which, after all, does nobody any harm, you had better have given it to me than have flung it into the Solway."
>
> "I hope, sir," answered Fairford, civilly, "you are in the habit of reading better books."
>
> "Faith," answered Nanty, "with help of a little Geneva text, I could read my Sallust as well as you can;" and snatching the book from Alan's hand, he began to read, in the Scottish accent. — "*Igitur ex divitiis juventutem luxuria atque avaritia cum superbia invasere: rapere, consumere; sua parvi pendere, aliena cupere; pudorem, amicitiam, pudicitiam, divina atque humana promiscua, nihil pensi neque moderati habere* ("The youth, taught to look up to riches as the sovereign good, become apt pupils in the school of Luxury. Rapacity and profusion went hand in hand. Careless of their own fortunes, and eager to possess those of others, shame and remorse, modesty and moderation, every principle gave way"[21]). — There is a slap in the face now, for an honest fellow that has been buccaniering! Never could keep a groat of what he got, or hold his fingers from what belonged to another, said you? Fie, fie, friend Crispus, thy morals are as crabbed and austere as thy style — the one has as little mercy as the other has grace. By my soul, it is unhandsome to make personal reflections on an old acquaintance, who seeks a little civil intercourse with you after nigh twenty years' separation. On my soul, Master Sallust deserves to float on the Solway better than Mother Midnight herself."

"Perhaps, in some respects, he may merit better usage at our hands," said Alan; "for if he has described vice plainly, it seems to have been for the purpose of rendering it generally abhorred."

"Well," said the seaman, "I have heard of the Sortes Virgilianae, and I daresay the Sortes Sallustianae are as true every tittle. I have consulted honest Crispus on my own account, and have had a cuff for my pains. But now see, I open the book on your behalf, and behold what occurs first to my eye! — Lo you there — *Catilina . . . omnium flagitiosorum atque facinorosorum circum se habebat* ("Catiline was surrounded by everyone who was evil and wicked"). And then again — *Etiam si quis a culpa vacuus in amicitiam ejus inciderat, quotidiano usu par similisque caeteris efficiebatur* ("If it happened that any as yet uncontaminated by vice were fatally drawn into his friendship, the effects of intercourse and snares artfully spread, subdued every scruple, and early assimilated them to their conductors"). That is what I call plain speaking on the part of the old Roman, Mr Fairford. By the way, that is a capital name for a lawyer."

"Lawyer as I am," said Fairford, "I do not understand your innuendo."

For Ewart, the Laird of the Solway Lochs is the modern equivalent of Catiline, and Fairford is either an innocent to be inevitably corrupted, or a confidence trickster who covers with a smooth exterior his activities, not only as conspirator, but also, in terms of the last remark, as smuggler, a follower of the euphemistically described Fair Trade. Although all this seems to pass Alan by, the idea that Redgauntlet is a modern Catiline is uppermost for the greater part of the novel, and is reinforced by the Satanic overtones of the family history related in Wandering Willie's Tale. In the final scene, however we are given a different impression; Redgauntlet's ultimate steadfastness comes to resemble that of another Roman of the late republic, the younger Cato (95-46 BC), who committed suicide rather than submit to Caesar. Lucan's epigraph, *Victrix causa deis placuit, sed victa Catoni* ("The victorious cause was pleasing to the gods, but the vanquished to Cato"), is, in effect, repeated in the final chapter;

"'It is the way of our house,' said Redgauntlet; 'our courage ever kindles highest on the losing side. I, too, feel that the catastrophe I have brought on must not be survived by its author.'" Yet again one recalls Horace:—

> *et cuncta terrarum subacta*
> *praeter atrocem animum Catonis*

("And all the world subdued, except for the unyielding mind of Cato.")

v

The first major novel to be generally classified as historical, *Waverley*, with its subtitle "'Tis Sixty Years Since", was published on 7th July 1814. On 29th July of the same year, Scott embarked from Leith to accompany the Commissioners for Northern Lights on what he called "a nautical tour round Scotland, visiting all that is curious on continent and isle". The trip lasted until 8th September, when Scott disembarked at Greenock and took the steam-boat to Glasgow on the first stage of his homeward journey. During the tour he kept a long diary, written primarily for the entertainment of himself, his family, and a few friends, but which incidentally reveals many of his imaginative and intellectual preoccupations at the time. Lockhart embodied it in volume III of his *Memoirs of the Life of Sir Walter Scott, Bart.*[22].

The diary was written at the beginning of Scott's career as a novelist, but also near the beginning of his career as an improving land-owner. The two are more closely linked than one might imagine. Scott had removed to Abbotsford in May 1812, and by the summer of 1814 his baronial mansion had substantially replaced its predecessor on the same site, the small poor farmhouse "with a common kail-yard on one flank, and a staring barn . . . on the other; while in front appeared a filthy pond covered with ducks and duckweed, from which the whole tenement had derived the unharmonious designation of Clarty Hole" (I quote Lockhart[23]). Scott himself, in other words, was responsible for the redemption of at least one part of Scotland from the clutches of the old agricultural system. His work as landlord played a significant part in the more general movement so often referred to in the earlier volume of this book.

The tension between an advancing and a retreating way of life formed part of the framework of Scott's very existence, and his temperament was of a kind likely to be strongly affected by it. On the one hand, he was a pragmatic lawyer, more concerned with things as they were, or would be in the near future, than with how they had been, or ought to be. And of course the political and intellectual background of his own life-time — The Enlightenment, the American and French revolutions, the rise of Napoleon and the long war with France, the preliminaries of the first Reform Bill — all projected on a European and world scale the same impulse towards revolutionary change visible on the face of the Border countryside which had helped to form him as an imaginative and thinking being. It is not surprising that revolution, the violent confrontation of an old with a new form of society, formed the staple of his creative output, even before the Waverley novels. The Last Minstrel, as his name indicates, is the last of his ancient order, and has survived into a different world; a vital part of the old Scotland disappeared in company with Marmion at Flodden. In *The Lady of the Lake* we have the reign of James V, with its confrontation of the old, represented by the House of Douglas and the Highlands, and the new, represented by the Lowlands and James himself.

Continuity, however, as well as revolution, was always present to Scott, and to a degree, his sense of continuity springs from the belief, in itself, as has been illustrated, characteristic of the Enlightenment, that the human mind at every historical period possessed certain common characteristics, and would invariably react in the same way, or at least on the same terms, to the same form of stimulus. "If we are asked therefore, Where the state of nature is to be found? we may answer, It is here: and it matters not whether we are understood to speak in the island of Great Britain, at the Cape of Good Hope, or the Straits of Magellan. While this active being is in the train of employing his talents, and of operating on the subjects around him, all situations are equally natural". Scott would have completed Ferguson's observation[24] by adding that it did not matter whether we speak in Edinburgh during the nineteenth century, Lanarkshire in the seventeenth, France in the fifteenth, or Constantinople in the twelfth century. The externals are different, but the central human instincts and properties remain the same. As a consequence, Scott could seldom think of the events of any single period solely in terms of that period. The Napoleonic wars, for instance, profoundly affected his imagination. He wrote a massive *Life* of Napoleon. But in some ways his deepest thoughts and feelings about the Emperor are to be found in the earlier verse-romances, which deal primarily with very different subjects. *Marmion* (1808) was written during the period of Napoleon's greatest success — the period which saw his victories at Ulm, Austerlitz, Jena, Eylau and Friedland, and the promulgation of the Berlin Decrees. For Britain it was a period of sustained disaster. The sub-title of *Marmion* is "A Tale of Flodden Field", and in the course of the poem it becomes clear that in the narrative of the greatest military defeat ever suffered by Scottish arms Scott saw a parallel to the current ebb of British fortunes in the Napoleonic wars. It was for this reason that he introduced the poem with the great elegy for Nelson and Pitt (Fox was added somewhat later):—

> But oh! my country's wintry state
> What second spring shall renovate?
> What powerful call shall bid arise
> The buried warlike and the wise;
> The mind that thought for Britain's weal,
> The hand that grasped the victor steel?
> The vernal sun new life bestows
> Even on the meanest flower that blows;
> But vainly, vainly may he shine
> Where glory weeps o'er Nelson's shrine;
> And vainly pierce the solemn gloom,
> That shrouds, O Pitt, thy hallowed tomb!
> (57-68)

The introduction to the third canto celebrates the exploits of the Duke of Brunswick (1735-1801) and Sir Ralph Abercromby (1734-1806), both of whom died heroically in the unsuccessful attempt to halt Napoleon's advance[25]. Rather less convincingly, the introduction to the fifth canto celebrates the prowess of the Edinburgh Volunteers:—

Nor deem that from thy fenceless throne
Strength and security are flown;
Still, as of yore, Queen of the North!
Still canst thou send thy children forth.
Ne'er readier at alarm-bell's call
Thy burghers rose to man thy wall,
Than now, in danger, shall be thine,
Thy dauntless voluntary line.

(93–100)

The passage immediately follows the description in Canto IV of the Scottish forces assembled on the Boroughmuir for the beginning of the Flodden campaign, and in this context the reference to the dauntless voluntary line has rather pessimistic overtones. These in turn correspond to the feelings of Scott and many of his contemporaries in 1806 and 1807.

Marmion deals with Flodden; the climax of *The Lord of the Isles* (1815) is Bannockburn. The Hebridean setting of the earlier cantos reflects the nautical tour of 1814. Scott's imagination however was kindled almost as much by the parallel between Bruce's liberation of Scotland in the period from 1307 to 1314 and the liberation of Europe from Napoleon between 1808, when the Peninsular War began, and 1814, when Napoleon abdicated. It cannot have escaped his notice that 1814 marked the quincentenary of Bannockburn. The parallel comes most closely to the surface in the Introduction to Canto Sixth:—

O who, that shared them ever shall forget
The emotions of the spirit-rousing time,
When breathless in the mart the couriers met,
Early and late, at evening and at prime;
When the loud cannon and the merry chime
Hail'd news on news, as field on field was won,
When Hope, long doubtful, soar'd at length sublime,
And our glad eyes, awake as day begun,
Watch'd Joy's broad banner rise, to meet the rising sun!

O these were hours, when thrilling joy repaid
A long, long course of darkness, doubts, and fears!
The heart-sick faintness of the hope delay'd,
The waste, the woe, the bloodshed, and the tears
That track'd with terror twenty rolling years,
All was forgot in that blithe jubilee!
Her downcast eye even pale Affliction rears,
To sigh a thankful prayer, amid the glee
That hail'd the Despot's fall, and peace and liberty.

Such news o'er Scotland's hills triumphant rode,
When 'gainst the invaders turn'd the battle's scale,
When Bruce's banner had victorious flow'd
O'er Loudon's mountain, and in Ury's vale;
When English blood oft deluged Douglas-dale,
And fiery Edward routed stout St John,
When Randolph's war-cry swell'd the southern gale,
And many a fortress, town, and tower was won,
And fame still sounded forth fresh deeds of glory done.

(1-27)

Scott, as poet, it is clear, saw the events of the past projected on
his own present. Equally, when he wrote of the present, he saw it
in terms of the past. In *The Vision of Don Roderick* (1811), the
events of the Peninsular War are foreseen by Roderick, the last
Visigothic king of Spain, who reigned briefly in 710 and 711. In
The Field of Waterloo (1815), Napoleon is addressed almost as if
he were James IV at Flodden—a James who had lacked the
decency to die in his last fight:—

Look, ere thou leavest the fatal hill,
  Back on yon broken ranks
Upon whose wild confusion gleams
The moon, as on the troubled streams
  When rivers break their banks,
And, to the ruin'd peasant's eye,
Objects half seen roll swiftly by,
  Down the dread current hurl'd;
So mingle banner, wain and gun,
Where the tumultuous flight rolls on
Of warriors, who, when morn begun,
  Defied a banded world.

(XV,8-19)

Verse-romance was thus an instrument which enabled Scott to see the past in terms of the present, and the present in terms of the past. It was an instrument, however, of limited range. The verse-romances were successful in their presentation of the more heroic, and more glamorous aspects of the Scottish past, but failed almost entirely to give an impression of humbler life, or of the distinctively Scottish present. They gave Scott no opportunity to exercise his command of Scots. The nineteenth century of the poems is the period of British and French imperial rivalry, in terms of which distinctively Scottish developments, and ordinary Scots men and women, appeared insignificant. Scott, who edited, admired and imitated Dryden, lacked Dryden's ability to use verse to transform the local and evanescent into the universal and permanent, while at the same time the local and evanescent was central to his imaginative experience. It was only when he turned from verse to prose, from the romance to the novel, that his imagination was expanded and liberated to deal with fine local detail of the more recent past and revolutionary present, the present which the Laird of Abbotsford and uncrowned King of Scotland was himself helping to shape. "Tis Sixty Years Since", the sub-title of *Waverley*, immediately reveals the change of emphasis—Scott had turned to events which had happened in Scotland within living memory, events which still exerted some influence on contemporary society, much as the 1914-18 War still has its effect on present-day Britain and Europe. Some of the ways in which he related past and present have been illustrated in the discussion of *The Antiquary*.

Scott's improvements at Clarty Hole shared in importance with the earlier raids into Liddlesdale in forcing him to become aware of the continuity between past and present in the Borders. The voyage with the Commissioners for Northern Lights helped to bring Scotland as a whole within his ken. The voyage took him to the Shetlands and Orkneys, along the north coast of the mainland and down the west coast, with visits to the Inner and Outer Hebrides, Northern Ireland and the islands of the Firth of Clyde. Scott, as antiquary and historian, was fascinated, but it is clear that Scott, the improving landlord, also found much of importance. In the northern islands particuarly, the older Scotland was alive and visible, as some passages from the account of the Shetlands will serve to illustrate.[26]

Scott arrived in Lerwick on August 4th, and almost immediately, as was his way, went for a long exploratory walk:—

> The ground is terribly encumbered with stones; the patches, which have been sown with oats and barley, bear very good crops, but they are mere patches, the cattle and ponies feeding among them and secured by tethers. The houses most wretched, worse than the worst herd's house I ever saw. It would be easy to form a good farm by enclosing the ground with Galloway dykes, which would answer the purpose of clearing it at the same time of stones; and as there is plenty of lime-shell, marle, and alga-marina, manure could not be wanting. But there are several obstacles to improvement, chiefly the undivided state of the properties, which lie *run-rig*; then the claims of Lord Dundas, the lord of the country; and above all, perhaps, the state of the common people, who, dividing their attention between the fishery and the cultivation, are not much interested in the latter, and are often absent at the proper times of labour. Their ground is chiefly dug with the spade, and their ploughs are beyond description awkward. An odd custom prevails—any person, without exception (if I understand rightly) who wishes to raise a few kail, fixes upon any spot he pleases, encloses it with a dry stone-wall, uses it as a kail-yard till he works out the soil, then deserts it and makes another. Some dozen of these little enclosures, about twenty or thirty feet square, are in sight at once. They are called planty-cruives . . .
>
> In our return, pass the upper end of the little lake of Cleik-him-in, which is divided by a rude causeway from another small loch, communicating with it, however, by a sluice, for the purpose of driving a mill. But such a mill! The wheel is horizontal, with the cogs turned diagonally to the water; the beam stands upright, and is inserted in a stone-quern of the old-fashioned construction. This simple machine is enclosed in a hovel about the size of a pig-stye, and there is the mill! There are about 500 such mills in Shetland, each incapable of grinding more than a sack at a time.

In his diary, Scott added a rough sketch to illustrate the operation of the mill.

Two days later he went to dine at the home of an improving landlord on the island of Bressay:—

> Young Mr. Mowat, son of my old friend, is an improver, and a *moderate* one. He has got a ploughman from Scotland, who acts as *grieve*, but as yet with the prejudices and inconveniences which usually attach themselves to the most salutary experiments. The ploughman complains that the Zetlanders work as if a spade or hoe burned their fingers, and though they only get a shilling a-day, yet the labour of three of them does not exceed what one good hand in Berwickshire would do for 2s.6d. The islanders retort, that a man can do no more than he can; that they are not used to be taxed to their work so severely: that they will work as their fathers did, and not otherwise; and at first the landlord found difficulty in getting hands to work under his Caledonian taskmaster. Besides, they find fault with his *ho*, and *gee*, and *wo*, when ploughing. "He speaks to the horse," they say, "and they gang— and there's something no canny about the man". In short, between the prejudices of laziness and superstition, the ploughman leads a sorry life of it; yet those prejudices are daily abaiting, under the steady and indulgent management of the proprietor. Indeed, nowhere is improvement in agriculture more necessary. An old-fashioned Zetland plough is a real curiosity. It had but one handle, or stilt, and a coulter, but no sock; it ripped the furrow, therefore, but did not throw it aside. When this precious machine was in motion, it was dragged by four little bullocks yoked abreast and as many ponies harnessed, or rather strung to the plough by ropes and thongs of raw hide. One man went before, walking backwards; with his face to the bullocks, and pulling them forward by main strength. Another held down the plough by its single handle, and made a sort of slit in the earth, which two women, who closed the procession converted into a furrow, by throwing the earth aside with shovels. An antiquary

> might be of opinion that this was the very model of the
> original plough invented by Triptolemus: and it is but
> justice to Zetland to say, that these relics of ancient
> agricultural art will soon have all the interest attached
> to rarity. We could only hear of one of these ploughs
> within three miles of Lerwick.

The most direct effect of Scott's visit to Shetland is to be seen
in *The Lord of the Isles,* and in one of his less successful novels,
The Pirate (1821)—there, most of all in the presentation of the
anachronistic but significantly named improver, Triptolemus
Yellowley. It is only necessary however to think of Cuddy
Headrigg, the ploughman in *Old Mortality,* to see the more
generalized effect which his experiences in the Shetlands and
elsewhere, sharpened by his labours as landlord of Abbotsford,
exercised on Scott's creative imagination. It was not merely, or
even primarily, the more glamorous incidents and people of the
past—Claverhouse, for instance, the Jacobite cause in general or
Prince Charles Edward in particular—which kindled Scott to his
most creative achievement. By the 'teens and 'twenties of the
nineteenth century, the glamour perhaps remained, but the
relevance had departed. Scott's concern was with the continuous
process and development which linked past with present. Above
all, perhaps, he was concerned with development as it affected
the land itself, as it affected Scotland, which he saw dominated
by the countryside and its people. Edinburgh was also part of
Scotland, but Scott's Edinburgh is a place reserved almost
exclusively for lawyers and mobs, a place from which to escape.
Several novels—one particularly recalls *The Antiquary* and
Redgauntlet—begin with a happy departure from Edinburgh.
Save in *Rob Roy,* Glasgow scarcely makes an appearance.

Scott only gradually, I believe, came to realize the full aptness
for his own purposes of the form which he tentatively adopted
in *Waverley. Waverley* almost certainly he wrote to be complete
in itself. By 1816 when he had completed *The Antiquary,* his
ideas had changed, as he indicates in the Advertisement prefixed
to that novel and already quoted.[27] Here clearly expressed is the
idea of historical progression through some fifty years, which is
to unite several volumes otherwise quite distinct, and emphasize
continuity as much as change. In the Advertisement he writes as
if with the completion of his trilogy he intended to give up the

novel. "I have now", he says, "only to express my gratitude to the public for the distinguished reception which they have given to works that have little more than some truth of colouring to recommend them, and to take my respectful leave, as one who is not likely again to solicit their favour."

In this way "The Author of Waverley" made, or pretended to make, his *congé*. A few months later, a work, apparently by a new author, appeared under the title of *Tales of My Landlord, Collected and Reported by Jedediah Cleishbotham, Schoolmaster and Parish-Clerk of Gandercleugh*. The four volumes, which composed the first series, contained *The Black Dwarf* and *Old Mortality*, and were afterwards succeeded by a second, third and fourth series, consisting of (2) *The Heart of Midlothian*, (3) *The Bride of Lammermoor* and *A Legend of Montrose*, and finally (4) *Count Robert of Paris* and *Castle Dangerous*. The complete set thus contained some of the best, as well as some of the weakest of Scott's writings. Throughout his life, the idea of a linked series obviously appealed to him; in addition to *Tales of My Landlord*, he produced *Tales of the Crusaders* (*The Betrothed, The Talisman*), two series of *Chronicles of the Cannongate* (series 1, *The Two Drovers, The Highland Widow, The Surgeon's Daughter*; series 2, *St. Valentine's Day or The Fair Maid of Perth*), four series of *Tales of a Grandfather*, and the series which derives a certain amount of mild fun from the interchanges between Captain Cuthbert Clutterbuck of Fairylodge, Kennaquhair, N.B., the Rev. Dr Dryasdust of York, and the mysterious Great Unknown, the Author of Waverley—(*The Monastery, The Abbot, Peveril of the Peak* etc.). The habit of regarding Scott's work, not as a group of individual works, but rather as a unified collection, the Waverley Novels perhaps derives from the existence within his *opus* of these significant, smaller, but still extensive, groupings.

Jedediah Cleishbotham claimed in his pompous schoolmasterly prose style to be no more than the editor of material which had in fact been collected and written up by his deceased assistant, Peter Pattieson, who in turn had gathered it from visitors to the Wallace Head Inn in the village of Gandercleugh, "the navel (*si fas sit dicere*) of this our native realm of Scotland; so that men from every corner thereof, when travelling on their concernments of business either towards our metropolis of law, by which I mean Edinburgh, or towards our metropolis and mart of gain, whereby I insinuate Glasgow, are frequently led to make Gandercleugh their abiding stage and place of rest for the night". Scott thus opened the way for a series of novels, each independent of, yet maintaining some kind of dependent relation to, the others. The device is old. In literary terms, the Wallace Head is a distant reflection of the Tabard Inn at Southwark, the meeting place of Chaucer's pilgrims; *Tales of My Landlord* is to be taken as in some sense a northern equivalent of *The Canterbury Tales*, the one representing medieval English society and the complexity of its interests at a time of intellectual and political crisis, the other that of Scotland during a period equally critical for its destiny. Scott is, in a sense, the last of the Scottish Chaucerians. In his tales, as in Chaucer's, comedy dominates, but the comedy is of a kind able to encompass tragedy and near-tragedy: it is human, even divine, comedy.

The dedication runs:— "To his loving Countrymen, whether they are denominated Men of the South, Gentlemen of the North, People of the West or Folk of Fife, these Tales, illustrative of ancient Scottish manners, and of the traditions of their respective districts, are respectfully inscribed, by their friend and liege fellow-subject, Jedediah Cleishbotham". In the national scope of the series as a whole, we may perhaps recognize one side-effect of the extended voyage with the Commissioners for Northern Lights.

The dedication lays particular emphasis on "ancient Scottish manners", yet the first readers must have been immediately struck by the expression of one distinctively modern aspect of Scottish life which forms the introduction to *The Black Dwarf*. The story is set in the Borders during the last years of Queen Anne's reign ("Ye had best bide content wi' auld Nanse for want of a better Queen" Hobbie tells the baffled conspirators in chapter 17), and demonstrates the final stages of Border life as it had been recorded in the ballads—"the auld riding days". The modern farmer and his shepherd are introduced not merely as sources of the story but to contrast the nineteenth with the eighteenth century:—

> "Hout awa' man," answered the farmer, "ye'll hae heard o' Canny Elshie the Black Dwarf, or I am muckle mistaen—A' the warld tells tales about him. but it's but daft nonsense after a'—I dinna believe a word o't frae beginning to end."

"Your father believed it unco stievely, though," said the old man, to whom the scepticism of his master gave obvious displeasure.

"Ay, very true, Bauldie, but that was in the time o' the blackfaces — they believed a hantle queer things in thae days, that naebody heeds since the lang sheep cam in."

"The mair's the pity, the mair's the pity," said the old man. "Your father, and sae I have aften tell'd ye, maister, wad hae been sair vexed to hae seen the auld peel-house wa's pu'd down to make park dykes; and the bonny broomy knowe, where he liked sae weel to sit at e'en, wi' his plaid about him, and look at the kye as they cam down the loaning, ill wad he hae liked to hae seen that braw sunny knowe a' riven out wi'the pleugh in the fashion it is at this day."

"Hout, Bauldie," replied the principal, "tak ye that dram the landlord's offering ye, and never fash your head about the changes o' the warld, sae lang as ye're blithe and bien yoursell."

"Wussing your health, sirs," said the shepherd; and having taken of his glass, and observed the whisky was the right thing, he continued, "It's no for the like o' us to be judging, to be sure; but it was a bonny knowe that broomy knowe, and an unco braw shelter for the lambs in a severe morning like this."

"Aye," said his patron, "but ye ken we maun hae turnips for the lang sheep, billie, and muckle hard wark to get them, baith wi' the pleugh and the howe; and that wad sort ill wi' siccan clavers, as was the gate lang syne, when the short sheep were in the fashion."

"Aweel, aweel, maister," said the attendant, "short sheep had short rents, I'm thinking."

Here my *worthy and learned* patron again interposed, and observed, "that he could never perceive any material difference, in point of longtitude, between one sheep and another."

This occasioned a loud hoarse laugh on the part of the farmer, and an astonished stare on the part of the shepherd. "It's the woo', man, — it's the woo, and no the beasts themsells, that makes them be ca'd lang or short. I believe if ye were to measure their backs, the short sheep wad be rather the langer-bodied o' the twa; but it's the woo'that pays the rent in thae days, and it had muckle need."

"Odd, Bauldie says very true, — short sheep did make short rents — my father paid for our steading just threescore punds, and it stands me in three hundred, plack and bawbee. — And that's very true — I hae nae time to be standing here clavering — Landlord, get us our breakfast, and see an' get the yauds fed — I am for doun to Christy Wilson's to see if him and me can gree about the luckpenny I am to gie him for his year-aulds. We had drank sax mutchkins to the making the bargain at St. Boswell's fair, and some gate we canna gree upon the particulars preceesly, for as muckle time as we took about it — I doubt we draw to a plea — But hear ye, neighbour," addressing my *worthy and learned* patron, "if ye want to hear ony thing about lang or short sheep, I will be back here to my kail against ane o'clock; or, if ye want ony auld-warld stories about the Black Dwarf, and sic-like, if ye'll ware a half mutchkin upon Bauldie there, he'll crack t'ye like a pen-gun. And I'se gie ye a mutchkin myself, man, if I can settle weel wi' Christy Wilson."

The main conflict of the *Black Dwarf* belongs to the early eighteenth century, when the heroic age of the Borderers as displayed, for instance, in the ballad *Jamie Telfer of the Fair Dodhead* was already a thing of the past. The nurse Annaple announces the harrying of Heugh-foot in the old style—"The steading's a' in a low, and the bonny stack yard lying in the reek ashes, and the gear a' driven away"—but when it comes to organising a pursuit of the marauders who are assumed to be English, no one now clearly remembers the proper method.

"And besides," said another old man, "I dinna believe there's ane now living that kens the lawful mode of following a fray across the border. Tam o'Whittram kend a' about it; but he died in the hard winter."

"Ay," said a third, "he was at the great gathering,

when they chased as far as Thirlwall; it was the year after the fight of Philiphaugh."

"Hoot", exclaimed another of these discording counsellors, "there's nae great skill needed; just put a lighted peat on the end of a spear, or hayfork, or siclike, and blaw a horn, and cry the gatherin-word, and then it's lawful to follow gear into England, and recover it by the strong hand, or to take gear frae some other Englishman, providing ye lift nae mair than's been lifted frae you.'"

(Chapter 7)

The last counsellor, although confident, is not, one must emphasize, strictly accurate. The fray, of course, peters out into almost nothing, and ends

"Hout, ay," said Elliot, "just let byganes be byganes, and a' friends again; deil ane I bear malice at but Westburnflat, and I hae gien him baith a het skin and a cauld ane."

(Chapter 17)

The Black Dwarf is not a distinguished novel, but in technique it is fascinating, operating, as it does, at three levels—that of the old ballads, the events and words of which are often echoed and parodied in the main narrative; that of assumed historical actuality in the early eighteenth century, when the old Borders and the old order, now represented by the Jacobites, were in decline, but still able to make trouble; and that, finally, of the nineteenth century, when the old life had been replaced by something apparently quite different. Each period is counterpointed against the others. Yet the sense of continuity is also strong. The old shepherd of the Introduction rides with his master as kinsman and equal; he is mounted on a Border pony, and wears the blue bonnet and long blue worsted hose which had characterized his fighting and marauding ancestors. The farmer has converted his feuds into the threat of legal proceedings, and, though he poses as a sceptic, it becomes clear that ancestral superstitions have not entirely departed from his mind and imagination—at heart he still believes in the Black Dwarf (who is not, incidentally, the dwarf who appears in the novel, but a figure of folk-belief). One part of Scott is saying and hoping that nothing essential to the life of the Borders has been lost in the transition from short to long sheep, or with the cessation of Border forays. The novel fails, not so much in its basic structure, as in the unconvincing presentation and characterization of the Black Dwarf himself, a figure whose natural habitat is the absurder kind of Gothic novel, more than the novel of social and intellectual change and contrast, which Scott for much of the book had successfully undertaken. He is too extreme a figure to be sheltered under the defence of melodrama offered for *The Antiquary*.

In *Old Mortality*, the most consistently successful of the series, the primary effect of the counterpoint is pastoral and elegaic; the figure of Old Mortality working among the tombs of the deserted country burial ground effectively distances the savagery of the Killing Times. The novel itself is concerned not merely with civil war and religion, but with reconciliation, symbolized by the wedding of old opponents, Cuddy Headrigg and Jenny Dennison, Henry Morton and Edith Bellenden, in each case to the discomfiture of rivals, Tam Halliday and Lord Evandale, who are politically more extreme than either successful suitor. So too there is much emphasis on the increase of knowledge and prosperity in the countryside. Near the beginning, Cuddie and Mause Headrigg are expelled from the employment of Lady Margaret Bellenden, who exclaims "I had rather that the rigs of Tillietudlem bare naething but windle-straes and sandy lavrocks than that they were ploughed by rebels to the king" (chapter 7). Cuddie's lament which appears a few pages later:— "I am no clear if I can pleugh ony place but the Mains and Mucklewhame—at least, I never tried ony other grund, and it wudna come natural to me"—is reminiscent of the complaints of the Shetlanders against the Border ploughmen. It is a different and more perceptive man who at the end of the book replies to the unrecognised Morton's compliment on the rich and peaceful countryside, "It's no to compleen o', sir, an we get the crap weel in . . . but if ye had seen the blude runnin' as fast on the tap o' that brigg yonder as ever the water ran below it, ye wadna hae thought it sae bonnie a spectacle" (Chapter 37: III.1). The Killing Time is seen as a kind of baptism of fire for the emergence of the new society.

Scott, however, is not complacent about the new society. *Old*

Mortality, basically, is the story of a Whig uprising in the West of Scotland, and, as such, could not be without its painful relevance to the period which immediately followed the Napoleonic Wars, when Castlereagh was Leader of the House of Commons and another rising of the Western Whigs presented a real and dangerous possibility. (In 1820 it became an actuality.) Scott was a Tory, but in *Old Mortality* his presentation of the moderate Whigs who adhere to Henry Morton is reasonably symphathe- tic, and it is these moderate Whigs who are the eventual victors in the struggle. Even in 1819, his reaction to revolution, although strong, avoided hysteria. During that year, in Lockhart's words,[28] "there prevailed a spirit of alarming insub- ordination among the mining population of Northumberland and the weavers of the west of Scotland". Scott's realization of the parallel with some of the events of *Old Mortality*, and the Covenanting period in general, is strikingly revealed in the letters which he wrote at this time.

> Glasgow is in a terrible state. The Radicals had a plan to seize on 1000 stand of arms, as well as a depot of ammunition which had been sent from Edinburgh Castle for the use of the volunteers. The Commander- in-Chief, Sir Thomas Bradford, went to Glasgow in person, and the whole city was occupied with patrols of horse and foot, to deter them from the meditated attack on the barracks. The arms were then delivered to the volunteers, who are said to be 4000 on paper; how many effective and trustworthy, I know not. But it was a new sight in Scotland on Sunday to see all the inhabitants in arms, soldiers patrolling the streets, and the utmost precaution of military service exacted and observed in an apparently peaceful city.

Scott's own company of volunteers were to be organised in a way which recalls the tournament of the Popinjay:— "And we will have shooting at the mark, and prizes, and fun, and a little whisky, and daily pay when on duty or drill"—and his com- ments on the possible defence of Berwick—"I defy the devil to pass the bridge at Berwick, if reasonably well kept by 100 men"—show that the earlier battle at Bothwell Brig was very much present to his mind. Scott as a magistrate was primarily concerned with the issue of law and order. As a novelist, his intellectual and imaginative sympathies were considerably further to the left. In many respects *Old Mortality* is a parable for Scott's contemporaries, a parable which has not lost its relevance to the present day.

The Introduction to *The Heart of Midlothian* provides another elaborate counterpoint. The central event of the novel, set in the late 1730's, is Jeanie Deans' long barefoot trudge from Edinburgh to London to plead for her sister's life. Her sister meanwhile is lodged in the Heart of Midlothian, the Tolbooth of Edinburgh under sentence of death by the strict and barbarous letter of a law, with which Jeanie has found herself unable to compromise. The contrast between law on the one hand and justice and mercy on the other is symbolised by the two Hearts of Midlothian, the Tolbooth in Edinburgh and Jeanie on the long road to London.

The first theme, which Scott, or rather Peter Pattieson, mischieviously takes up in his introductory chapter, is travel, the journey, and the wonders and perils of modern rapid transport as compared with that of the eighteenth century. "Mail-coach races against mail-coach and high-flyer against high-flyer, through the most remote districts of Britain. And in our village alone, three post-coaches, and four coaches with men armed and in scarlet cassocks, thunder through the streets each day." The comparison with the journey of Jeanie Deans is obvious. Progress, however, brings new perils on the road, and it is as a result of a mail-coach crash that Peter Pattieson meets the two lawyers and the debtor recently released from the Heart of Midlothian, from whom at the Wallace Head he gathers the material which forms his own *Heart of Midlothian*. The Tolbooth, he also learns, is on the point of demolition, while the released debtor, Mr. Dunover, is on a lesser scale as much a victim of the law as was Jeanie Deans' sister Effie. Continuity is primarily represented by the constancy of injustice, and misfortune, as evident in the case of Mr. Dunover as in that of Effie Deans—and also by the kindliness of the lawyers which in a minor way parallels the more heroic conduct of Jeanie.

Nor is this all. Contrast is at least as important as continuity. The most important passage of the introductory chapter is the 'Last Speech, Confession and Dying Words' of the condemned

Edinburgh Tolbooth, or rather the development of the theme by
the young advocate, Hardie:—

> "I have understood", said I, encouraged by the
> affability of my rattling entertainer, "that less of this
> interest must attach to Scottish jurisprudence than to
> that of any other country. The general morality of our
> people, their sober and prudent habits—"
> "Secure them", said the barrister, "against any great
> increase of professional thieves and depredators, but not
> against wild and wayward starts of fancy and passion,
> producing crimes of an extraordinary description,
> which are precisely those to the detail of which we
> listen with thrilling interest. England has been much
> longer a highly civilised country; her subjects have
> been very strictly amenable to laws administered with-
> out fear or favour, a complete division of labour has
> taken place among her subjects, and the very thieves
> and robbers form a distinct class in society, subdivided
> among themselves according to the subject of the
> depredations and the mode in which they carry them
> on, acting upon regular habits and principles, which
> can be calculated and anticipated at Bow Street, Hatton
> Garden, or the Old Bailey. Our sister kingdom is like a
> cultivated field, — the farmer expects that, in spite of
> all his care, a certain number of weeds will rise with the
> corn, and can tell you beforehand their names and
> appearance. But Scotland is like one of her own
> Highland glens, and the moralist who reads the record
> of her criminal jurisprudence, will find as many curious
> anomalous facts in the history of mind, as the botanist
> will detect rare specimens among her dingles and
> cliffs."

"The history of mind" and in particular the history of the
abnormal or non-typical mind, is what Scott here emphasises,
and the metaphor which he employs is the contrast between the
enclosed cornlands of the Agricultural Revolution and the
unenclosed profusion of a Highland glen. As the novel advances,
however, one becomes more and more aware that an almost
medieval element of biblical allegory is implied by the contrast.

Justice and mercy are the main themes of the novel, and time and again a parallel with the thematic development of Shakespeare's *Measure for Measure* becomes apparent. From this point of view, the old Scotland and its criminal jurisprudence becomes identified with Old Law of preventive justice; the new and improved Scotland with the New Law of mercy, as the concepts are developed in Pauline theology. The Pauline Old Man appears in the Porteous riots and the condemnation of Effie Deans; the first stages of the transition from Old to New are represented by the end of Scottish independence in 1707, the second by Jeanie Deans' mission of mercy, and the theme is completed by the eventual settlement of Davie and Jeanie Deans and Reuben Butler is the pastoral landscape of Dumbartonshire. The novel turns on two reprieves or redemptions; that of Porteous, which leads to a recrudescence of the Old Law, and that of Effie which goes far to establishing the New. Time and again the dialogue returns to this point:—

> "I am judging," said Mr. Plumdamas, "that this reprieve wadna stand gude in the auld Scots law, when the kingdom *was* a kingdom."
>
> "I dinna ken muckle about the law," answered Mrs. Howden; "but I ken, when we had a king, and a chancellor, and parliament-men o' our ain, we could aye peeble them wi' stanes when they werena gude bairns."
>
> (Chapter 4)

Stoning as a punishment decidedly belongs to the Old Law. With this, contrast Jeanie's speech to Queen Caroline:—

> "O, madam, if ever ye kend what it was to sorrow for and with a sinning and a suffering creature, whose mind is sae tossed that she can be neither ca'd fit to live or die, have some compassion on our misery!—Save an honest house from dishonour, and an unhappy girl, not eighteen years of age, from an early and dreadful death! Alas! it is not when we sleep soft and wake merrily ourselves that we think on other people's sufferings. Our hearts are waxed light within us then, and we are for righting our ain wrangs and fighting our ain battles.

But when the hour of trouble comes to the mind or to the body—and seldom may it visit your Leddyship—and when the hour of death comes,that comes to high and low—lang and late may it be yours!—Oh my Leddy, then it isna what we hae dune for oursells, but what we hae dune for others, that we think on maist pleasantly. And the thought that ye hae intervened to spare the puir thing's life will be sweeter in that hour, come when it may, than if a word of your mouth could hang the haill Porteous mob at the tail of ae tow."

(Chapter 37: IV.i.)

Jeanie brings the Queen, who herself represents one aspect of the old regime, if not quite the Old Law, to the general level of suffering humanity, and in this, as in her entire phraseology and cast of thought, she shows the Calvinist ancestry which had done so much to shape the old Scotland. Redemption from the old is by way of the old, raised to the highest point of humanity. Equally, however, as Jeanie realises, the condemnation of Effie results from Calvinist church government in its less enlightened aspects.

"Stand up, young woman," said the Queen, but in a kind tone, "and tell me what sort of a barbarous people your countryfolk are, where child-murder is become so common as to require the restraint of laws like yours?"
. . .

"Some think it's the Kirk-Session—that is—it's the—it's the cutty-stool, if your Leddyship pleases," said Jeanie, looking down and curtseying.

"The what?" said Lady Suffolk, to whom the phrase was new, and who besides was rather deaf.

"That's the stool of repentance, madam, if it please your Leddyship," answered Jeanie, "for light life and conversation, and for breaking the seventh command."

(Chapter 37: IV.i.)

The Kirk-Session, in other words, is responsible for the situation which led to Effie's condemnation, even if, at the same time, the teaching of the Kirk produced Jeanie to redeem her sister.

One aspect of the Old Law is caricatured by the learned leather-merchant, Bartholomew Saddletrees, while the Cameronian, Davie Deans, represents the teaching and practice of the Kirk in its most traditional form. It is his way of life which is responsible for the downfall of his daughter Effie, and for the refusal of Jeanie to perjure herself even to save her sister's life. But Jeanie's courage and endurance is an even more significant part of her Cameronian inheritance. And Deans exhibits in himself the Cameronian adaptability to the new order when he becomes the successful and effective superintendent of the Duke of Argyle's fancy-farm in Dumbartonshire. (Here again, the novel returns to the Agricultural Revolution.) On his death he leaves a fortune of £1500, which with Jeanie's contribution, enables the Butlers to buy the estate of Craigsture. One of her sons becomes a soldier, the other a lawyer; her daughter marries a Highland laird. Even if the process is enlightened, and typical of Scotland in the later eighteenth century, the last pages of the novel are more prosaic, even prosy, than the earlier chapters. The new Scotland is duller than the old. Scott certainly felt, however, that his Scotland needed a substantial infusion of plain, prosperous prose. The contrast of the Butlers with the Catholic, Jacobite Stauntons is self-explanatory.

Although *The Bride of Lammermoor* turns on the same contrast of old and new—the Master of Ravenswood versus Sir William Ashton—I can see minimal artistic point in the Introduction, the description of the painter, Dick Tinto. That to *A Legend of Montrose*, however is in some ways the most striking of all, because here Scott uses, as his tragic counterpoint to Montrose and the veteran of the wars of Gustavus Adolphus, Dugald Dalgettie, a discharged and disabled Highland veteran of the Peninsular War, Sergeant More McAlpin, who has been forced as a result of the Highland Clearances, to take up residence in Gandercleugh.

> He retired with the intention of enjoying this in-
> come [his pension and prizemoney] in the wild High-
> land glen, in which, when a boy, he had herded black
> cattle and goats, ere the roll of the drum had made him
> cock his bonnet an inch higher, and follow its music for

nearly forty years. To his recollections, this retired spot was unparalleled in beauty by the richest scenes he had visited in his wanderings. Even the Happy Valley of Rasselas would have sunk into nothing upon the comparison. He came—he revisited the loved scene; it was but a sterile glen, surrounded with rude crags, and traversed by a northern torrent. This was not the worst. The fires had been quenched upon thirty hearths—of the cottage of his fathers he could but distinguish a few rude stones—the language was almost extinguished—the ancient race from which he boasted his descent had found a refuge beyond the Atlantic. One southland farmer, three grey-plaided shepherds, and six dogs, now tenanted the whole glen, which in his youth had maintained, in content, if not in competence, upwards of two hundred inhabitants.

Emigration, depopulation, sheep taking the place of men—the perennial lament of the Highlands in modern times gives a new poignancy to a narrative primarily concerned with what Neil Munro was afterwards to call the Little Wars of Lorne.

It is probably worth while to compare the technique adopted by Scott in *Tales of My Landlord* with that of his younger contemporary John Galt, in *Annals of the Parish* and *The Provost*. Galt's work is discussed in some detail in the next chapter. Here, it is enough to say that his method is generally autobiographical. His minister, Mr. Balwhidder, and his Provost Pawkie, have themselves lived through revolutionary times, and at the end of their lives set down an account of what they have seen, heard and experienced. The method has some advantages. It is more direct than that of Scott, and at the same time allows a fair number of subtleties, as for instance in Mr. Balwhidder's short-sighted but appropriate recollections of the period of the French Revolution. Under 1788 he records the building of a cotton-mill in his parish, and the first "signs of decay in the wonted simplicity of our country ways". He mentions in passing that the affairs of the French were then gathering towards a head. Under 1789, the year of the Revolution, the French receive not a single mention. "This I have always reflected upon as one of our blessed years', Mr. Balwhidder remarks. "It was not remarkable for any extraordinary occurrence." A stage-coach however makes its first appearance in the parish, where a notable sermon was also preached in a new and Anglified style by a visiting clergyman. In 1790 a bookshop was opened, and a daily newspaper made its first appearance. Infidelity increased, despite the building of a bridge over the Brawl burn—"a great convenience, in the winter time, to the parishioners that lived on the north side; for when there happened to be a speat on the Sunday, it kept them from the kirk, but I did not find that the bridge mended the matter, till after the conclusion of the war against the democrats, and the beginning of that which we are now waging with Boney, their child and champion."

The French Revolution is present, however muted, and Mr. Balwhidder's limited parochial point of view serves marvellously to put even the French Revolution into the more extended perspective of intellectual and industrial change.

Galt was a remarkable man and accomplished novelist, whose work has not yet had its due. He was able, moreover, to tackle what Scott did not attempt, the growth of industrialism in Scotland and elsewhere, and the establishment of emigrant Scots overseas in Canada and the United States. His sense of change is as acute, perhaps more acute, than that of Scott. On the other hand, possibly because he spent so much of his life outside Scotland, and so in a sense lacked roots in the community, Galt in a measure fails to give us the sense of long-term continuity and growth within Scotland, which as I have tried to indicate is so characteristic of Scott. In the full world of the nineteenth century, Mr. Balwhidder and Provost Pawkie are clearly survivals, anachronisms; the narratives of Peter Pattieson belong to the new world without any sense of total rupture with the old.

Galt's novels will be discussed in the next chapter. Scott's artistic accomplishments I have several times described as one of the reconciliation between new and old. In the end, however even Scott's charity was unable to embrace every feature of the new world. The Whig revolt of the seventeenth century is paralleled by that of the nineteenth. Sergeant More McAlpin is not a figure of reconciliation, and the final impression left by *The Heart of Midlothian* is surely the continued presence of injustice and evil in the new as in the old world.

NOTES

During the past quarter-century, a series of interesting, sometimes provocative, books and essays, primarily on Scott as novelist, have appeared. These include Alexander Welsh, *The Hero of the Waverley Novels* (New Haven and London, 1963) Thomas Crawford, *Scott* (Edinburgh, 1965): D.D. Devlin (ed.), *Walter Scott* (Nashville and London, 1969): R.C. Gordon, *Under Which King?* (Edinburgh and London, 1969): A. Norman Jeffares (ed.), *Scott's Mind and Art* (Edinburgh, 1969): Angus and Jenni Calder, *Scott* (New York, 1971): David Daiches, *Sir Walter Scott and his World* (London, 1971): A. Bell (ed.), *Scott Bicentenary Essays* (Edinburgh and London, 1973): Robin Mayhead, *Walter Scott* (London, 1973): Ian Campbell (ed.), *Nineteenth Century Scottish Fiction* (Manchester, 1979. This book is also of interest for the later chapters of the present work.): Mary Lascelles, *The Story-Teller Retrieves the Past* (Oxford, 1980): A.N. Wilson, *The Laird of Abbotsford. A View of Sir Walter Scott* (Oxford, 1980): Jane Millgate, *Walter Scott. The Making of the Novelist* (Toronto and Edinburgh, 1984).

Three studies, primarily of biographic interest, should also be mentioned: Edgar Johnson, *Sir Walter Scott. The Great Unknown* (2 vols., London, 1970): Carola Oman, *The Wizard of the North* (London, 1973): D. S. Hewitt (ed.), *Scott on Himself* (Edinburgh, 1981). W.E.K. Anderson has produced a good edition of *The Journal of Sir Walter Scott* (Oxford, 1972).

The most accessible edition of Scott's poetry is still J. Logie Robertson, *The Poetical Works of Sir Walter Scott* (London, 1904, and many reprints).

A new edition of the novels, under the General Editorship of Dr Hewitt, is now under preparation.

1. *The Theory of Moral Sentiment* appeared in 1759; *An Inquiry into the Nature and Causes of the Wealth of Nations* (2 vols.) in 1776.

2. For the importance of Hartley, see especially "David Hartley and Nature's Education", chapter 8 of Basil Willey, *The Eighteenth Century Background* (London, 1940: Pelican ed., 1972).

3. The phrase is taken from chapter 1 of *The Heart of Midlothian*. See above, p.101.

4. See especially chapter 1, "Prelude to the Eighteenth Century".

5. *Scott Bicentenary Essays*, pp.134-46. It is substantially incorporated in chapter 4 of his book, *Walter Scott*.

6. "Scott's Achievement as a Novelist", reprinted in *Scott's Mind and Art*, pp.21-52. The phrase quoted will be found on p. 38.

7. The phrases quoted are loosely based on *The Alchemist*, II.iii.189-98.

8. p.32. *The History of John Bull* is edited by Alan W. Bower and Robert A. Erickson (Oxford, 1976).

9. 19 vols. (Edinburgh, 1814).

10. *ed.cit.*, p.viii.

11. The most recent edition is by A.M. Stewart, *The Complaynt of Scotland* (STS, Edinburgh, 1979).

12. Stewart, p.49.

13. A.M. Kinghorn and A. Law (eds.), *The Works of Allan Ramsay* III (STS, Edinburgh and London, 1961), pp. 7-31. The father's name, Duniwhistle, represents Gaelic *duin' uasal*, "a gentleman": it is part of Ramsay's general

view of Scottish history, and specifically of his Jacobitism, that he gives the ancestral figure in his poem, the giver of the symbolic bonnets, a distinctively Gaelic name. Compare in Scott's novel the relationship of Rob Roy to Baillie Nicol Jarvie, on which I comment in *Progress and Poetry*, p.72.

14. *ed. cit.*, VI (STS, Edinburgh and London, 1974), p.104.

15. H. Bergson, *Laughter*, trs. of *Le Rire, Essai sur la signification du comique* (1900), in W Sypher (ed.), *Comedy* (New York, 1956), pp.61-190. The quotation will be found on p.69.

16. Sypher, *op.cit.*, pp.69-70.

17. "*Ulysses*, Order and Myth", *The Dial* (November, 1923), pp.480-83.

18. *The Dickens World* (Oxford, 1941), p.90.

19. See especially pp.5, 102-105, 134ff.

20. E. Fraenkel, *Horace* (Oxford, 1957), p.217.

21. This and the later passages translated are quoted by Scott in footnotes as the work of his friend, the improver Sir Henry Stewart of Allanton (1759-1836). *The Works of Sallust, with Original Essays* appeared in two volumes in 1806.

22. (Edinburgh and London, 1837), pp.136-277.

23. Volume II, p.358.

24. Duncan Forbes (ed.), *An Essay on the History of Civil Society 1767* (Edinburgh, 1966), p.8.

25. Karl Wilhelm Ferdinand, Duke of Brunswick, had his first military experience as an ally of Prussia during the Seven Years War (1756-63). He was commander of the allied Austrian and German army assembled to crush the French Revolution. He was in command of the Prussian army when he was mortally wounded at the battle of Auerstedt (1806).

Sir Ralph Abercromby also served in the Seven Years War. His sympathies with the American cause led him to take no part in the War of American Independence (1775-83). After his return to the army, he was one of the few successes in the disastrous Dutch campaign of 1793-5. In 1795 he became the very effective commander-in-chief of the British forces in the West Indies: subsequently he held command posts in Ireland and Scotland, and was second-in-command to the Duke of York in the Dutch expedition of 1799. In 1801 he commanded the expedition sent to expel the French from Egypt, organised a brilliant landing at Aboukir Bay, and was mortally wounded in the course of an unsuccessful surprise attack on his troops near Alexandria.

Scott, or rather his supposed interlocutor, William Erskine, sees either soldier as the possible hero of a modern epic:—

> Or deem'st thou not our later time
> Yields topic meet for classic rhyme?

$$(43-4)$$

Interestingly, perhaps disappointingly, he sets this scheme in contrast to the historical dramas—*Basil* and *De Montfort*—of Joanna Baillie (1762-1851), whom he regarded as the successor of Shakespeare in this field. His own later novels display an obvious and powerful relationship to the

Histories and other plays. See Mary Lascelles, "Scott and Shakespeare", first of the Sir Walter Scott Lectures for 1960, *University of Edinburgh Journal*, Spring Number, 1961, pp.23-33: W. Brewer, *Shakespeare's Influence on Sir Walter Scott* (Boston, 1925: reprint, Boston, 1974).

26. pp.143-5, 152-3.
27. Above, p.49.
28. Volume 4, chapter x. pp.318, 324, 330, 328. See also below, pp.163-4.

CHAPTER III

JOHN GALT

Scott was never much of a traveller. He belonged to the more conservative east of Scotland; his natural haunts were the monuments and antiquities of Edinburgh and Tweeddale, from which normally he felt little inclination to remove himself. To turn from him to John Galt (1779-1839) is to become aware of a contrast. Galt's roots were in the commercial and radical west, which formed the scene of many among his novels, and usually served for the rest as ultimate background. Personally, however, he was a traveller whose journeys furth of the British Isles made those even of Childe Harold himself seem provincial. For the most part, the immediate purpose of these journeys was commercial. But Galt did not limit himself to such purposes. His outlook was philosophic and historical; he was a business man, but also a student of *The Wealth of Nations* and *The History of Civil Society*. In short, he was an active unit of the historic nation, and thus tended to see everything in terms first of theory (he was always a theoretic historian), and, second, of his own national history.

This latter activity might take several forms all of which may be illustrated from the books which precede his novels. One is straightforward comparison. "The distant appearance of the Acropolis somewhat resembles that of Stirling Castle, but it is inferior in altitude and general effect."[1] Sometimes, and generally in a distinctively English rather than Scottish context, the effect is more oblique. In the instance to be quoted Galt begins from the pupils at a Turkish school established in the ancient Greek city of Argos:—

> "I have not yet had an opportunity of learning whether these schools are wholly for the instruction of Turkish boys, or whether they have been instituted also

110

for the pious purpose of bringing up any neglected Christian children in the gospel according to Mahomet.

All the youths brought up at the academy prove Mahomedans just in the same manner as all the students in the English universities become members of the Church of England. There is, however, some difference between the Turkish system and the English, if it embrace the conversion of youth to the tenets of the state religion. For at Oxford and Cambridge, where the youth are sent to be taught the true doctrines of the church, which are supposed not to be well taught any where else, it is very wisely required that they shall have not only pre-resolved to become members of the church, but that they shall actually be members—an arrangement which cannot be too much admired, as it has the effect, by excluding dissenters and catholics, of preserving the emoluments of the colleges to a much smaller number of persons. This system in the present age is the more worthy of being allowed to remain unaltered; for the number of dissenters is rapidly increasing, and if they were to be allowed to enter the universities, they might turn out the dealers in advowsons and fellowships, as the money-changers were of old expelled from the temple."[2]

Galt's third method has the appearance of contrast rather than comparison, but the contrast implies a comparison which often possesses a greater intrinsic importance:—

"Although I am very willing to allow the antients to have been very extraordinary persons, yet you know that I have always thought but little of their great affairs, and particularly of their famous characters, compared to the great affairs and the famous characters of the moderns. Aristides and Pericles, I own, were very able and respectable magistrates, and they may have been endowed by Nature with virtues and talents which would have fitted them for the rule of kingdoms, equal, in all the complexity of interests, to those of France and Britain; but the petty circumstances in which they were placed, surely render them, in a comparative estimate, but of moderate rank; otherwise, we do injustice to those whom we value, only by what they actually have done, without regarding what they might have performed, had their circumstances been more fortunate. However, with respect to the Grecian mind in general, I confess myself puzzled. By no hypothesis within my power of framing, can I account for that extraordinary excellence, in art and literature, which the Greeks so unquestionably attained, except by embracing the notion that the world has its stages of age like man; and supposing that the antients lived in the youth of the world, when all things were more fresh and beautiful than in the state in which we see them. We have the unquestionable authority of Homer, for the decline of human strength; and the reveries of Plato, and the other philosophers of Greece, are evidences of the juvenility, in their time, of the reason of man!"

The letter breaks off at this ambiguous point, but Galt began his next with the same subject:—

"Either you or I were in good luck, by the occurrence of an interruption, which obliged me to terminate my last letter abruptly. I found myself beginning to speculate; and God knows what nonsense you might have been obliged to read, had I been permitted to go on. As I cannot re-unite the spider-thread of theoretical reflection, which was then broken, I must soberly resume my narrative."[3]

Galt may or may not have been edging towards the admission that the art of statesmanship, as much as that of poetry or history or sculpture, may find its supreme expression in an early but very limited form. He may even have been moving towards some hypothetical equation of the magistrates of classical Athens with the Scottish burgh officials of his own experience. The language of the second extract just quoted seems to indicate at least that his mind was moving in the general area of speculative or theoretical history, where he was himself soon to produce his two chief studies of local accomplishment on the diminutive scale, *Annals of the Parish* and *The Provost*. The earliest version of the former seems to belong to 1813, the year in which *Letters from the Levant* was published. *Letters from the Levant*, in turn, certainly contains a multitude of references which involve parallels between the petty circumstances under which power was exercised in Greece, whether classical or modern, and eighteenth or nineteenth century Scotland and England.

The effect sometimes is merely diminishing. "On the shore, below them, another of the three ports of Athens is seen—and such a port! But it was large enough for the wherries and pinnaces of the Greeks—those boats, which the inhabitants of colleges translate ships of the line, to the confusion of all the means of forming distinct ideas of the real achievements of the antients."[4] He describes the battle of Salamis as "a battle of boats".[5] (Galt's father, we recollect, was owner and master of a West Indiaman; his own standards in shipping matters were thus likely to be high.) Of the Archbishop of Athens, he says: "His palace would, in Scotland, rank as a manse of the first class, and in England as a respectable parsonage. But the primate of all England does not exact a tithe of the reverence which is levied by the prelate".[6] He uses an interesting negative scale for the classification of Castro, the principal city on the island of Aegina:—

> "Assuming that the most despicable borough in all Scotland is zero in the scale of towns, I conceive that a Sicilian town of equal quantities must be many degrees lower. Castro, in the Isle of Egina, is about as much inferior to a Sicilian town of equal quantities as such a Sicilian town is inferior to the most despicable borough in all Scotland."[7]

The conclusion of all this debunking, reminiscent of Henry Ford at his most militant, is: "A multitude of minute circumstances in description is very apt to give an impression of greatness to small affairs. The circumstantiality with which the Greek historians have narrated all the little events, and even scandal, of their respective towns, has had the effect of making a magnified idea of every thing concerning them."[8]

Magnified or not, the technique used by Galt in his later works of fiction benefited by the earlier experience of Greek actualities seen in their relationship to Greek historical writing. In its way, *Annals of the Parish* is the Scottish equivalent of Thucydides' account of the period of the Peloponnesian War.

Galt did not limit his speculations to the Greeks. In *The Life and Administration of Cardinal Wolsey* (1812), he explained his interest in the rather unexpected figure of the self-made Renaissance prince of the English church by way of the relationship between a particular kind of man, and a particular stage in the development of society—terms very applicable to the West of Scotland in Galt's own time, which with some minor modification might be applied to the action of *The Provost*, *The Entail*, or *Lawrie Todd*, and which also have some relevance for Galt's own self-image:—

> "This state of the clergy and nobility, of manners, and learning, and trade, afforded ample scope for the exercise of an ambitious, resolute, ostentatious mind. The following narrative is an attempt to delineate the operations of a character indubitably of this description, and to exhibit a view of the influential events, by which it was governed, in a period full of great emergencies, and fraught with changes affecting the interests, perhaps, of the whole human race,—a period which, like the present momentous age, may be regarded as one of those vast occasional eddies in the mighty current of human affairs, by which homes and inheritances are overwhelmed and swept away, but which, as the violence subsides, never fail to leave, behind, inestimable riches for the use and improvement of society."[9]

The first draft of *Annals of the Parish* was, as we have seen, written not long after the publication of *Cardinal Wolsey*. In the final form, published in 1821, the book deals with the society of a single Ayrshire parish in the period from 1760 to 1810, 'the present, momentous age' which saw both the personal reign of George III, and the personal ministry of the narrator, the Rev. Micah Balwhidder. The great outside works of the king and the small world of the parish are drawn together by Balwhidder's more or less innocent eye, and each gives significance to the other. Like Cardinal Wolsey, Balwhidder is a churchman, but he is one who lacks the ambitious, resolute, ostentatious mind of his mighty predecessor. Such minds, however, do exist, on the parochial scale as in the outside world, and the changes which take place locally are largely brought about by men like Mr Kibbock, the improving farmer, and Mr Cayenne, the mill-owner, whose minds are built on the Wolsey pattern. The period of the book overlaps that which Scott attempted in his first three novels, and as Galt was the younger by almost a decade, the chronology assumed relative to the life of the author is almost equivalent. *Annals of the Parish* is a historical novel in the same sense as *Waverley, Guy Mannering* and *The Antiquary*.

I have already commented on the development in narrative technique between Fielding and Scott. Galt carries the process one stage further by the directness and rich texture of his fictitious autobiography:—

> "In the same year, and on the same day of the same month, that his Sacred Majesty King George, the third of the name, came to his crown and kingdom, I was placed and settled as the minister of Dalmailing. When about a week thereafter this was known in the parish, it was thought a wonderful thing, and everybody thought of me and the new king as united in our trusts and temporalities, marvelling how the same should come to pass, and thinking the hand of Providence was in it, and that surely we were pre-ordained to fade and flourish in fellowship together; which has really been the case, for in the same season that his Most Excellent Majesty, as he was very properly styled in the proclamations for the general fasts and thanksgivings, was set by as a precious vessel which had received a crack or a flaw, and could only be serviceable in the way of an ornament, I was obliged, by reason of age and the growing infirmities of my recollection, to consent to the earnest entreaties of the Session, and to accept of Mr. Amos to be my helper."[10]

The narrator is at once placed; he is an old man writing for younger contemporaries; a retired, egalitarian, Presbyterian and unconsciously self-important ("me and the new king") clergy-man, who can remember a time when news took a week to travel from London to rural Ayrshire. His language with its biblical overtones, marked alliteration, and Scots legal and colloquial idiom ("In the same year, and on the same day of the same month", "the third of the name", "placed and settled", "trusts and temporalities", "thinking the hand of Providence was in it", "set by") clearly stems from education in a Scottish university at a period before the Enlightenment and the rise of polite letters had reached their full effect. The word "pre-ordained" emphasises Balwhidder's moderate but entirely ortho-dox Calvinism. At the same time, the passage emphasises that the narrator's powers, like those of George III, have begun to decline, and so in a sense warns the reader that his own approach to *Annals* must make allowance for human frailty, that a more enlightened intelligence must analyse and fill the gaps in the recollections of an old man somewhat bewildered and left behind by the stirring events of the later eighteenth and early nineteenth centuries. Balwhidder is an anachronism, a survival from earlier days, who nevertheless has observed the events of the modern world. The very inadequacy of his responses sometimes defines the shape of events more penetratingly than investigations which to surface appearance are more subtle.

Balwhidder belongs, however tenuously, to the present of the novel; he draws on his store of memory and observation to bear witness to "the work of a beneficent Providence, even in the narrow sphere of my parish."[11] Even for Balwhidder, that is to say, his parish is no more than part of the general Calvinistic, Providential scheme. The reader may not share his Calvinism, but Galt assumes that at worst he will be prepared to substitute the idea of progress, or at least of a predestined progressive tendency in history, the reality of which may be seen on a small scale in Dalmailing, on a larger scale in the American and French revolutions, the growth of industry, the fall of the old local aristocracy, and the rise of an educated working class, all of which help to shape the course of events in the parish as in the outside world.

To the end of his life, Galt remained a Calvinist, whose doctrines had undergone some surface modification by New-tonian physical science. In Calvin's theology, predestination and providence were central and related doctrines; sometimes at least, predestination was regarded as a special application of the divine providence. Providence, in turn, operated in three ways, through the order of nature, by special external acts, and by the interior operation of the Holy Spirit. "The world is governed by God, not only in that he maintains the course of the world in being such as he established it all at once; but in that he has a particular care for each creature . . . It is a perversity to want to hide and obscure . . . the special providence of God, which is so well and plainly shown to us by clear and certain testimonies of scripture that it is a wonder how anyone can doubt it."[12]

In this tradition, Galt saw himself as a consistent predestinarian who, when he analysed the hypotheses to which he gave willing intellectual assent, was forced to deny the doctrine of a special or particular providence. His verses include such extended philosophical pieces as the posthumous *The Demon of Destiny* (1839). "I proclaim myself openly a predestinarian", he wrote in a chapter of *The Literary Life of John Galt* (1834), a chapter entitled "Fatalism and Particular Providence", in which he continues:—

> "In the order of things and the succession of events, the providence of God is constantly seen; and such is the harmony of the universe, that the smallest occurrence affects its whole frame and system.
>
> The simplest form in which we can contemplate providence, is by considering the whole universe as one machine. It consists of parts, each an entire thing of itself, endowed with distinct qualities, and placed in such a situation with respect to others, that it is constantly acted upon by them, and reacts upon them at the same time. Every part is subject to the principles or laws of its own particular organization, as well as to those of the universe, and every part is essential to the accomplishment of the object for which the whole was formed.
>
> The tact of human sense is not sufficiently fine to discover the principle of motion, we only know of its existence by effects; but there is no fact in existence of which the mind is more assured, than that every thing hath both an individual and a universal motion. The individual motion consists of augmentation or diminution of growth or of decay; and the universal motion consists of the revolutions which the thing as a part of

the universe performs, in connexion with the other parts.

If, therefore, the universe consists of things in motion, arranged according to a plan, it must also be allowed that the action of one thing upon another will produce an effect previously determined. This is the law of necessity, philosophical fatality, religious predestinarianism; but it is not according to the doctrine of a particular Providence."[13]

In *Annals of the Parish* especially Galt is concerned with the smallest occurrences in relation to the general body of world events. The relationship is established, not in terms of the principle of motion, but in terms of effects—how small occurrences affect, and still more how they are affected by, the whole frame and system of society. That is why the novels of a widely travelled man, who spent much of his life outside Scotland, concern themselves so markedly with Scottish local affairs, and the local affairs of Scotsmen overseas. Galt recognised the significance of small events in the destinal scheme.

The idea of a particular providence nevertheless loomed large in his imagination and dominated much of his writing. In *Annals of the Parish* this is readily perceptible. The coincidence, for example, of the succession of George III with Balwhidder's appointment to Dalmailing is regarded by the parishioners as a particular intervention of the hand of providence. Balwhidder himself realises only imperfectly the interconnections of the events which he describes; his limited perspective leads him to treat secondary, and even tertiary causes as if they had been prime movers. He regards them, in fact, as instances of a particular providence. Some critics hold that Balwhidder's outlook represents the limitations of Galt's own. Dr. Craig, for instance, has observed[14] that "because the minister is as conservative and credulous as many of his parishioners, and because everything is felt through his mentality, all other possible life is diminished to his kind of understanding." The remark is, in a way, a naive tribute to the art which conceals art, and to Galt's complete realisation of the minister's character, but even a brief analysis of a few sentences has been enough, I believe, to show the inadequacy of Dr Craig's response. Galt's use of language inevitably directs the reader to a more extended and philosophical perspective, with a distinctively Calvinistic slant. Fictitious autobiography is the perfect narrative technique for the production of such effects.

Galt's treatment of the commercial and industrial developments which followed the opening of the Ayrshire coalfields will demonstrate his methods. For Balwhidder everything springs from apparent chance and personal contingency—a dearth of fuel in the winter of 1765 and an accident to Lord Eglesham in March 1767. Admittedly, under 1762 the coal trade between Irville and Ireland is already mentioned, and Balwhidder suggests rather than states that the fuel shortage caused the new pits to be opened. It would probably be accurate to say that he regarded the opening of the pits as the providential remedy for the hardships of the preceding winter. Notably, and significantly for his work as a whole, he makes Providence an ally of commercial prosperity in a way which corresponds very closely to ideas set out a century later by R H Tawney in *Religion and the Rise of Capitalism:*—[15]

> "In the winter there was a dearth of fuel, such as has not been since; for when the spring loosened the bonds of the ice, three new coal-heughs were shanked in the Dowray moor, and ever since there has been a great plenty of that necessary article. Truly, it is very wonderful to see how things come round; when the talk was about the shanking of thir heughs, and a paper to get folk to take shares in them, was carried through the circumjacent parishes, it was thought a gowk's errand; but no sooner was the coal reached, but up sprung such a traffic, that it was a God-send to the parish, and the opening of a trade and commerce, that has, to use an old bye-word, brought gold in gowpins amang us." (Year 1765)[16]

For Balwhidder, the paper which is mentioned seems almost to lead an independent existence; at least he gives no sign of realizing that the proposals which it contained were produced as the result of human forethought and commercial ingenuity, operating, one presumes, outwith the immediate neighbourhood of the parish. The parish is the centre of all human activity; beyond it lies the field of providential operation, which sometimes acts through intermediaries—kings, governments and speculators—almost as remote as Providence itself. But this view is confined to Balwhidder. The reader is compelled to realise its inadequacies when he accepts the full implications of the reference to the paper; Galt assumes a thorough acquaintance with joint-stock companies and their shareholders.

Coal when it is mined, must be distributed, and inevitably the distribution depends on a satisfactory system of transport. The sequel to the opening of the local pits was the construction of a turnpike road to bypass the perils of the Vennel of Dalmailing:—

> "The king's highway, as I have related in the foregoing, ran through the Vennel, which was a narrow and a crooked street, with many big stones here and there, and every now and then, both in the spring and the fall, a gathering of middens for the fields, insomuch that the coal carts from the Dowray-moor were often reested in the middle of the causeway, and on more than one occasion some of them laired altogether in the middens, and others of them broke down." (Year 1767)[17]

At no point in his narrative does Balwhidder comment on the most striking feature of this entry, the casual way in which he accepts middens on the king's highway as a natural hazard. One may deduce from chapter XXVII of *The Provost* that by 1810, the date at which Balwhidder is writing, such middens had elsewhere become rarities:—

> "But new occasions call for new laws. The side pavement, concentrating the people, required to be kept cleaner, and in better order, than when the whole width of the street was in use, so that the magistrates were constrained to make regulations concerning the same, and to enact fines and penalties against those who neglected to scrape and wash the plainstones forenent the houses, and to denounce, in the strictest terms, the emptying of improper utensils on the same; and this, until the people had grown into the habitude of attending to the rules, gave rise to many pleas, and contentious appeals and bickerings, before the magistrates."[18]

In *The Provost* the apparent date of the new laws is 1805. Gudetown, however, was a royal burgh, Dalmailing a mere clachan, which might well be laggard in matters of public hygiene. Whatever the true assessment, Balwhidder, unlike Provost Pawkie, belongs to the past by virtue of his casual acceptance of the middens.

The middens become vitally connected with transport improvements when, as the result of an encounter with the coal-carts, Lord Eglesham's carriage is accidentally overturned into one of them. For Balwhidder, this is both the proximate and ultimate cause by which a turnpike was instituted; it is a particular act of Providence:—

> "His lordship was a man of genteel spirit, and very fond of his horses, which were the most beautiful creatures of their kind that had been seen in all the country side. Coming, as I was noting, to see the new lands, he was obliged to pass through the clachan one day, when all the middens were gathered out reeking and sappy in the middle of the causeway. Just as his lordship was driving in with his prancing steeds like a Jehu at the one end of the Vennel, a long string of loaded coal carts came in at the other, and there was hardly room for my lord to pass them. What was to be done? His lordship could not turn back and the coal carts were in no less perplexity. Every body was out of doors to see and to help, when, in trying to get his lordship's carriage over the top of a midden, the horses gave a sudden loup, and couped the coach, and threw my lord, head foremost, into the very scent-bottle of the whole commodity, which made him go perfect mad, and he swore like a trooper that he would get an act of parliament to put down the nuisance—the which now ripened in the course of this year into the undertaking of the trust road . . .
>
> But to return to the making of the trust-road, which, as I have said, turned the town inside out. It was agreed among the heritors, that it should run along the back side of the south houses; and that there should be steadings feued off on each side, according to a plan that was laid down, and this being gone into, the town

gradually, in the course of years, grew up into that orderlyness which makes it now a pattern to the countryside—all which was mainly owing to the accident that befel the Lord Eglesham, which is a clear proof how improvement came about, as it were, by the immediate instigation of Providence, which should make the heart of man humble, and change his eyes of pride and haughtiness into a lowly demeanour." (Year 1767)[19]

Galt's irony (not Balwhidder's) is unmistakable, but Balwhidder certainly has a point—Lord Eglesham's accident hastened the institution of the turnpike. The narrative, none the less, shows that road improvements had been meditated for some little time, and even without the accident would certainly have been instituted. Under the year 1765, for instance, the year in which the new pits on the Douray moor were opened, we find what is probably intended to be a direct consequence, that the king's road through the Vennel had been mended. In 1767, the year of the accident, the minister noted that "there had been, for many a day, a talk and sound of an alteration and amendment".[20] Talk and action are not the same thing, but it is fairly clear once more that Balwhidder has attributed to particular Providence a change which in fact resulted from general economic forces.

In isolation, this treatment of mining and transportation is remarkable enough. In context, it is still more remarkable. Galt consistently indicates universals by way of apparent contingencies often assumed by Balwhidder to indicate the intervention of providence. The Agricultural Revolution, for instance, is insinuated by way of Balwhidder's marriage to Miss Lizy Kibbock, the second Mrs Balwhidder, daughter of Mr Kibbock of the Gorbyholm, a pioneer of new farming methods. Under the year 1761, a phrase—"the very bairns on the loan"—sufficiently indicates that the playground of the old-fashioned farm was the patch of ground near the steading on which during summer cows were milked in the open air. Equally the reference under 1765 to Mr. Kibbock's Delap-cheese which "spread far and wide over the civilized world", by its very hyperbole demonstrates the establishment of new dairying methods with a new magnitude of commercial operation. Nor were Mr

Kibbock's innovations confined to dairying. He improved his arable land by plantation, and by enclosure, to do away with the old system of in-field and out-field.

> "Mr Kibbock, her father, was a man beyond the common, and had an insight of things, by which he was enabled to draw profit and advantage, where others could only see risk and detriment. He planted mounts of fir-trees on the bleak and barren tops of the hills of his farm, the which everybody, and I among the rest, considered as a thrashing of the water, and raising of bells. But as his tack ran his trees grew, and the plantations supplied him with stabs to make *stake* and *rice* between his fields, which soon gave them a trig and orderly appearance, such as had never before been seen in the west country." (Year 1765)[21]

By way of his second wife and her inherited talents, Balwhidder himself came to share in the profits of new enterprise, indeed, to become rich, without himself ever seeming to realise what exactly had happened. Only to a very limited extent does he grasp the purpose of plantation and enclosure, which he seems to regard as intended primarily to enable the countryside to vie scenically with Italy and Switzerland. That he had some awareness, at least of the wider geographical context, is suggested by the reference in the annal for 1766 to Mr Coulter, who had gained his skill in farming in the Lothians, where the process of improvement had then advanced farther than in Ayrshire. As his name indicates, Mr Coulter was a specialist in ploughing methods, who had replaced the old Scottish plough with a more up-to-date and efficient implement, and who practised crop-rotation, which in turn implies enclosure. Balwhidder appreciates the increase in prosperity caused by the new methods, but again what he emphasises is the increase in visible beauty—the effect on his own eyes. "Nothing could surpass the regularity of his rigs and furrows—Well do I remember the admiration that I had, when, in a fine sunny morning of the first spring after he took the Breadland, I saw his braird on what had been the cow's grass, as even and pretty as if it had been worked and stripped in the loom with a shuttle." (Year 1766)[22]

Galt certainly did not intend his readers to dismiss

Balwhidder's observation entirely. As I hope to show later, he held that improvement led to an increase in natural beauty as well as an increase in prosperity. It remains doubtful however that an increase in natural beauty was one of Mr Coulter's immediate objectives.

Galt's general attitude to progress and improvement, like Balwhidder's, is receptive and even welcoming, but, through Balwhidder, he expresses some awareness of human consequences which were sometimes less pleasant. Balwhidder's visit to Glasgow in 1791 is a failure:—

> "But although there was no doubt a great and visible increase of the city, loftier buildings on all sides, and streets that spread their arms far into the embraces of the country, I thought the looks of the population were impaired, and that there was a greater proportion of long white faces in the Trongate, than when I attended the Divinity class. These, I was told, were the weavers and others concerned in the cotton trade, which I could well believe, for they were very like in their looks to the men of Cayenneville; but from living in a crowded town, and not breathing a wholesome country air between their tasks, they had a stronger case of unhealthy melancholy. I was, therefore, very glad, that Providence had placed in my hand the pastoral staff of a country parish, for it cut me to the heart to see so many young men, in the rising prime of life, already in the arms of a pale consumption. 'If, therefore,' said I to Mrs Balwhidder, when I returned home to the Manse, 'we live, as it were, within the narrow circle of ignorance, we are spared from the pain of knowing many an evil; and, surely, in much knowledge, there is sadness of heart.'
>
> But the main effect of all this was to make me do all in my power to keep my people contented with their lowly estate; for in that same spirit of improvement, which was so busy everywhere, I could discern something like a shadow, that shewed it was not altogether of that pure advantage, which avarice led all so eagerly to believe. Accordingly, I began a series of sermons on the evil and vanity of riches, and, for the most part of

the year, pointed out in what manner they led the
possessor to indulge in sinful luxuries, and how in-
dulgence begat desire, and desire betrayed integrity and
corrupted the heart, making it evident, that the rich
man was liable to forget his unmerited obligations to
God, and to oppress the laborious and the needful
when he required their service." (Year 1791)[23]

This was strong doctrine for the period of the Terror, and
partly as a consequence Balwhidder himself fell into melancholia,
which in 1792 almost led him to suicide. Galt takes care to
emphasize how the home industry of the second Mrs Balwhidder, in itself typical of the new era, was a further, more
personal, cause of the break-down:—

"About the end of this year, I fell into a dull way:
My spirit was subdued, and at times I was aweary of
the day, and longed for the night, when I might close
my eyes in peaceful slumbers. I missed my son Gilbert,
who had been a companion to me in the long nights,
while his mother was busy with the lasses, and their
ceaseless wheels and cardings, in the kitchen. Often
could I have found it in my heart to have banned that
never-ceasing industry, and to tell Mrs Balwhidder,
that the married state was made for something else than
to make napery, and bittle blankets; but it was her
happiness to keep all at work, and she had no pleasure
in any other way of life, so I sat many a night by the
fireside with resignation; sometimes in the study, and
sometimes in the parlour, and, as I was doing nothing
Mrs Balwhidder said it was needless to light a candle."
(Year 1791)[24]

As usual, Galt makes his point by imagery and indirections,
but certainly Balwhidder's mental illness has the same ultimate
source as the physical consumption of the Glasgow workers, and,
in the world outside the novel, Robert Fergusson's religious
mania.
Whatever their social and intellectual implications, all these
developments are matters in the first place of economic history.
Social and intellectual history however are not neglected, and

Galt uses the same indirect methods as elsewhere. In purely social history, the major event, described under the year 1766, is the destruction by fire of the local great house, the Breadlands. Galt here exemplifies the decline of the old social order, the *ancien regime*, for the house is never rebuilt, and the policy is eventually let out as a farm to Coulter. The fire is the climax, but no more than the climax, of an earlier process of change. Already, after the death of the Laird of Breadland in 1761, his widow and family had removed to Edinburgh, letting the house to Major Gilchrist, a returned Indian nabob, and his sister Miss Girzie, Lady Skimmilk. The Gilchrists represent an early stratum of the *nouveau riche*; their social origin is obscure, and during the Major's period of service, Miss Girzie "had been in a very penurious way as a seamstress in the Gorbals of Glasgow."[25] Even before the fire, that is to say, the Breadlands had already in some degree ceased to be the centre of secular life in the parish. The old Laird too had been Balwhidder's patron, but after his death, the powers of patronage shifted to the more distant and Anglified figure of Lord Eglesham, and after his murder in 1781, they seem altogether to disappear. From 1785 the local grandee is the returned American loyalist, Mr Cayenne, who becomes an industrialist, the founder of Cayenneville with its mills and radical weavers. He has little more interest in Balwhidder's orthodox Calvinism than have his imported work-people, whether utilitarians, non-conformists or Irish Catholics. The long-term results are clear. In 1780, it is still possible for the parish to be convulsed by reports of the troubles which in London led to the anti-Catholic Gordon riots. In 1804, however, an Irish priest reintroduced the Mass to the parish without disturbance; in 1806 a dissenting meeting house was opened. The externals of Presbyterianism suffered a corresponding diminution. Under 1764, the story of Nichol Snipe's humiliation in church reveals the disciplinary powers of the old kirk. By 1779 Balwhidder's sermon at the General Assembly in Edinburgh is clearly thought old-fashioned, and in 1789, although the elderly people of the parish feel that the sermon delivered by young William Malcolm is too Anglified, "the younger part of the congregation were loud in his praise, saying, there had not been heard before such a style of language in our side of the country."[26] In 1804 the Session agreed that church censures should be commuted with fines.

Lady Macadam's jointure house, first mentioned in 1763, is the nearest approach in the parish to a second great house, and in a less spectacular way it suffered a change as great as that of the Breadlands. On the death of Lady Macadam, shortly after the murder of Lord Eglesham in 1781, the house stood empty until 1785, when it was briefly occupied by Mr Cayenne. In 1787 he moved to a new house. By then, as a consequence of developments along the turnpike road, the jointure house had come to be in the middle of town. Since 1764 the village had boasted a change-house (ale-house) but by 1787 the general increase of prosperity and the growing number of travellers on the road, made the establishment of an inn a practical possibility. For this purpose, a large unoccupied building in the centre of town had obvious attractions, and as a result the jointure house became The Cross Keys Inn. The social implications are manifold.

Galt does not confine his social investigations to the upper levels of society. By 1760, for instance, the belief in witchcraft which had led to the spectacular trials and executions of the later sixteenth and seventeenth centuries, and which is present, although not greatly emphasized in *Ringan Gilhaize*, had virtually disappeared, save at the level of popular superstition. Here, as Burns's *Tam o' Shanter* has already illustrated, it retained a latent vigour, which might even on occasion lead to the threat of public action. *Annals of the Parish* is an imaginative account of the Enlightenment as it affected a small country parish, and Galt twice indicates the survival of pre-Enlightenment fears about witches. In the annal for 1762, Balwhidder mentions the death of Mizy Spaewell at the pagan seasonal festival of Samhain (Hallowe'en). She is obviously regarded as a white witch:—

> "Mizy had a wonderful faith in freats, and was just an oracle of sagacity at expounding dreams, and bodes of every sort and description—besides, she was reckoned one of the best howdies in her day; but by this time she was grown frail and feckless, and she died the same year on Hallowe'en, which made every body wonder, that it should have so fallen out for her to die on Hallowe'en." (Year 1762)[27]

Equally obviously, Nanse Birrel, whose death is mentioned in the annal for 1766, is a black witch, finally driven to suicide by her diabolic master:—

> "An aged woman, one Nanse Birrel, a distillator of herbs, and well skilled in the healing of sores, who had a great repute among the quarriers and coalliers—she having gone to the physic well in the sandy hills, to draw water, was found with her feet uppermost in the well, by some of the bairns of Mr Loremore's school; and there was a great debate whether Nanse had fallen in by accident head foremost, or, in a temptation, thrown herself in that position, with her feet sticking up to the evil one; for Nanse was a curious disconten-ted blear-eyed woman, and it was only with great ado that I could get the people keepit from calling her a witchwife." (Year 1766)[28]

"Calling her a witchwife" is probably a euphemism for "treating her as a witchwife" and ducking her. The "people" are the ordinary villagers and farmworkers, as opposed to the more uncanny quarriers and coalliers, who worked in the depths of the earth. The magic physic well in the sand hills is itself a probable survival from pre-Christian times.

After 1766, although *Annals* still records dreams, prodigies and superstitions, there is no hint of actual witchcraft.

To summarize—from one point of view *Annals of the Parish* indeed belongs to the parish. Few aspects of life there are ignored, and they are consistently presented from a point of view which itself belongs to the parish. The location of the parish, however, makes internal events typify what is happening in the wider world, if not from China to Peru, at least from India to the United States—the wider world too, which under the influence of the Enlightenment was beginning to change from an agrarian to an industrial economy. The book thus achieves something like universality. It is the immediacy of the intensely local combined with the universal which gives *Annals of the Parish*, like all Galt's best work, a vividness and intellectual range, which can sometimes seem more valuable than all but the very best of Scott.

ii

It would be easy to extend the discussion of *Annals of the Parish*, but for the moment one main point will suffice — the relationship between the social and economic developments

analysed and the society of the Reformation period in which
these developments had their origin. R.H Tawney's account[29]
of Puritanism and the rise of English capitalism is very
relevant:—

> "'The capitalist spirit' is as old as history, and was
> not, as has sometimes been said, the offspring of
> Puritanism. But it found in certain aspects of later
> Puritanism a tonic which braced its energies and
> fortified its already vigorous temper. At first sight, no
> contrast could be more violent than that between the
> iron collectivism, the almost military discipline, the
> remorseless and violent rigours practised in Calvin's
> Geneva, and preached elsewhere, if in a milder form,
> by his disciples, and the impatient rejection of all
> traditional restrictions on economic enterprise which
> was the temper of the English business world after the
> Civil War. In reality, the same ingredients were present
> throughout, but they were mixed in changing propor-
> tions, and exposed to different temperatures at different
> times. Like traits of individual character which are
> suppressed till the approach of maturity release them,
> the tendencies in Puritanism, which were to make it
> later a potent ally of the movement against the control
> of economic relations in the name either of social
> morality or of the public interest, did not reveal
> themselves till political and economic changes had
> prepared a congenial environment for their growth.
> Nor, once those conditions were created, was it only
> England which witnessed the transformation. In all
> countries alike, in Holland, in America, in Scotland, in
> Geneva itself, the social theory of Calvinism went
> through the same process of development. It had begun
> by being the very soul of authoritarian regimentation.
> It ended by being the vehicle of an almost Utilitarian
> individualism. While social reformers in the sixteenth
> century could praise Calvin for his economic rigour,
> their successors in Restoration England, if of one
> persuasion, denounced him as the parent of economic
> licence, if of another, applauded Calvinist communities
> for their commercial enterprise, and for their freedom

> from antiquated prejudices on the subject of economic
> morality. So little do those who shoot the arrows of the
> spirit know where they will light."

Scottish developments differed significantly from those in
England, but even so small an example from fiction as Davie
Deans's admonition to his daughter in *The Heart of Midlothian* —
"If you neglect your wardly duties in the day of affliction, what
confidence have I that ye mind the greater matters that concern
salvation?"[30] — shows that they had something in common.

Annals of the Parish commences at a period when the 1690
settlement and the conditions of the later seventeenth century
had suffered the minimum of disturbance — when in Ayrshire at
least religion had scarcely begun the transformation to capitalism. Galt makes it very clear that Scotland in general, and the
parish in particular, were prepared by the prevailing Calvinism
for the changes which overtook them during Balwhidder's
ministry. Calvinism itself is a factor which Galt does not over-
emphasize, but which is certainly, even universally, present.
Covenanting stubbornness and individualism go far to explain
the success of such people as Mr Kibbock, Mr Cayenne, and the
second Mrs Balwhidder. In *Annals of the Parish* however Galt
more assumes than analyses these qualities.

In 1823 Galt published his three-volume *Ringan Gilhaize* with
its subtitle "The Times of the Covenanters", the novel in which
he extended his historical scope to analyse the Calvinistic
character, and some of its effects on Scotland. The distinctive
technique developed in *Annals of the Parish* assumed further
importance. In *Annals of the Parish*, Galt as ultimate narrator
almost invariably operated on a level quite distinct from that of
Balwhidder, the assumed narrator, and so enabled the reader to
gain the minister's perspective, as well as that of Galt, on the
emergence of more enlightened times from what in Scotland
was still the last stage of Reformation conflicts. This double
perspective is the chief source of irony. A similar technique
recurs throughout the series of fictitious autobiographies — *The
Provost*, (1822), for instance, *Lawrie Todd*, (1830) *The Member*
(1832) and *The Radical* (1832) — which Galt produced in the
twenties and thirties of the nineteenth century. In *Ringan
Gilhaize* it received its most symphonic development — again,
in a novel which deals with a revolutionary change in social

structure and intellectual history, the transformation of the
hierarchical Catholic Scotland of the earlier sixteenth century, to
the impoverished, obsessed, egalitarian middle class Calvinistic
society of the late seventeenth century, the society which fifty
years later had prepared itself to be again transformed by the
Agricultural and Industrial revolutions. The period covered—
from the 1550s to 1690—is beyond the reach of any single
human memory, and in the first part of the book Galt adopts not
a double but a triple perspective, relating in the person of the
seventeenth century Covenanter and Cameronian, Ringan
Gilhaize, the events of the mid-sixteenth century, of which he
had gained knowledge by conversations in boyhood with his
grandfather, Michael Gilhaize, who died, he relates, at the
advanced age of ninety one years, seven months and four days, at
a time when he was himself eight years old.

In the first part of the book, Galt tells the story of Michael
Gilhaize by the mouth of Ringan; in the second, Ringan
describes his own experiences. In the earlier section the reader
remains conscious of Ringan as intermediary, but Galt successfully distinguishes between the style of grandfather and grandson. "It is a thing past all contesting", Ringan begins, "that, in
the Reformation, there was a spirit of far greater carnality
among the champions of the cause than among those who in
later times so courageously, under the Lord, upheld the un-
spotted banners of the Covenant", (I:i)[31] and the presence or
absence of carnality in itself sufficiently distinguishes the two
parts. At the beginning, for instance, there are virtually no
Biblical quotations; the second part abounds with precise Biblical
references. "My father chose the lxxvi Psalm, and when it was
sung he opened the Scriptures in Second Kings, and read aloud,
with a strong voice, the xxiii chapter, and every one likened
Josiah to the old King, and Jehoahaz to his son Charles, by whose
disregard of the Covenant the spirit of the land was then in such
tribulation"(II.xii).[32] The most notable series of references occurs
in the third volume, where Ringan, at least partially recovered
from the madness which followed the murder by dragoons of his
wife and daughters, and the destruction of his home at Quharist,
consults the Word on his first personal encounter with the
outlawed Cameronians. The son to whom he refers, is Joseph,
his only surviving child:—

"But though my spirit clove to theirs, and was in unison with their intent, I could not but doubt of so poor a handful of forlorn men, though it be written, that the race is not to the swift nor the battle to the strong, and I called to my son to bring me the Book, that I might be instructed from the Word what I ought at that time to do, and when he had done so I opened it, and the twenty-second chapter of Genesis met my eye, and I was awed and trembled, and my heart was melted with sadness and an agonising grief. For the command to Abraham to sacrifice Isaac his only son, whom he so loved, on the mountains in the Land of Moriah, required me to part with my son, and to send him with the Cameronians; and I prayed with a weeping spirit and the imploring silence of a parent's heart, that the Lord would be pleased not to put my faith to so great a trial.

I took the Book again, and I opened it a second time, and the command of the sacred oracle was presented to me in the fifth verse of the fifth chapter of Ecclesiastes—

'Better is it that thou shouldst not vow, than that thou shouldst vow and not pay.'

But still the man and the father were powerful with my soul; and the weakness of disease was in me, and I called my son towards me, and I bowed my head upon his hands as he stood before me, and wept very bitterly, and pressed him to my bosom, and was loath to send him away.

He knew not what caused the struggle wherewith he saw me so moved, and he became touched with fear lest my reason was again going from me. But I dried my eyes, and told him it was not so, and that maybe I would be better if I could compose myself to read a chapter. So I again opened the volume, and the third command was in the twenty-sixth verse of the eighth chapter of St Matthew:

'Why are ye fearful, O ye of little faith'" (III.xix,175-7)[33]

The direct consequence of Ringan's adherence to his own particular providence, as he interprets it, is the death of Joseph and the mutilation of his body. Ringan hears of it when he is imprisoned with other Presbyterians in the Edinburgh Tolbooth:—

> "At that moment a shriek of horror rose from all then looking out, and every one recoiled from the window. In the same instant a bloody head on a halbert was held up to us. — I looked — I saw the ghastly features, and I would have kissed those lifeless lips; for O! they were my son's." (III.xx, 195)[34]

Galt is fully capable of tackling the savageries of seventeenth century history, and indeed, for a modern reader, one of the most convincing aspects of the book is the depiction of the way in which a totalitarian society affects its adherents and, still more, its opponents. It was this realism, presumably, which denied the book any popularity with Galt's contemporaries, and ensured its neglect by the Victorian and Edwardian reading public. But although the twentieth century has become more accustomed to cruelty, in life as in literature, there is still little sign of new interest.[35] It is obsession, however, rather than cruelty, which gives point to the first passage quoted. Galt, as has been mentioned, was a predestinarian within the Newtonian system of mechanics. Ringan is a predestinarian of more theological ancestry, who believes to obsession that he is singled out by a particular providence to play the role which he completes with the assassination of Claverhouse after the victory of Killiecrankie. The entire course of his life — when he listened to his grandfather's stories of the Reformation, when he took part in the Pentland raid, when he was wounded by Claverhouse at Drumclog, when the members of his family one by one were destroyed — is directed, he believes, to a single end, the destruction of the prelatical House of Stewart, and its most dedicated upholder, Claverhouse.

The process began long before Ringan's birth in the struggle waged by John Knox and the Lords of the Congregation against the Queen Regent and her daughter, Queen Mary, but the completion is delayed for more than a century and Ringan Gilhaize is reserved to strike the final blow:—

"I took off my bonnet, and kneeling with the gun in
my hand, cried, 'Lord, remember David and all his
afflictions;' and having so prayed, I took aim as I knelt,
and Claverhouse raising his arm in command, I fired.
In the same moment I looked up, and there was a
vision in the air as if all the angels of brightness, and the
martyrs in their vestments of glory, were assembled on
the walls and battlements of heaven to witness the
event, — and I started up and cried, 'I have delivered
my native land!' But in the same instant I remembered
to whom the glory was due, and falling again on my
knees, I raised my hands and bowed my head as I said,
'Not mine, O Lord, but thine is the victory!"
(III.xxxiii,308)[36]

Gilhaize's belief is of course central to the Calvinism which
gained control over Scotland, not so much in the time of John
Knox as in that of his spiritual heir, Andrew Melville (1545-
1622). Melville spent much of his early life in Geneva, and his
Second Book of Discipline [37] (1578) was the effectual instrument
by which the church in Scotland became Calvinist rather than
merely Protestant. Biblical oracles were regarded by men like
Gilhaize as the means by which God communicated his purpose
to the elect; these texts, chosen apparently at random, were
central to the predestinal scheme as it affected certain individuals,
highly-favoured, not in terms of worldly prosperity or happiness, but simply because God has chosen and shaped them to be
his particular instruments. God shapes Ringan Gilhaize, partly
by the influence of his grandfather, and to a lesser extent his
father; still more by the harsh series of events which make up his
life, and which, in his own words, turn his spirit into iron and his
heart into stone — the flight from Rullion Green, his various
imprisonments and exiles, his wound at Drumclog, the destruction of his family. All this is justified, as it were, because it
resulted finally in the expulsion of the Stewarts, and in particular
because it prepared Ringan to become the assassin of Claverhouse, the only man capable of restoring the Stewart fortunes, a
man, too, who in Cameronian eyes had sold himself into the
power of Satan. In one sense, the death of Claverhouse is almost
like that of Evandale in *Old Mortality*, a cowardly murder; from
another, it is the climax of the struggle between the powers of

darkness and light. The latter certainly is how Gilhaize himself views it.

In his own eyes, Gilhaize, like his fellow Cameronians, avoids carnality because he acts in full submission to the will of God, and is prepared to abrogate all claims of the flesh, even when the claims are on behalf of his own youngest, and last surviving, son, the appropriately named Joseph.

In his own eyes — but one must bear in mind the double, and even triple, perspective of the novel. Gilhaize sees his task as war with the worshippers of the Beast and his Image, a war to which Galt, as opposed to Gilhaize, owed no allegiance whatsoever. Galt was aware of the extent to which the Calvinistic elect were capable of self-deception and even hypocrisy. The reader is not intended, for instance, to take even a passage like the following simply at face value. Gilhaize sees some part of the truth, and he retains the reader's full sympathy, but he certainly exaggerates the importance of his own actions:—

> "Many a time yet, when I remember that night, do I think with wonder and reverence of our condition. An infirm grey-haired man, with a deranged head and a broken heart, going forth amidst the winter's wind, with a little boy, not passing thirteen years of age, to pull down from his throne the guarded King of three mighty kingdoms, — and we did it, — such was the doom of avenging justice, and such the pleasure of Heaven. But let me proceed to rehearse the trials I was required to undergo before the accomplishment of that high predestination." (III.xviii)[38]

The last word, of course, is particularly significant, but almost equally significant is the reference to the deranged head. Throughout the book, as will have become evident, the suggestion recurs that Gilhaize is not wholly responsible for his actions, that in some degree he is mentally deranged. As a consequence of the discovery that his wife and daughters have been raped and murdered by the dragoons, he becomes for six or eight months clinically mad. Even during his childhood there were such incidents as his over-reaction to his father's account of the reading of the liturgy in Edinburgh — "I . . . was thrilled with an unspeakable fear; and all the dreadful things, which I had heard my grandfather tell of the tribulations of his time, came upon my spirit like visions of the visible scene, and I began to weep with an exceeding sorrow."(II.x.)[39] Later (II.xxviii)[40], there is his equally violent, if prophetic, reaction to the discovery of the dead child after Rullion Green, and to his escape, with his wife's help, from prison (III.iii)[41] —a violence showing, I suggest, his own subconscious urge to the destruction of his family and friends. Gilhaize combines strong family affection with what might almost be regarded as a schizophrenic impulse towards solitariness and destruction, an urge which readily identifies itself with the "purification" which was central to the Protestant Reformation in its more extreme forms. A significant phrase which occurs almost at the end of the book, is "The godly people of Edinburgh . . . rose, as it were with one accord . . . and purified the chapel, even to desolation" (III.xxviii)[42] — that is, they reduced it to ruins. Gilhaize purifies his life in an almost identical way.

Nor is this the only way in which Galt qualifies Gilhaize's opinion of his own principles and actions. Occasionally his methods approach caricature, as in the snatch of dialogue between Nanse Snoddie and Robin Fullarton:—

> "'What's te prelates, Robin Fullarton?' said auld Nanse Snoddie turning round to John's son, who was standing behind his father.
>
> 'They're the red dragons o' unrighteousness,' replied the sincere laddie with great vehemence.
>
> 'Gude guide us!' cried Nanse with the voice of terror; 'and has the King daur't to send sic accursed things to devour God's people?'" (II.x.)[43]

The sheer ignorance of anything but biblical texts which underlies Nanse's reaction is not without relevance for the Covenanters as a group. Galt too is at pains to emphasise the narrow limits, social and geographic as well as intellectual, of the world within which the Covenanters exist. Michael Gilhaize had moved freely, and as a matter of course, over the length and breadth of Scotland. He was acquainted with queens, regents, archbishops and earls, and was equally familiar with a baillie's family in Crail and the expelled nuns who established the maidenly character of the Kirkgate in Irvine. It was Michael nevertheless who chose of set policy to limit the outlook and experience of his descendants when he settled at Quharist in Ayrshire. His intentions were good. The corruptions of courtly life were already beginning to affect him when he saw the group of Edinburgh labourers who gave form to his resolution:—

> "Hitherto he had never noted, or much considered, the complicated cares and trials wherewith the lot of man in every situation is chequered and environed; and when he heard these bondmen of hard labour, jocund after sound slumbers and light suppers, laughing contemptuously as they beheld the humiliating sight, which divers gallants and youngsters, courtiers of the court, degraded with debauch, made of themselves as they stumbled homeward, he thought there was surely more bliss in the cup that was earned by the constancy of health and a willing mind, than in all the possets and malvesia that the hoards of ages could procure. So he composed his spirit, and inwardly made a vow to the Lord, that, as soon as the mighty work of the redemption of the Gospel from the perdition of papistry was accomplished, he would retire into the lea of some pleasant green holm; and take, for the purpose of his life, the attainment of that happy simplicity which seeks but the supply of the few wants with which man comes so rich from the hands of his Maker, that all changes in his natural condition of tilling the ground and herding the flocks only serve to make him poorer by increasing." (I.xvii.)[44]

This passage typified the change from the old pre-Reformation Scotland to the new Israel, and it is not accidental that the paragraph immediately following describes the arrival of John Knox and his servant in Edinburgh. Galt, in the person of Gilhaize, is indicating the extent to which — and the motives for which — post-Reformation Scotland deliberately turned its back on the cosmopolitan sophistication of the pre-Reformation period to become local, introverted and Hebraic. Once again the idea of purification to desolation has some relevance. The seventeenth century world of Ringan Gilhaize is a harsher version of the parochial world in which the Rev Micah

Balwhidder later took up his ministry, and it was by the action of Michael Gilhaize and others like him that the world of *Annals of the Parish* came into being. Quharist, the name of Gilhaize's home, means "Where is it?", and so emphasizes the obscurity of the place on which so much of the action of the novel centres. The experience of *Ringan Gilhaize* includes a gradually increasing sense of claustrophobia. The obsessional quality in Ringan himself gains much of its power from this sense.

Not all Scotland is presented as insane or obsessed. The voice of reason is most nearly represented by Deacon Fulton of Paisley, who helped Gilhaize and Esau Wardrop to escape from the council chamber where they had been imprisoned after the Pentland rising:—

> "'True, true, we are a' Covenanters,' replied the deacon, 'and Gude forbid that I should e'er forget the vows I took when I was in a manner a bairn; but there's an unco difference between the auld covenanting and this Lanerk New-light. In the auld times, our forebears and our fathers covenanted to show their power, that the king and government might consider what they were doing. And they betook not themselves to the sword, till the quiet warning of almost all the realm united in one league had proved ineffectual; and when at last there was nae help for't, and they were called by their conscience and dangers to gird themselves for battle, they went forth in the might of the arm of flesh, as weel as of a righteous cause. But, sirs, this donsie business of the Pentland raid was but a splurt, and the publishing of the Covenant, after the poor folk had made themselves rebels, was, to say the least o't, a weak conceit." (III.vi)[45]

I have already commented that Ringan Gilhaize at no point totally loses the reader's sympathy, and it is noteworthy that here even the unfanatical voice of reason is in favour of action. It is the manner, not the fact, to which the deacon raises objections, and he is prepared to assist the prisoners' escape after their capture. In the context of the book however it becomes clear that the deacon's rationality offers no immediately effective instrument for the restoration of liberty in Scotland. The existence of such men encourages hope for the future; on the other hand, it is by men like Gilhaize that a time is created in which the deacon's commonsense will have scope to flourish, a time such as is analysed in *Annals of the Parish*, *The Provost* and *The Entail*. Deacon Fulton is a more attractive character than Mr Kibbock, Provost Pawkie or Claude Walkinshaw, but their spiritual kinship is clear. And although Ringan Gilhaize is a half-mad fanatic the vision of the future which he sees before Rullion Green has in it a strong element of truth. "I yet had a blessed persuasion that the event would prove in the end a link in the chain, or a cog in the wheel, of the hidden enginery with which Providence works good out of evil." (II.xxv.)[46] For Galt, the events of the Covenant, and the personalities of the Covenanters, were the necessary prelude to the awakening of the later eighteenth century. Gilhaize was not the chosen instrument of a particular providence, but he was one of the many links by means of which the general destinal forces of the world worked towards their ultimately benevolent conclusions.

iii

Galt's Newtonian concept of predestination and progress is presented, partly by means of, partly in opposition to, the concept as held by the central characters in his novels. The effect varies. An adverse criticism of *Annals of the Parish*, for instance, might base itself on the lack of a central dynamic. Balwhidder is a simple believer in predestination, who observes great social changes which he is content to ascribe to a benevolent but inscrutable Providence. Human participation in, and cooperation with, the acts of Providence is reduced to a minimum, or is left to such insight and understanding as the reader himself may bring. *Ringan Gilhaize* has a more obvious narrative impulse. The narrator himself is central to the action, the dynamic of which is provided by the gradual growth under persecution, and eventual fulfilment, of his obsession with the predestined vengeance of God, and the replacement of one social order with another. As ultimate narrator, Galt accepts the idea of predestination, but interprets it in a way quite distinct from that of Gilhaize. In a fictitious autobiography, however, Galt himself can have no representative; his points are made indirectly by the tone and arrangement of individual episodes. In *The Entail* (1822) Galt temporarily abandons fictitious autobiography for the external narrator more or less in the style of the earlier Scott. The effect is not always happy. He could not wholly avoid his usual autobiographical style, and consequently sometimes allowed his narrator to appear as an individual in a way which clashes with the more usual impersonal tone of the narrative. When Watty marries Betty Bodle, for instance, the narrator is introduced as a twenty three year old guest at the ceremony, for no other purpose, it would appear, than to allow him to give an account of bed-room happenings with which in real life no one but a family acquaintance could have been familiar. It is typical of Galt to be concerned about such a detail, but generally, unless problems of this kind are thrust upon the reader, they offer no difficulties and the intrusion of a definite narrative personality may well, as here, give rise to discomfort. The function of the external narrator is not to heighten the effect of realism but to give perspective, to enable the reader to see the principal characters at once internally, from their own point of view, and externally, from the point of view of their, and our, society and surroundings.

The change nevertheless had some artistic justification. In *Ringan Gilhaize* Galt was mainly concerned with the internal developments which shaped Gilhaize, and which, more generally, shaped and prepared the Lowland Scottish character for the developments of the eighteenth century. By the end of the book, however, these developments have scarcely begun. There is no need for the reader to concern himself with anything beyond what is implied by the complexities of Gilhaize's mind. In *The Entail* Galt dealt with characters who are significant not only in themselves, but in relation to a past, which they cannot recover, a present, which is opposed to their style of life, and a future, which they cannot control. A long period of time is involved, one too which could not easily be covered autobiographically by the use of such a narrative device as Galt found for *Ringan Gilhaize*. *Annals of the Parish* had been much concerned with the external world, but for that work an autobiographical technique had been appropriate, simply because Balwhidder had little personal effect on the sequence of the events which he recorded. For the action of *The Entail*, no corresponding office, and so no possible convincing observer was available. The only method appropriate was that of the impersonal external narrator.

In despite of, or perhaps as the result of, its greater narrative power, *The Entail* is as much a theoretical history as *Annals of the Parish*. The theme of both works is the emergence of the new Scotland from the old, but in *The Entail* the scene is no longer a quiet country parish, but the great mercantile and industrial city of Glasgow. As in *Ringan Gilhaize*, obsession is the unconscious instrument of social change. Claud Walkinshaw, the central figure, begins adult life as a packman, but rises eventually to considerable commercial success. From childhood, however, his mind has been set on a return to the pre-commercial world of the seventeenth century by the redemption of the heritable estate of the Walkinshaw family, the lands of Grippy and Kittleston-heugh, lost by Claud's grandfather as a result of the failure of the first major Scottish attempt at new enterprise, the Company of Scotland, and its ill-fated venture, the Darien scheme (1695-1700). The effects of this obsession are sordid and inhuman, but Galt retains some sympathy for Walkinshaw by tracing, with considerable insight, its rise to the exhortations of Maudge Dobbie, the old bairnswoman of the family, who brings him up, despite her extreme poverty, to venerate ancestral rights and despise mere commercial success. His obsession in other words, is not primarily for his individual advantage:—

> "'Na; Claudie, my lamb, thou maun lift thy een
> aboon the trash o' the toon, and ay keep mind that the
> hills are standing yet that might hae been thy ain; and
> so may they yet be, an thou can but master the pride o'
> back and belly, and seek for something mair solid than
> the bravery o' sic a Solomon in all his glory as yon
> Provost Gorbals.'" (I.i.)[47]

What matters here is more than the mere fact that Claud's motives, later in the book, are in a warped sense disinterested and even self-sacrificing. The form of Maudge's exhortation is that of the Calvinist sermon, based closely on biblical texts. Within a single sentence she contrives to make references to at least three scriptural passages, with the additional irony that all are from the Sermon on the Mount — "Take no thought for your life, what ye shall eat, or what ye shall drink; nor yet for your body, what ye shall put on", "Lay not up for yourselves treasures upon earth", and "Consider the lilies of the field, how they grow; they toil not, neither do they spin: And yet I say unto you, That even

Solomon, in all his glory was not arrayed like one of these." Her misunderstanding is more or less on a level with Nanse Snoddie's in *Ringan Gilhaize*. The ethics, such as they are, belong not to the New Testament, but to a distortion of the worst of the Old. The dominant note is a confused bibliolatry, very characteristic of the novel, and of the intermediate stages of the development from Calvinism to capitalism as described by Tawney. Pauline and biblical terms are remembered, but their application has been forgotten. "No, no, Mr Keelevin, we're no now in a state o' nature but in a state o' law", Claud says (I.xviii)[48] to his lawyer, who has protested against the terms of the entail which gives the book its title. The Pauline implications are clear. Bondage to the law is idol-worship, which implies damnation, as Claud discovers when it is too late to make any human amends:—

> "'O man!' exclaimed the hoary penitent, 'ye ken little o' me. Frae the very dawn o' life I hae done nothing but big and build an idolatrous image; and when it was finished, ye saw how I laid my first-born on its burning and blazing altar. But ye never saw what I saw — the face of an angry God looking constantly from behind a cloud that darkened a' the world like the shadow of death to me; and ye canna feel what I feel now, when His dreadful right hand has smashed my idol into dust.'" (II.vii)[49]

Ringan Gilhaize drew a false parallel between his own actual sacrifice of his son and Abraham's sacrifice of Isaac, which God averted. In reality he came closer to Claud, who sees himself accurately as a Moloch-worshipper, sacrificing his child to an idol afterwards proved false and overthrown. The power of the figure derives partly from its Old Testament associations (II Kings xxiii, 10), but partly also from its more general application to the unbridled commercial activity of the new capitalism.

Galt has prepared the way for Claud's conversion. When he first formed the resolution to disinherit Charles, his eldest son, and reconstitute his family's ancient estate by a marriage between his second son Walter and the heiress, Miss Betty Bodle, he received a scriptural oracle, in some ways closely resembling that of Ringan Gilhaize:—

"He opened the book with a degree of superstitious trepidation, and the first passage which caught his eye was the thirty-second verse of the twenty-seventh chapter of Genesis. He paused for a moment; and the servants and the family having also opened their Bibles, looked towards him in expectation that he would name the chapter he intended to read. But he closed the volume over upon his hand, which he had inadvertently placed upon the text, and lay back on his chair, unconscious of what he had done, leaving his hand still within the book.

'We're a' ready,' said Mrs Walkinshaw; 'whare's the place?'

Roused by her observation from the reverie into which he had momentarily sunk, without reflecting on what he did, he hastily opened the Bible, by raising his hand, which threw open the leaves and again he saw and read, —

'And Isaac his father said unto him, Who art thou? and he said, I am thy son — thy first-born, Esau;

And Isaac trembled very exceedingly.'

'What's the matter wi' you, gudeman? said the Leddy; 'are ye no weel?' as he again threw himself back in his chair, leaving the book open before him. He, however, made no reply, but only drew his hand over his face, and slightly rubbed his forehead.

'I'm thinking, gudeman,' added the Leddy, 'as ye're no used wi' making exercise, it may be as weel for us at the beginning to read a chapter until oursels'.

'I'll chapse that place,' said Walter, who was sitting opposite to his father, putting, at the same time, unobserved into the book a bit of stick which he happened to be sillily gnawing." (II.xix.)[50]

Walter, who thus inserts a marker in his father's Bible just when his elder brother, Charles, has been disinherited in his favour is the *fatuus* who after his father's death is himself to be ousted by the third brother George. The biblical element is as strong as anything in *Ringan Gilhaize*, but the tone of the passage is markedly different. The theologically based conviction of the seventeenth century has in the eighteenth been replaced by superstitious fear. Later still, when George meets his end, even superstition has virtually disappeared from the novel. (Mrs Eadie is one of Galt's relatively few errors in literary tact, and need not be taken too seriously.) Galt's sense of intellectual history is faultless. Yet the insistence on predestination remains. Superstitions are no more than superstitions, but still they have a knack of corresponding with the orderly and dispassionate working of the enlightened universe which Galt saw subsuming his narratives.

The process of law in general, more specifically the operation of the entail on the lands of Grippy, symbolizes the regular operation of the Providential system, despite the efforts of human beings to bend it to their own interests — to create a particular providence for themselves. The direct result of Claud's disinheritance of Charles, and of George's legal machinations to have his brother declared *fatuus*, is to ensure in George's default of heirs male, that James, son of the disinherited Charles, shall succeed. Charles was disinherited because he followed the dictates, not of interest, but of natural feeling, when he married the penniless Isabella Fatherlans. His children inherit his capacity for natural feeling, as a consequence of which James refused to marry George's daughter Robina. The eventual succession of James marks the replacement of the old order of obsession and superstition by the new law of natural feeling and reason. This is combined with the material progress of the Enlightenment, and it seems probable that Galt intended the marriage of James with Ellen Frazer to symbolise the harmonious union of Lowland with Highland in the new Scotland.

In its emphasis on law, *The Entail* in some degree resembles *The Heart of Midlothian*. Corrupt lawyers — the writers Pitwinnoch and Pilledge, and the advocate Threeper — are particularly associated with the figure of George. Two others stand in complete contrast. One is Mr Keelevin, whose attempts to dissuade Claud from executing the entail have already been mentioned. Still more important is Leddy Grippy, Claud's wife, herself the daughter of a legal controversialist, and in her way a minor prophet. The legal, biblical and theological overtones of her speech are one of the main means by which Galt keeps the theme of predestination to the fore. Here, for instance, is her outcry when her supposed legal acumen has ensured James's succession to the estates:—

"'O Bell, Bell — when I think o't — it's a judgment — it's a judgment, Bell Fatherlans, aboon the capacity o' man! Really, when I consider how I hae been directit — and a' by my own skill, knowledge, wisdom and understanding — it's past a' comprehension. What would my worthy father hae said had he lived to see the day that his dochter won sic a braw estate by her ain interlocutors? — and what would your gudefather hae said, when he was ay brag bragging o' the conquest he had made o' the Kittlestonheugh o' his ancestors — the whilk took him a lifetime to do — had he seen me, just wi' a single whisk o' dexterity, a bit touch of the law, make the vera same conquest for your son Jamie Walkinshaw in less than twa hours?'" (III.xxviii.)[51]

The Leddy is triumphantly confused. The dominant impulses of her mind attempt to claim full responsibility and credit for her achievement while simultaneously she contradicts her own words by regarding herself as the 'directit' instrument of a particular providence. She is right to claim that she has been directed, but it is not by a particular providence, nor by her skill, knowledge, wisdom and understanding; it is by the ultimately benevolent but impersonal forces which are bringing a new society into being.

In one's experience, however, the tragic frustrations of the earlier action tend to predominate over the final resolution. No one would readily describe *The Entail* as an optimistic novel.

iv

"Such is the system of Providence, the base propensities of individuals yield beneficial results to the species, and particular evils always engender general good." So Galt wrote at the end of his study of Cardinal Wolsey.[52] Wolsey himself he seems to have regarded as an instance of the triumph and tragedy of the mercantile genius under the revolutionary circumstances which linked the sixteenth in such close parallel with the eighteenth and the early nineteenth centuries. The rise of the merchant class he regarded as the central political fact of the period which saw both the first exploitation of the New World and the success of the Protestant Reformation; the prosperity, based on overseas enterprise of that class, he saw as the immediate cause, at least of the English Reformation, and the continuing dominance of that class was, he believed, a necessary consequence of the success of the Reformation. "Avarice overcame Ambition in the councils of princes; and sovereigns, and subjects, alike, eager to participate in the golden regions of the West, promoted the moral independence of man by cultivating the means of commerce."[53] The avarice of Henry VII amassed the wealth which made the careers of Wolsey and Henry VIII possible; the misuse of that wealth led to the corruption of both, and so eventually to the English reformation and the triumph of the mercantile classes.

The development of *The Entail* is clarified if the parallel with the sixteenth century is kept in mind. The novel operates at the level, not of kings and cardinals, but merchants and shopkeepers. The technique distantly resembles Burns's peasant mock-heroic in *Tam o' Shanter*.[54] Claud corresponds to Henry VII. The more generous qualities of Wolsey and Henry VIII are exemplified in Charles and James, the more sordid in George. Over Claud, the mere fact of hereditary landed possession exercises a diabolic fascination to the virtual exclusion of every other human faculty. Once he has regained possession of the Kittlestonheugh, he does very little with it. His only improvement is to execute the deed of entail which binds it by way of Wattie to the heirs-male of his body, as he hopes, for ever. In Glasgow he aspires to no dignity higher than that of a shopkeeper. The Glasgow merchants at this early stage are represented by Provost Gorbals and his lady:—

> "The Provost was a man in flourishing circumstances, and he was then walking with his lady to choose a scite for a country-house which they had long talked of building. They were a stately corpulent couple, well befitting the magisterial consequence of the husband.
>
> Mrs Gorbals was arrayed in a stiff and costly yellow brocade, magnificently embroidered with flowers, the least of which was peony; but the exuberance of her ruffle cuffs and flounces, the richness of her lace apron, with the vast head-dress of catgut and millinery, together with her blue satin mantle, trimmed with ermine, are items in the gorgeous paraphenalia of the Glasgow ladies of that time, to which the pencil of some abler limner can alone do justice.

The appearance of the Provost himself became his dignity, and corresponded with the affluent garniture of his lady: it was indeed such, that, even had he not worn the golden chain of his dignity, there would have been no difficulty in determining him to be some personage dressed with at least a little brief authority. Over the magisterial vestments of black velvet, he wore a new scarlet cloak, although the day had been one of the sultriest in July; and, with a lofty consequential air, and an ample display of the corporeal acquisition which he had made at his own and other well furnished tables, he moved along, swinging at every step his tall golden-headed cane with the solemnity of a mandarine." (I.l.)[55]

Maudge Dobbie's hostility is not altogether surprising. But it is Mrs Gorbals who sets up Claud as a packman, and his own efforts thereafter enable him to become a shopkeeper. By way of the shop he amasses the considerable wealth used by George to further his own more spectacular projects.

George becomes a merchant when "the general merchants of the royal city began to arrogate to themselves that aristocratic superiority over the shopkeepers which they have since established into an oligarchy, as proud and sacred, in what respects the reciprocities of society, as the famous Seignories of Venice and of Genoa."[56] His success in the role of merchant, and his pride as a land-owner, are emphasised with dramatic irony by Leddy Grippy:—

> "'Dear keep me, Geordie!' said she, 'what's in the wind noo, that ye hae been galloping awa in your new carriage to invite Bell Fatherlans and her weans to Grippy?'
>
> George, eager to prevent her observations, interrupted her, saying —
>
> 'I am surprised, mother, that you still continue to call the place Grippy. You know it is properly Kittlestonheugh.'
>
> 'To be sure,' replied the Leddy, 'since my time and your worthy father's time, it has undergone a great transmogrification; what wi' your dining-rooms, and

what wi' your drawing-rooms, and your new back
jams and your wings.'

'Why, mother, I have but as yet built only one of the
wings,' said he.

'And enough too,' exclaimed the Leddy. 'Geordie,
tak my word for't, it'll a' flee fast enough away wi' ae
wing.'" (II.xxiv.)[57]

James aspires to a station higher still:—

"The early habits and the tenor of the lessons he had
received were not calculated to insure success to James
as a merchant . . . The bias of his character, the visions
of his reveries and the cast of his figure and physiognomy, were decidedly military. But the field of
heroic enterprise was then vacant — the American war
was over, and all Europe slumbered in repose, unconscious of the hurricane which was then gathering."
(II.xxviii.)[58]

A few pages later, Galt relieves the heroics, and places James
unmistakeably in the new age by the industrial figure with
which he symbolises the young man's feelings as he returns from
Grippy. "His whole bosom was a flaming furnace — raging as
fiercely as those of the Muirkirk Iron Works that served to
illuminate his path." (II.xxxiv.)[59]

v

"If we admit that man is susceptible of improvement, and has
in himself a principle of progression, and a desire of perfection, it
appears improper to say, that he has quitted the state of his
nature, when he has begun to proceed."[60] This, one of the main
tenets of Ferguson's *History of Civil Society*, Galt accepted with
no more than a few ironic reservations, and incorporated in his
imaginative work. The significance of the improvements in
Glasgow and the west of Scotland was not limited to material
prosperity, or rather, on the occasions when it was, the improvement generally served to conceal some human corruption.
Genuine improvement involved a corresponding improvement
in human nature, an improvement in which general Nature also
participated. Galt, for instance, was able to see the beauty of
industrial furnaces seen by night — his perception here is almost
Turneresque. The relation of Nature, human nature and impro-

vements he establishes by the vignettes of Glasgow and the surrounding countryside which occur at turning points in the novel. Galt's attitude to Glasgow is almost like that of Thomson to London, discussed in the first volume of this book.[61]

Claud Walkinshaw first met Provost Gorbals and his lady at Whitehill, on the eastern outskirts of the city as it existed in the early eighteenth century. The Provost was contemplating the move from city to country which Claud rather than he was destined to perform:—

> "It was only in the calm of the summer Sabbath evenings that she (Maudge Dobbie) indulged in the luxury of a view of the country; and her usual walk on these occasions, with Claud in her hand, was along the brow of Whitehill, which she perhaps preferred, because it afforded her a distant view of the scenes of her happier days; and while she pointed out to Claud the hills and lands of his forefathers, she exhorted him to make it his constant endeavour to redeem them, if possible, from their new possessors, regularly concluding her admonitions with some sketch or portrait of the hereditary grandeur of his ancestors.
>
> One afternoon, while she was thus engaged, Provost Gorbals and his wife made their appearance." (I.i.)[62]

Maudge's theme — redemption of the past — is a major part of the novel, the working out of which is made almost impossible by the overlegalistic form which she gives it, and by the grossly materialistic intrusion of the city magistrate and his wife. The opposition which she establishes between city and country, although real enough, is expressed in false terms, which dominate the novel almost to the end. Twice, however, the city is described in a harmony with Nature, which clashes sharply with the course of events described immediately afterwards, although not with the conclusion of the novel. The first is when Charles has agreed to the postponement of his marriage to Isabella, occasioned by the ruin of her father after the collapse of the Ayr Bank[63] in 1772:—

> "The year was waning into autumn, and the sun setting in all that effulgence of glory, with which, in a

serene evening, he commonly at that season terminates his daily course behind the distant mountains of Dumbartonshire and Argyle. A thin mist, partaking more of the lacy character of a haze than the texture of a vapour, spreading from the river, softened the nearer features of the view, while the distant were glowing in the golden blaze of the western skies, and the outlines of the city on the left appeared gilded with a brighter light, every window sparkling as if illuminated from within. The colour of the trees and hedges was beginning to change, and here and there a tuft of yellow leaves, and occasionally the berries of the mountain ash, like clusters of fiery embers, with sheaves of corn, and reapers in a few of the neighbouring fields, showed that the summer was entirely past, and the harvest time begun." (I.xv.)[64]

The only phrase here with darker overtones is the final one. The calm landscape however soon modulates into the vernacular fury of Mrs. Jarvie, directed at the innocent and penniless Bell Fatherlans:—

"'The goun's ruin't — my gude silk to be clippit in this nearbegaun way — past a' redemption. Gang out o' the gait, ye cutty, and no finger and meddle wi' me. This usage is enough to provoke the elect; as 'am a living soul, and that's a muckle word for me to say, I'll hae the old craighling scoot afore the Lords. The first cost was mair than five and twenty guineas. If there's law and justice atween God and man, she shall pay for't, or I'll hae my satisfaction on her flesh.'" (I.xv.)[65]

Mrs Jarvie misuses the Scottish national motto, "Wha daur meddle wi' me", and unconsciously equates herself with Shylock. But her outburst is chiefly characterized by her mercantile and Calvinist self-righteousness and certainty of salvation. Even in her passion, Mrs Jarvie takes it for granted that she is one of the elect, whose redemption (unlike that of the gown) cannot be affected by anything internal or external — not even by a false oath — and who is certain that the law and justice of God will always decide in her favour. At some level of her mind she is a

Justified Sinner, whereas, by definition, the penniless Bell Fatherlans is a reprobate. It is to rescue her from such unnatural
encounters that Charles marries Bell, with consequences that are
unfortunate in everything but the final outcome.

The second passage occurs when James, at the crisis of his
fortune, sets out from the city to confront his uncle George at
Kittlestonheugh. The general description is more threatening but
the final emphasis is hopeful—

> "The weather was cloudy but not lowering — a
> strong tempest seemed, however, to be raging at a
> distance; and several times he paused and looked back
> at the enormous masses of dark and troubled vapour,
> which were drifting along the whole sweep of the
> northern horizon, from Ben Lomond to the Ochils, as
> if some awful burning was laying waste the world
> beyond them; while a long and splendid stream of hazy
> sunshine, from behind the Cowal mountains, brigh-
> tened the rugged summits of Dumbuck, and, spreading
> its golden fires over Dumbarton moor, gilded the brow
> of Dumgoin, and lighted up the magnificent vista
> which opens between them of the dark and distant
> Grampians.
>
> The appearance of the city was also in harmony with
> the general sublimity of the evening. Her smoky
> canopy was lowered almost to a covering — a mist
> from the river hovered along her skirts and scattered
> buildings, but here and there some lofty edifice stood
> proudly eminent, and the pinnacles of the steeples
> glittering like spear-points through the cloud, sug-
> gested to the fancy strange and solemn images of
> heavenly guardians, stationed to oppose the adversaries
> of man." (II.xxx.)[66]

In both these instances, the modern city is described. When
Charles learns that Claud has disinherited him, the emphasis
shifts to the grotesque and hostile medieval aspects of the city,
and in particular to the "Pictish" cathedral. (The reader will
remember Claud's conversation with Cornelius Luke, quoted in
Progress and Poetry,[67] about the classical architecture of the new
St. Andrew's Church):—

"The scene and the day were in unison with the tempest which shook his frame and shivered his mind. The sky was darkly overcast. The clouds were rolling in black and lowering masses, through which an occasional gleam of sunshine flickered for a moment on the towers and pinnacles of the cathedral, and glimmered in its rapid transit on the monuments and graves in the church-yard. A gloomy shadow succeeded; and then a white and ghastly light hovered along the ruins of the bishop's castle, and darted with a strong and steady ray on a gibbet which stood on the rising ground beyond. The gusty wind howled like a death dog among the firs, which waved their dark boughs like hearse plumes over him, and the voice of the raging waters encouraged his despair." (II.i.)[68]

At once ironically and appropriately, the novel ends with the motto which appears on the city coat of arms, "Let Glasgow Flourish!"

vi

The assumed date at which the action in each of the novels so far discussed takes place always considerably precedes that of publication. *Annals of the Parish*, for instance, ends in 1810, but the book first appeared in 1821. The effect of distancing contributes, as in Scott, to the perspective of the novel, but at the same time more or less eliminates the possibility of reportage, often present and powerful elsewhere in Galt, who was among other things a good professional journalist. Part at least of the interest in *The Ayrshire Legatees* (1821, but first published as a serial in *Blackwood's Edinburgh Magazine* between June 1820 and February 1821) rises from the apparently first-hand accounts, sent home from London by the Pringles, of the action for divorce, unsuccessfully instituted by the king, George IV, against Queen Caroline, and heard (1820) in the House of Lords. Dr Pringle becomes a supporter of the Queen, whom he describes in a letter to Mr. Micklewham:—

"Mrs Pringle and me, by ourselves, had a fine quiet canny sight of the queen, out of the window of a pastry baxter's shop, opposite to where her majesty stays. She

seems to be a plump and jocose little woman; gleg,
blithe and throwgaun for her years, and on an easy
footing with the lower orders — coming to the
window when they call for her, and becking to them,
which is very civil of her, and gets them to take her
part against the government.[69]

Galt indicates motive here by the same indirect method used
in *Annals of the Parish*. Dr Pringle's reasons for patronising a
particular baker's shop are tolerably clear. Already before the
assumed opening of the novel respect for royalty as an institution
has been diminished by the bad relationship between the King
and the Queen. Dr Pringle unconsciously continues the process,
in particular by his choice of adjectives, gleg, blythe and
throwgaun — a choice, the very appropriateness of which sets
the Queen more fittingly in an Irvine parlour than in a royal
palace or at the bar of the House of Lords. The effect of her
conscious appeal to the masses is itself somewhat diminishing.

Dr Pringle found a place outside the House of Lords on the
day when the action was finally dismissed. His words again
emphasize the Queen's common humanity at the expense of
traditional dignity. The position and emotions of a woman
prevail over her role as vindicated royal consort, and force even
Dr Pringle to join the crowd in an expression of sympathy:—

> "I was in the House of Lords when her majesty came
> down for the last time, and saw her handed up the
> stairs by the usher of the black-rod, a little stumpy
> man, wonderful particular about the rules of the
> House, insomuch that he was almost angry with me for
> stopping at the stair-head. The afflicted woman was
> then in great spirits, and I saw no symptoms of the
> swelled legs that Lord Lauderdale, that jooking man,
> spoke about, for she skippit up the stairs like a lassie.
> But my heart was wae for her when it was all over, for
> she came out like an astonished creature, with a wild
> steadfast look, and a sort of something in the face was
> as if the rational spirit had fled away; and she went
> down to her coach as if she had submitted to be led to a
> doleful destiny. Then the shouting of the people began,
> and I saw and shouted too in spite of my decorum,

> which I marvel at sometimes, thinking it could be
> nothing less than an involuntary testification of the
> spirit within me."[70]

Galt presents the trial in a way which differs only in social level of expression from that used by Scott in *Waverley* to narrate, say, events during the battle of Prestonpans.[71] These last are seen through the eyes of Edward Waverley, and centre on the death of his friend and former commanding officer, Colonel Gardiner. The Colonel, like the Queen, is a genuine historical figure. Correspondingly, the real events of the divorce action are seen through the fictitious eyes of the Pringles. In either case, the effect is to heighten the human as well as the historical reality of the scene. Journalism is involved, but in itself the method is proper to the novelist rather than the conscientious reporter, who aims, or ought to aim, at an impersonal view of events. Instead, everything is here dramatised — is seen through the eyes of a spectator, whose individual tastes, sympathies and prejudices affect both what is seen and the way in which it is experienced. The event in itself may or may not be of historical importance, but the emphasis is on actuality as realised by a participant or bystander. The dramatization may involve satire, which need not be limited to a single target — the narrator within the fiction, or the events which he records — but may extend over both to include a whole society.

This last is the case with *The Ayrshire Legatees*. Galt's treatment of the Pringles is obviously satirical, but so too is his treatment of London society and the King and Queen. In *Progress and Poetry* I noted as one consequence of the political events of the seventeenth and early eighteenth century that "in Scotland and England alike, the outward show of an hierarchical and hereditary society continued long after rational or empirical justification had become impossible. Respectable society as a consequence became in some measure pervaded by elements of guilt and hypocrisy"(p.3). Such elements are Galt's targets in *The Ayrshire Legatees*, the success of which depends on the extension of "historical" methods to the treatment of contemporary issues. This also occurs elsewhere in his writing.

The movement towards the historical treatment of the present in his novels is paralleled elsewhere, for instance, in his biographical writings. *The Life and Administration of Cardinal Wolsey*, an early work, has already been mentioned; it deals with the fairly remote past. Later ones — in particular *The Life of Lord Byron* (1830) — deals with notable people of Galt's own generation and acquaintance; they are seen from Galt's point of view, but he also attempts to judge them from the anticipated perspective of history. "I shall consider him, if I can", he says[72] of Byron, "as his character will be estimated when contemporary surmises are forgotten, and when the monument he has raised to himself is contemplated for its beauty and magnificence, without suggesting recollections of the eccentricities of the builder."

The aim does not mean that the personal eccentricities of the subject are ignored:—

> "Perhaps I regarded him too curiously, and more than once it struck me that he thought so. For at times, when he was in his comfortless moods, he has talked of his affairs and perplexities as if I had been much more acquainted with them than I had any opportunity of being. But he was a subject for study, such as is rarely met with — at least, he was so to me; for his weaknesses were as interesting as his talents, and he often indulged in expressions which would have been blemishes in the reflections of other men, but which in him often proved the germs of philosophical imaginings. He was the least qualified for any sort of business of all men I have ever known; so skinless in sensibility as respected himself, and so distrustful in his universal apprehensions of human nature, as respected others. It was, indeed, a wild, though a beautiful error of nature, to endow a spirit with such discerning faculties, and yet render it unfit to deal with mankind." (Chapter XXVII)[73]

The unromantic emphasis on business is part of Galt's characteristic style, but otherwise it is almost as if Boswell had been reincarnated to deal with Byron rather than Johnson or Rousseau.

Galt also produced an Edinburgh edition (1822) of Alexander Graydon's *Memoirs of a Life Chiefly Passed in Pennsylvania within the last sixty years*, which had been published eleven years previously in Harrisburg, Pennsylvania. Graydon had been a soldier, and afterwards a British prisoner-of-war during the

American struggle for independence. He had witnessed the Presidencies of Washington and Adams. He was a contemporary, who had lived the life of a private man in a remote part of the world, yet had seen and taken part in events of world-wide significance. His career was precisely of the kind to stimulate Galt's mind and imagination.

Apart from *The Ayrshire Legatees*, four of Galt's tales (neither *The Steamboat* nor *The Gathering of the West*, published in 1822 and 1823 respectively, is properly to be regarded as a novel) deal with spectacular public events, seen from a point-of-view immediately private, but entailing a reconsideration of the course of recent history. The final episode of *The Steamboat* brings Dr and Mrs Pringle back to London, where in company with Mr Thomas Duffle they attend George IV's coronation. *The Gathering of the West* deals with the sight-seeing tours made for various more or less specious reasons by the citizenry of Greenock, Paisley and Glasgow to Edinburgh on the occasion of the King's visit in 1822. *The Member* and *The Radical*, late novels, both published in 1832, deal, from opposed political stand-points, with events leading to the Reform Bill of that year. *The Last of the Lairds* (1826), as recently restored to us by Professor I.A. Gordon, distils much of the essence of these tales: the elegiac title suggests the end of an era; the Laird's literary and philosophical work is inspired by his visit to Edinburgh to see the King; his downfall is the result of pressure from the world of trade and commerce, and his partial salvation is a side-effect of the corrupt voting system brought to an end by the Reform Bill.

In *Annals of the Parish* and *The Provost*, Galt treated the personal reign of George III as dominated by revolutionary change — on the whole, for the better. In the series of later tales just listed his views are somewhat different. George IV represents the survival of the old order in a corrupt and degenerate form, soon to be replaced by a new, which will still be corrupt, but in a way which seems unlikely to improve on its predecessor. The King's death in 1830 marks the great divide. Archibald Jobbry, the unreformed and unregenerate M.P., whose parliamentary memoirs form *The Member*, becomes almost eloquent on the subject:—

> "Whilst this change and enlargement of my mind
> was going on, his Majesty King George IV, that

gorgeous dowager, departed this life; an event of a
serious kind to me, and to those with whom I acted;
for although our grief on the occasion was not of a
very acute and lachrymose description, it was nevertheless heartfelt; for he stood in our opinion as the last of
the regal kings, that old renowned race, who ruled
with a will of their own, and were surrounded with
worshippers.

'Never more,' said I, 'shall we have a monarch that
will think his own will equivalent to law. His successors hereafter will only endeavour to think agree-
ably to their subjects; but the race of independent kings
is gone for ever.' In a word, the tidings of his death,
though for some time expected, really smote me as a
sudden and extraordinary event. Had I heard that the
lions had become extinct on the face of the earth, I
could not have been more filled, for a season, with
wonder and a kind of sorrow."[74]

Mr Jobbry's lament may be interpreted in more ways than
one, any of which, however, corresponds in some degree with
the appearances which the King makes in Galt's earlier books,
whether he is sueing unsuccessfully for divorce, enjoying the
tawdry pageantry of his coronation (which Mr Duffle compares[75] unfavourably with the popular Glasgow ceremony of
King Crispin's coronation "on the 12th of November,
A.D.1818"), or failing to present himself in person to his adoring
subjects in Edinburgh. Here is the first of many disappointments
suffered on that occasion by Mrs Goroghan from Greenock:—

"She dressed with all possible expedition, and took
care not to forget an umbrella, for the day was at this
period overcast, and symptoms of rain began to spot
and speckle the pavement. In this she had for once the
advantage of the M'Auslans, for they having set off
with Mrs Lorn, immediately after breakfast, were then
seated on the scaffold; and the morning being fine
when they left Edinburgh, they were not prepared for
the pitiless and disloyal rain that commenced about an
hour before the squadron came to anchor, and continued with unabating violence all the evening and

night, by which not only the M'Auslans and Mrs Lorn
were wetted to the skin, but a grand bonfire, which
had been poetically imagined of volcanic magnitude,
on the summit of Arthur's Seat, was so drookit, that in
the evening when it was lighted, as a signal to all the
land that the King was come, it scowled as sulkily and
sullenly as if it had been kindled by the foul breath of a
radical."[76]

The phrase "the King was come" has Jacobite overtones,
which Walter Scott had already exploited in his song "Carle,
now the King's come",[77] subtitled "New words to an auld
spring", and dated "On the occasion of George IV's visit to
Scotland, August, 1822". The "auld spring" was a Jacobite song,
a complete version of which had been contributed by Burns to
The Scots Musical Museum (1790)[78], while an earlier adaptation,
"Peggy, now the King's come" was to be found in Ramsay's
The Gentle Shepherd, II.iii:—[79]

> Peggy, now the King's come,
> Peggy, now the King's come:
> Thou may dance, and I shall sing,
> Peggy, since the King's come.
> Nae mair the hawkies shalt thou milk,
> But change thy plaiding-coat for silk,
> And be a lady of that ilk,
> Now, Peggy, since the King's come.

The immediate reference is pre-Jacobite — to the restoration of
Charles II, which is also to bring about the restoration of Peggy
and Patie to the social status in which they had been born. For
Ramsay himself, however, writing after the Hanoverian succession, Jacobite overtones were necessarily present. Burns's
version is more directly insurrectionary:—

> An somebodie were come again,
> Then somebodie maun cross the main,
> And every man shall hae his ain,
> Carl an the king come.

When a Stewart returns, that is to say, the House of Hanover
must leave. In the passage from *Tom Jones* quoted in chapter 1,[80]

the Jacobite Squire Western refers to an English variant of the same song.

For Scott the new version marks the redirection of traditional loyalties towards the Union, and towards a king who was Hanoverian only by ancestry, and whose right had been established by the passage of time. Galt's irony, compounded as it is by the sinister image — "the foul breath of a radical" — which ends the sentence, calls everything into question. The feeble bonfire shows how unvolcanic questions of succession, and even of kingship, have become; the real point at issue is radicalism and reform. He parodies Scott's own adaptation somewhat later on in *The Gathering of the West*[81] "A celebrated Edinburgh poet . . . had made the following most capital song, published at Blackwood's Emporium of Loyalty, Literature, and Libels, and which we would give our lugs if we could have made ourselves:—

THE KING'S MUSTER

> Little wat ye wha's coming,
> Little wat ye wha's coming,
> Little wat ye wha's coming,
> Now the King himsel's coming.
> There's coaches coming, steam-boats lumming,
> Targets coming, turtles scumming,
> Bow-street and Lochaber's coming,
> Wi' pipes to make a braw bumming.
> > Little ken ye wha's coming,
> > Clans and Clowns and a's coming.

The rowdiness and vulgarity of the occasion is heightened by the presence of the police in the form of the London Bow-street Runners and the Edinburgh City Guard with their Lochaber axes.

In *The Literary Life of John Galt* (1834), he allowed himself a rare direct comment on coronation and royal visit[82]:—

> "In one respect the tomfoolery of the coronation of George IV. was not, however, altogether 'a vain show' in my eyes, and, when not tickled with the kything of the ridiculous, I had occasional moments of sedate reflection which assumed the gravity of philosophy. It

seemed to me that such things now did not harmonize with our natural national character . . . At the time, the coronation afforded me inconceivable pleasure, for I could only see things, bating the occasion, worthy to provoke heart-easing laughter; the remembrance, however, like many other sweets, sours in the rumination. It did more to lessen my respect for the tricks of state than anything I ever witnessed.

If the coronation disclosed the folly that sits in high places, the gathering to see the King in Edinburgh fully matched it, by showing the depths of absurdity to which the mass will descend. Certainly the sight was gay and jocund, but it was a nation in its 'Sunday clothes.' What kings should seek to see, is not how their subjects can appear when put to a stress, but how they daily do when in fabrication of those things which are the sinews and muscles of power. Had George the Fourth's performance of Crispianus in the Scottish metropolis been a truly royal avatar, as it was given out to be, he would at least have given one day to the inspection of the hospitals, of the receptacles of the houseless, and of the haunts and habitations of the miserable and forlorn. I have an utter loathing of royal visitations to the bright side of things, and for many a year have seen in them that flattering which too many think it is the business of kings to receive. The Edinburgh citizens cuckoo about George the Fourth calling them gentlemen, and their town a city of palaces, as if he had not read enough of other places to know the truth, and thought but of outdoing them in cajolery."

Galt's attitude is partly a matter of his local cast of mind. His roots were not in Edinburgh, but in the shires of Renfrew and Ayr. The title, *The Gathering of the West*, is ironically reminiscent of Covenanting times, when, in spite of the Ayrshire origin of the House of Stewart, the Western whigs, with Ringan Gilhaize, rose to overthrow Charles II. In Edinburgh, the reception of George IV was stage-managed (largely by Walter Scott)[83] until it appeared almost as if he were a benevolent reincarnation of the Stewart line come to proclaim the virtues of Union and

Protestant succession. To correct this error of perspective, an occasional but recurrent image in Galt's writing is the brutality exercised on behalf of the reigning monarch's grandfather against supporters of the Stewarts. One of the London sights viewed by Dr Pringle was "the Temple Bar, where Lord Kilmarnock's head was placed after the Rebellion"[84], placed, that is to say, after he had been publicly executed in accordance with the cruel ceremonies prescribed by the English law of treason. Dr Pringle naturally sees the event in terms of an Ayrshire family, but Galt himself was less restricted; the image recurs even in *The Life of Lord Byron*, when the journey made by the poet and his companions to the court of the Albanian vizier Ali Pashaw is described:—

> "On entering Joannina, they were appalled by a spectacle characteristic of the country. Opposite a butcher's shop, they beheld hanging from the boughs of a tree a man's arm, with part of the side torn from the body. — How long is it since Temple-bar, in the very heart of London, was adorned with the skulls of the Scottish noblemen who were beheaded for their loyalty to the son and representative of their ancient kings!"[85]

England and the Hanoverians are identified with the atrocities of an Albanian who was little more than a brutally successful bandit chieftain.

This however is a comparatively minor part of Galt's total attitude. "I was surely born a radical", he says at the beginning of the chapter of the *Literary Life* from which I have just quoted, and, as should now begin to become clear, that assessment, which he qualifies only to a very limited degree, is borne out by much in the novels and tales. His personal involvement and partial identification with the Covenanters was extended to include the democratic ambitions of the weavers and others — this despite the fact that their activities often made as acute an appeal to his sense of the ludicrous as did coronation or royal visit. Not always, however. In 1791 Mr Balwhidder, no less, is regarded as a "black-neb" by many of the heritors, and it is clear from the 1793 entry that the feelings of the minister at least were more for the radicals than for Mr Cayenne:—

"On the Monday following, Mr Cayenne, who had been some time before appointed a justice of the peace, came over from Wheatrig-house to the Cross Keys, where he sent for me and divers other respectable inhabitants of the clachan, and told us that he was to have a sad business, for a warrant was out to bring before him two democratic weaver lads, on a suspicion of high treason. Scarcely were the words uttered, when they were brought in, and he began to ask them how they dared to think of dividing, with their liberty and equality principles, his and every other man's property in the country. The men answered him in a calm manner, and told him they sought no man's property, but only their own natural rights; upon which he called them traitors and reformers. They denied they were traitors, but confessed they were reformers, and said they knew not how that should be imputed to them as a fault, for that the greatest men of all times had been reformers. — 'Was not,' they said, 'our Lord Jesus Christ a reformer?' — 'And what the devil did he make of it?' cried Mr Cayenne, bursting with passion; 'Was he not crucified?'

I thought, when I heard these words, that the pillars of the earth sunk beneath me, and that the roof of the house was carried away in a whirlwind. The drums of my ears crackit, blue starns danced before my sight, and I was fain to leave the house and hie me home to the Manse, where I sat down in my study, like a stupified creature awaiting what would betide. Nothing, however, was found against the weaver lads; but I never, from that day, could look on Mr Cayenne as a Christian, though surely he was a true government-man."[86]

The effect is complex. The previous day, Mr Balwhidder had preached against the excesses of the Terror in France. He can easily distinguish, however, between Parisian revolutionaries and Ayrshire weavers. Almost without realising it, he identifies the government with Mr. Cayenne, and both as un-Christian and oppressive. One recollects the sermon which he preached before the Commissioner at the General Assembly of 1779, and which

Lord Eglesham regarded as going rather beyond the bounds of modern moderation. Galt shows how, even in a placed minister, strict religious conservatism might be combined with a radicalism, only partly conscious, which, as he sees it, is an inherited feature of the West of Scotland mind — the first kythings, almost, of the later Red Clydeside.

The fortunes of the radicals, and the curious ways in which their beliefs might develop, always concerned him. Lawrie Todd, the hero of the late (1830) novel of the same name, begins as a democrat of the French Revolutionary period who is forced as a consequence to go to America. He returns a rich man, who retains some of his old sympathies, modified by experience in a new land.

The so-called Radical War of 1820 is mentioned in *The Gathering of the West* and *The Radical*. Galt shows insight, combined with a measure of contempt for the pusillanimity shown by most survivors of the affair, and the realisation that the best of them would soon abandon even what was left of their beliefs to pursue the wealth to be gained from new and burgeoning industries.

The course of events during the 1820 uprising is summarised thus by Dr Ferguson in the fourth volume of the *Edinburgh History of Scotland*:—[87]

"Not only was radical literature, such as Wooler's periodical *The Black Dwarf*, being widely disseminated, but numerous local radical unions were also springing up in the manufacturing counties of the west with a central committee in Glasgow. There a plot of some kind was undoubtedly being hatched which its projectors hoped would be co-ordinated with risings in England; but it was scotched by the arrest of its leaders in February 1820. After that date the government knew that there was little danger of a serious outbreak, but it gladly availed itself of a mysterious incident that diverted Glasgow on 2 April 1820. Bills were placarded calling upon the people to support a provisional government. To help the new 'government' (which failed to materialise) the weavers went on strike, but the expected *sansculotte* hordes did not appear. Possibly egged on by government agents a few men rose in arms. A small band from Strathaven in Lanarkshire, which included an old jacobin James 'Perley' Wilson, marched on Glasgow; but on the outskirts they could not find the promised reinforcements and dispersed quietly to their homes. Some of the Calton weavers trudged eastwards to join up with some non-existent English rebels who were said to be marching to seize the Carron Ironworks; but at Bonnymuir near Falkirk the Calton rebels were scattered by cavalry. Thus ended the mysterious so-called 'Radical War' of 1820. Forty-seven prisoners were tried for treason by a commission of oyer and terminer, and of these three — Wilson, John Baird and Andrew Hardie — were executed".

The march of the Calton weavers to defeat at Bonnymuir roughly parallels that of the Covenanters to Rullion Green in 1666, and in *The Gathering of the West* is parodied by the expedition of the Paisley weavers to Edinburgh, after their radical political philosophy has been overthrown by the mere rumour of the royal presence. The first chapter to deal with them, headed "Paisley Bodies", begins with a reference to the Radical War and its aftermath:— "Among other extraordinary effects of the radical distemper which lately raged in the West, was a solemn resolution on the part of a patriotic band of weavers' wives, to abjure tea and all other exciseable articles; in conformity to which, and actuated by the fine frenzy of the time, they seized their teapots, and marching with them in procession to a bridge, sacrificed them to the Goddess of Reform, by dashing them, with uplifted arms and an intrepid energy, over into the river, — and afterwards they ratified their solemn vows with copious libations of smuggled whisky."

The men prove even less dedicated. In the face of temptation, their radical tradition is upheld by a single figure only, that of Clattering Tam, "an eminent member of the Radical Association", who eventually abandons the discussion, "stalking away with long strides, his hands in his pockets, and his elbows looking out at the holes in his sleeves". The victor in the argument is the more respectable Peter Gauze, "a short, well-set man, who, by a certain air of activity in his manner, and neatness in his dress, compared with the others, indicated that he was one of those clever and shrewd fellows, who, by the exercise of their natural sagacity, rise from the loom into the warehouse, and ultimately animate the vast machinery of the cotton-mills"[89] — in other words, a potential James Coats, whose family later was to make the Paisley cotton industry a dominating force in world trade. Galt fails to develop the character of Peter Gauze, who does no more than applaud the arrival of the King from a rowing boat, and come to an understanding with Miss Nanny Eydent, the Irvine seamstress, but the figure contains at least the embryo of another study of self-made commercial man, a Claude Walkinshaw or Provost Pawkie, born in a later generation.

Galt sometimes allows characters in his later novels to advance distinctively radical doctrines, which nevertheless receive reluctant agreement from the moderate Tories to whom they are addressed. The best example is probably to be found in the penultimate chapter of *The Member*. After an agricultural riot, forcibly suppressed by dragoons, Mr Jobbry joins Mr Blount, a local landlord and Tory MP, in an investigation of the causes and circumstances. One of the people consulted is "a Mr Diphthong, who was a schoolmaster well known in that part of the country to have much to say with the common people". Mr Diphthong singles out as a major cause of the trouble the failure of the (English) Poor Law to distinguish between charitable assistance given by the parish to aged and infirm paupers, and the employment, on road works, for instance, offered by the parish to able-bodied labourers, otherwise unemployed. ("It would be just as equitable," he claims, "to call the bricklayers who are now building the new church paupers, as those poor men who are breaking stones for the improvement of the highways.") His first suggestion therefore is to recognise officially the distinction between the two.

> "'Still,' replied Mr Blount, 'that would only be calling six half-a-dozen. There is a surplus population, or, in other words, a want of employment. How is that to be remedied?'
> 'By two ways — emigration and public works.'
> 'But where are the means to execute public works?'
> 'Circulation. Property must be taxed: the proceeds of this tax must be devoted to the employment of the

labourers, for public advantage or ornament. From them the money will flow to the dealers, thence to those they employ, and so pervade the community.'

'But, Mr Diphthong,' quo' I, 'Don't you see that the effect of that would be to bring down the large properties?'

'I do,' said he; 'but is not this better than to put an end to the rent of landlords, which is the present tendency of public opinion?'

'Really, Mr Diphthong, you put the matter in a very alarming light: is there no alternative?'

'I think not,' said he; 'the great properties have had their day: they are the relics of the feudal system, when the land bore all public burdens. That system is in principle overthrown, and is hastening to be so in fact. The system that it will be succeeded by is one that will give employment to the people — is one that will gradually bring on an equalisation of condition.' —

At this I started, for I saw by it that he was of the liberty and equality order; and grieved I was that men of his degree could talk so glibly on subjects that puzzle the highest heads in the land. But I said nothing: his sentiments, however, remain with me; and I cannot get the better of what he propounded about the feudal system being at an end, and of the system by which he thinks it is to be succeeded."[90]

Mr Jobbry's acquiescence is compelled, as he sees it, not so much by the strength of the argument, as by its correspondence with the direction in which he senses that public affairs are moving. The conversation immediately precedes, and contributes to hasten, his retirement from Parliament, for he sees it confirmed, first, by the trivial circumstances (defeat on the Civil List, "the snuff-money of a few old shaking-headed dowagers") which led in 1830 to the resignation of the Tory Duke of Wellington as Prime Minister[91]; secondly, by his feeling that his successors in office, the Whigs, are "backed and supported by a far stronger faction than themselves, — a faction who are looking forward to frighten them from their stools at the first expedient uproar of difficulty"[92] — the radicals, that is to say, and advocates of Corn Law reform, who, for Whigs in the 1830s may be regarded as equivalent to Militant Tendency for the Labour Party in the 1980s. The immediate extension of the franchise to half-a-million from a total population of twenty-two million opens what for Mr Jobbry are terrifying prospects. "The one-and-twenty millions and a half will not be long content with such a fractional representation as it is proposed to give them; for what is the reform intended to do, unless it be to work out the abolition of rents and tithes? Less than that, I fear, will not satisfy the radicals; nor less than that, sooner or later, will a reform parliament, after it has again reformed itself, be found obliged to concede.'"[93]

Galt makes Mr Jobbry unusually clear-sighted, but it would certainly be wrong to assume that he completely shared the retired MP's distaste for the prospect. The total evidence of novels and autobiographical writings suggests that he regarded it with some relish.

One of the most striking features in all the books under discussion is Galt's realisation of a change, not predominantly in the externals, the comfort and prosperity, of modern life, but rather in the cast of mind which accompanied them. The change, misunderstood to a degree though it may be by the characters who discuss it, is clearly signalled in the novels. A decade earlier than Mr Jobbry, Provost Pawkie was already aware of it, as the following remarkable passage demonstrates:—

> "Things in yon former times were not guided so thoroughly by the hand of a disinterested integrity as in these latter years. On the contrary, it seemed to be the use and wont of men in public trusts, to think they were free to indemnify themselves in a left-handed way, for the time and trouble they bestowed in the same. But the thing was not so far wrong in principle, as in the hugger-muggering way in which it was done, and which gave to it a guilty colour, that by the judicious stratagem of a right system, it would never have had. In sooth, to say, through the whole course of my public life, I met with no greater difficulties and trials, than in cleansing myself from the old habitudes of office. For I must, in verity, confess, that I myself partook, in a degree, of the caterpillar nature; and it

was not until the light of happier days called forth the wings of my endowment, that I became conscious of being raised into public life for a better purpose than to prey upon the leaves and flourishes of the common-wealth. So that, if I have seemed to speak lightly of those doings, that are now denominated corruptions, I hope it was discerned therein, that I did so, rather to intimate that such things were, than to consider them as in themselves commendable. Indeed, in their notations, I have endeavoured, in a manner, to be governed by the spirit of the times in which the transactions happened, for I have lived long enough to remark, that if we judge of past events by present motives, and do not try to enter into the spirit of the age when they took place, and to see them with the eyes with which they were really seen, we shall conceit many things to be of a bad and wicked character, that were not thought so harshly of by those who witnessed them, nor even by those who, perhaps, suffered from them; while, therefore, I think it has been of a great advantage to the public to have survived that method of administration in which the like of Baillie M'Lucre was engendered, I would not have it understood that I think the men who held the public trusts in those days a whit less honest than the men of my own time. The spirit of their own age was upon them, as that of ours is upon us, and their ways of working the wherry entered more or less into all their trafficking, whether for the commonality, or for their own particular behoof and advantage."[94]

Provost Pawkie bases his *apologia* on a historicism and cultural relativism more often to be found in the last than in the first quarter of the nineteenth century, and differing considerably from the universalism, masked by temporal and cultural peculiarities, characteristic of Scott and Hume. Both the latter would, I think, have been antagonized by the overtly metaphysical phrase, "the spirit of the age", although in the 1820's it was becoming fashionable; under that title Hazlitt, for instance, published (1825) a series of essays on contemporary figures. The new spirit necessarily involved the disappearance of such relics of the feudal system (to adopt Mr Diphthong's words) as Baillie M'Lucre and his methods of adminstration.

One reason for the Provost to adopt this metaphysical style was, of course, simply the opportunity it gave for constructive hypocrisy. The sentence in which he claims to think that the men of a previous generation were not a whit less honest than the men of his own time is deliberately ambiguous, more so than the direct remark made earlier that the behaviour of his predecessors was not so much wrong in itself, as in the manner of performance. The Provost is in essentials no different from any of them. The Shakespearian image of caterpillar and butterfly links him in his office to Bushy, Bagot and Green, the caterpillars of the commonwealth in Shakespeare's *Richard II*, and to the question put by the servant in the garden scene:—

> Why should we in the compass of a pale
> Keep law and form and due proportion,
> Showing, as in a model, our firm estate,
> When our sea-walled garden, the whole land,
> Is full of weeds, her fairest flowers chok'd up,
> Her fruit-trees all unprun'd, her hedges ruin'd,
> Her knots disorder'd, and her wholesome herbs
> Swarming with caterpillars?
>
> (III.iv.,40-47)

The growth of wings, the transformation of caterpillar into butterfly, hints at a change for the better, but even here there is a muted suggestion that the Provost was given wings only to spread them — to extend his depredations, that is to say, over a wider range, and under a more prepossessing outward appearance. The Provost is a conscious disciple of Machiavelli, using words to conceal rather than reveal his true meaning.

He behaves in this way, however, because the meaning which he hopes the words will convey possesses in fact a certain validity. Things have changed. The age has a new spirit, which no longer finds the bare-faced manipulations of a Baillie M'Lucre acceptable. Partly, no doubt, this results from generally higher standards of morality, but the new age is also more sanctimonious than the old, demanding that unpleasant necessities should at all costs be decently veiled. The feudal system and

M

Richard II have gone, but they have been succeeded by the more hypocritical "policy" of modern Bolingbrokes.

An incidental result of this development is that communication between people of the two kinds, the new and the old, becomes increasingly difficult. The Provost and the Member are both Tories, still spiritually more at ease in the old world, and personally more or less unaffected by the new tendency. Clear signs of it, however, are visible elsewhere — in *Annals of the Parish*, for instance, where Mr Balwhidder, that unconscious radical, is often totally misunderstood by others, or finds himself incapable of understanding them. His difficulties, oddly enough, though the fact is explicable, are least with the democrats, greatest with the industrialist, Mr Cayenne, who in turn more often than not himself fails to communicate with either. This last has already been illustrated by one entry, that for 1793, which deals with the two weaver lads accused of high treason. The reasons for his failure to come to any kind of mutual understanding with Mr Balwhidder may in turn be illustrated by the annal for 1785. Mr Balwhidder, it will be recollected, invited three divines, Mr Keekie of Loupinton, Mr Sprose of Annock and Mr Waikle of Gowanry, to preach at his summer occasion or celebration of Holy Communion:—

> "I invited Mr Keekie of Loupinton, who was a sound preacher, and a great expounder of the "kittle" parts of the Old Testament, being a man well versed in the Hebrew and etymologies, for which he was much reverenced by the old people that delighted to search the Scriptures. I had also written to Mr. Sprose of Annock, a preacher of another sort, being a vehement and powerful thresher of the word, making the chaff and vain babbling of corrupt commentators to fly from his hand. He was not, however, so well liked, as he wanted that connect method which is needful to the enforcing of doctrine. But he had never been among us, and it was thought it would be a godly treat to the parish to let the people hear him. Besides Mr Sprose, Mr Waikle of Gowanry, a quiet hewer out of the image of holiness in the heart, was likewise invited, all in addition to our old stoops from the adjacent parishes.
>
> None of these three preachers were in any estimation

with Mr Cayenne, who had only heard each of them
once; and he happening to be present in the Session-
house at the time, inquired how we had settled. I
thought this not a very orderly question, and I gave
him a civil answer, saying, that Mr Keekie of Loupinton would preach on the morning of the fast day, Mr
Sprose of Annock in the afternoon, and Mr Waikle of
Gowanry on the Saturday. Never shall I or the elders,
while the breath of life is in our bodies, forget the
reply. Mr Cayenne struck the table like the clap of
thunder, and cried, 'Mr Keekie of Loupinton, and Mr
Sprose of Annock, and Mr Waikle of Gowanry, and all
such trash, may go to —— and be ——! and
out of the house he bounced, like a hand-ball stotting
on a stone."[95]

The preachers were all, like Mr Balwhidder himself, Calvinist
metaphysicians, products, one assumes, of the Orthodox University of Glasgow. The democrats in turn had their own metaphysics, derived from Godwin, Bentham and Tom Paine. Mr
Cayenne is by nature too inarticulate to give any connected
account of the intellectual distress which they made him suffer,
but in terms of cultural history, he occupies the middle ground
between the two — essentially he is a man of the Enlightenment,
with all the dislike of *a priori* reasoning natural to his kind. As an
American as well as an industrialist, he would seem to belong
more to the new than to the old world. As against this, he is an
American Tory refugee from the Revolution, and in this sense
belongs not so much to the old as to the intermediate state,
represented by that other Tory condemner of metaphysics,
David Hume. From the point of view of such a man, the
ministers and weavers are all metaphysicians of one kind or
another, all equally unbearable.

Mr Balwhidder is less successful with the men than with the
women when in his sermons he attempts to harmonize the rival
systems:—

"As there was at that time a bruit and a sound about
universal benevolence, philanthropy, utility, and all the
other disguises with which an infidel philosophy appro-
priated to itself the charity, brotherly love, and well-

doing inculcated by our holy religion, I set myself to task upon these heads, and thought it no robbery to use a little of the stratagem employed against Christ's Kingdom, to promote the interests thereof in the hearts and understandings of those whose ears would have been sealed against me, had I attempted to expound higher things. Accordingly, on one day it was my practice to shew what the nature of Christian charity was, comparing it to the light and warmth of the sun that shines impartially on the just and the unjust — shewing that man, without the sense of it as a duty, was as the beasts that perish, and that every feeling of his nature was intimately selfish, but that, when actuated by this divine impulse, he rose out of himself and became as a god, zealous to abate the sufferings of all things that live. — And, on the next day, I demonstrated that the new benevolence which had come so much into vogue, was but another version of this Christian virtue. — In like manner I dealt with brotherly love, bringing it home to the business and bosoms of my hearers, that the Christianity of it was neither enlarged nor bettered by being baptized with the Greek name of philanthropy. With well-being, however, I went more roundly to work. I told my people that I thought they had more sense than to secede from Christianity to become Utilitarians, for that it would be a confession of ignorance of the faith they deserted, seeing it was the main duty inculcated by our religion to do all in morals and manners, to which the new-fangled doctrine of utility pretended."[96]

The fact that is is possible for Mr Balwhidder to preach such sermons demonstrates how close in fact his position is to that of the philanthropists and Utilitarians.

Mutual incomprehension shows itself most clearly in *The Radical*, the political autobiography of Nathan Butt, who was briefly a member of the first Reform Parliament on the Government side, and was unseated by an investigating committee for flagitious perjury in his election campaign. The end of the memoir leaves him still hoping to be returned for the next Parliament.

Nathan's apprehension of the spirit of the age is more lurid
(indeed, almost preternatural in its effect) than anything revealed
to Provost Pawkie. It appears to him as a demon rather than an
undefined spirit. "It seemed to me as if the world had been, from
time immemorial, in backsliding confusion; and my heart
burned with a vehement ardour to arrest the chaos into which it
was fatally hurrying. But in that moment, the demon of the age
— that genius of the oppression which so saddens the earth —
was hovering at hand."[97] The demon, however, is not a solitary
power; he takes his place in a dualistic theology, and as a
consequence has to endure opposition, the nature of which
strengthens Nathan's political hopes, at the same time as it clouds
his intellect and language. During the early stages of the French
Revolution, for instance, "the ruling demon of society and the
genius of nature were . . . fighting in the mid heavens; and the
latter could not but sooner or later prevail. 'Thrones and
sovereignties,' said I, 'the resources of empires, hierarchies, and
orders, and the progeny of artificial life, may for a time
withstand the eternal goddess; but as sure as the moon waxes to
the round bright full, she will vindicate her jurisdiction, and
gladden the earth.'"[98]

This is not so much the language of philosophy as of religion,
if not superstition, and several passages demonstrate that Nathan,
like Ringan Gilhaize a century and a half previously, is in fact
prone to superstitious fears — for example, when he is frightened by the candles gleaming from the windows of the house in
which his uncle lies dying.[99] Certainly he sees the world as
governed by powerful and warring eternal principles, sometimes
personified, sometimes not, one of which has an absolute claim
on his services, "It did not appear that it could, for a moment, be
admitted that legislation should be regulated by expediency, or
made subservient to temporary exigencies. 'It must,' I exclaimed,
'be regulated by eternal principles; and it is because it has been
for so many ages adapted to the wants of occasion, rather than to
the necessities of nature, that it has been, instead of a protection
to mankind, an over-flowing fountain of bitter waters.'"[100] The
similarity between Nathan and Ringan Gilhaize is again
perceptible.

Nathan is as conscious as the Provost of a change in the human
mind, though he expresses it in different terms. These correspond, however, no less than the words of the Provost, to the

facts of the world, as interpreted by his own political beliefs. Rather than one contradicting the other, they represent opposite sides of the same coin, light directed from two different directions on a single object. The Provost sees the change as from open to decently concealed corruption. Nathan gives the radical assessment:—

> "It appeared to me, by this study that a moral transmutation was taking place, at least equal in importance to that political change which had at first attracted my attention. The olden and the reverenced were no longer regarded with the same sentiment as in other times; and men's minds, instead of considering what might be for the good of society, began to question whether society itself, organised as it was by error, could be of any good at all. I frequently wondered how it came to pass that mankind ever consented to endure artificial arrangements subservient of the rights of nature; for there can be no doubt that the arrangements which result from the social structure are corrosive of individual powers and endowments. Privilege is but a poor substitute for faculty; and it is as much the nature of society to subvert individual faculty, as it is of education to extinguish original genius."[101]

Both see a new moral imperative, to which they must adapt their lives. Nathan's, which involves the abandonment of all previously accepted standards in favour of an absolute individualism, stands much further, apparently, from the social norm. In its application, however, as seen in the methods used to gain him a seat in Parliament, the difference becomes almost negligible.

Not surprisingly, most people find conversation with Nathan difficult, especially on matters which they see as significant, but he does not — or sees as having a significance quite distinct from their own. For his father, an attorney, dialogue becomes all but impossible. Much the same is true of his mother, and later his wife. His maternal uncle, in whose household he suffers banishment, is more flexible, but even he succeeds only for a time:—

> "When I had resided some time, better than a year, with my uncle, he said to me, as we were sitting

together one Sunday evening by the fire-side, he looking over some family papers, and I reading Godwin's Political Justice, a work in the highest style of man:

'Nathan Butt,' said he, 'our family is not very numerous, and in course of nature, bating my sister, you are the nearest, as the eldest of her children, to me of kin; and should you survive me, I have thought that it would be a prudent thing of you, and a great satisfaction to me, were you to make a prudent marriage. I see it is not necessary that fortune should be an essential ingredient in the choice, but it can be no detriment.'

To this I replied, 'That I was very sensible of the kindness with which he treated me; but, sir,' I added, 'marriage is what I have never thought of: indeed, to speak plainly, I have great objections to incur an obligation, to which the world has attached so many restraints, at variance with the freedom which mankind have derived from nature.'

'Pooh, pooh, Nathan,' cried my uncle, 'I am serious; don't talk such stuff now; we are not on an argument, but an important business of life.'

'I assure you, sir,' was my sedate answer, 'I have never been more serious. Marriage, sir, is one of those artificial compacts invented by priests and ecclesiastics to strengthen their moral dominion.'

'I shall not dispute with you, Nathan,' replied my uncle, 'that marriage does bring grist to the church's mill, but we are not to judge of it merely by the tax which we pay for its blessings; therefore say nothing on that head. Men and women must have some law to regulate them in their domicile, and as no better has yet been enacted, we must conform to what is.'

'In Paris, sir,' said I, 'it is no longer —'

'Nathan Butt,' said my uncle, rather sternly, 'I am speaking to you on a very important subject; therefore don't trouble me with any thing about your French trash, and the utility of living in common like the beasts that perish.'

I had never heard Mr Thrive express himself in this

manner before: hitherto he had only laughed, as it were, at what he called my Jacobin crotchets; but I could discern that a feeling of a more sensitive kind affected him on this occasion. He was a rich man — his favour was therefore worth cultivating; and I frankly acknowledge that this consideration had great weight with me. But principle should be above corruption; and I felt at the moment that I was yielding to the deleterious influences of the artificial social state, when, for a moment, I thought it might be for my interests to accede to what was evidently his intention. However, I rallied, and frankly told him that I never intended to marry.

'You are a fool,' cried he, 'and may live to repent it:' and abruptly gathering up his papers and rising, said, before leaving the room, 'Reflect, Nathan, well on this short conversation. I do not look for an old head on young shoulders, and you are not destitute, on some occasions, of common sense; reflect on this, I say, for a week, and next Sunday evening we shall resume the conversation.'"[102]

Mr Thrive, it is apparent, has been prepared to discuss Nathan's Jacobin ideas on the level of friendly abstraction, but it is clear that the possibility of applying them to life in Great Britain has not occurred to him. He distinguishes in a very English way between "argument" and "important business of life", a distinction which means nothing to Nathan until he realises that for himself it may have substantial material consequences. They have engaged in their previous discussions, which Nathan, engrossed as he is in *Political Justice*, begins by seeing as now merely continued, on a basis of more or less complete mutual misunderstanding. Mr Thrive enjoys the mental stimulus of argument, but, as his death-bed shows, conforms as much as any other of Nathan's relatives to traditional religious beliefs. Nathan is committed to his principles, although, as his marriage almost immediately demonstrates, not to the extent of abandoning his possible inheritance.

Nathan conspicuously fails to apprehend how others think and feel when his uncle and his mother are on their death-beds. Particularly notable is the dry restraint with which both events are treated by Galt; the point-of-view throughout remains that of the would-be philosopher and revolutionary, puzzled by the reactions of others and the emotions which he observes in himself, but resolute to overcome both. The technique employed is not unlike that of Swift in his "Argument against abolishing Christianity" and "A Modest Proposal":—

> "I then left the room, and went to my own chamber, where, after a season, I grew impatient at my softness, and cried out, with a grudge, 'Why is it that man alone should be molested with such scenes?' But, do what I would, and resolutely as I nerved myself, I could not check the current of my thoughts and tears. This was undoubtedly an unbecoming imbecility; and for a time, in spite of myself, I was obliged to give way to the mood that fell upon me. In the sequel, however, I recovered my self-possession; and it is salutary to reflect how soon, after the grave has closed on the truest of friends — a parent — a man regains his accustomed wont. No doubt the shrinking sense of grief is afterwards felt occasionally in the lone and the sad hour, and I have not been without the experience of its icy touch; but sorrow is not a habitude of nature, and, to confess the fact, I really thought that the demise of my worthy mother left me freer to pursue the course of my endeavours to improve the condition of man; for while she lived, my dread of giving any cause of uneasiness to her made me shy to undertake many enterprises of pith and moment that the heritage of the world so wofully requires."[103]

A parallel delicacy of touch and language is apparent when Nathan's wife refuses to allow him any part in the ceremonies when his son is baptized. Neither can understand the beliefs of the other, for which, nevertheless, each is prepared to make every allowance (in the case of the mother, save the ultimate one). Each finds the other strangely deficient, and indeed it is obvious that as a group Nathan's relatives fear for his sanity, while he in turn takes refuge from what he sees as human incomprehensibility in the beauty of Nature, the goddess to whom he has devoted his powers. On this occasion, however, even she proves ineffective:—

"At all times since my childhood I have been a lover of Nature; and when my feelings have been chafed by the effect of the existing system, I have sought solace and soothing from the beauty and calm of the landscape. But on this occasion its wonted sweet influences were stale; for in my bosom there was a bitter controversy, in which conscious rectitude, and adherence to my own notions of the right, would not intermingle. Something decisive was, however, requisite; and at last calling to mind how much nobler it is to sacrifice one's own sentiments to those which are dear to others, I resolved to make no farther objection either to the fees or the baptismal performance; and accordingly returned home in this benevolent resolution, where, finding my wife alone in our bedchamber, I bade her wipe her tears, and do in the whole affair as she thought fit, adding; 'I am ready to do my part — the father's part in the ceremony — since to you and the old people it is so important.'

Instead of returning me my answer, she began to weep still more grievously, which seemed very inexplicable; and I expressed my regret, with some surprise, that she should receive my concession with so little satisfaction.

'O Nathan!' cried she, 'speak not to me in this manner: although you are my husband, the father of my child, and one whom I have vowed at the holy altar to love and obey — it will yet make me turn from you with feelings that I dare not entertain. Your concession fills me with horror. In the ceremony you have no part; and it is the dreadful thought, that it is I who must object to you, which makes these tears to flow.'

'What do you mean?' cried I; 'you are incomprehensible.'

'Ah! in that lies much of my grief. Your irreligious opinions — I will call them by no harsher name — disqualify you to take the Christian vows. Your father and uncle are to stand in your place.'

'Come, come,' said I, somewhat disconcerted; 'this is carrying the joke too far: I assure you, my dear, that I will do what I ought, and all that you can desire.'

'But you shall not. No, Nathan, it is I that bar you from the altar. You are not fit to take upon you the sacred obligations for your own child. Your father and uncle must incur them for you.'"[104]

The first effect is to make the reader question Nathan's intellectual credibility. If his first adherence is really to principle, his gesture of nobility might appear no more than hypocrisy. The reference to fees adds to this suspicion. On the other hand, his devastating use of the phrase "carrying the joke too far" indicates the depth of his own belief in the hypocrisy of society; in offering to join in the ceremony, he sees himself as harmlessly joining the others in what all reasonable people see as make-believe, a joke. And of course he cannot understand his own feelings, the "bitter controversy" in his bosom, any more than he can the attitude adopted by others.

vii

Mr Diphthong depressed Mr Jobbry by his reference to the relics of the feudal system, in which the land had borne all public burdens. Nineteenth century society was increasingly dominated by ready money; the possession of land might confer prestige, but effectually, as Adam Smith had indicated,[105] even here what counted was the return on purchase-price or assumed value to be obtained from rents based on likely returns from sale or produce. Trade and manufacture were directly based on cash. After the Napoleonic wars, as land-values fell, there was a corresponding reduction in rent-income to the landlords, the agricultural interest. The downfall of many among them may be traced to wadsets, mortgages, which they undertook to resolve what they mistakenly thought of as temporary cash-flow difficulties. (The phrase itself, of course, is modern.) Merchants meanwhile, especially those whose connections were with the East India Company, and, initially to a lesser degree, manufacturers, were flush with cash, and eager to establish themselves in landed respectability. At the same time, agricultural discontent, which sometimes took violent forms, inflicted considerable financial and moral pressure on hereditary proprietors.

The Last of the Lairds (1826, but in authentic published form 1976) is a mock-elegy in prose on the feudal system of land tenure, strangled by the cash-nexus, an elegy written in a tone somewhat reminiscent of Fergusson's "Elegy, On the Death of Scots Music" or Burns's "Poor Mailie's Elegy". The occasion is provided by the experiences of one old-established Renfrewshire proprietor, named in the sub-title as Malachi Mailings Esq., of Auldbiggings. The name corresponds to his situation, and serves to orchestrate the elegiac theme of the book. Malachi is the title of the last among the Old Testament prophets before the new dispensation, and this indicates the laird's succession and ancestry. It also introduces the series of biblical reminiscences which helps to shape the work as a whole. Mailings, his surname, shows the source of such income as he still has — a mailing is "a piece of arable ground held on lease by a *mailer* (a cotter), a tenancy of land, a kind of smallholding" (SND). The term was already obsolescent when Galt wrote, and carries with it a strong suggestion that the Laird's estate was unimproved. This is confirmed by the territorial appellation, Auldbiggings, "old buildings", and by the description of the dilapidated Place and policies with which the book opens.

Malachi, the Laird, is unusual in that he has himself felt the influence of the new Political Economy, which theoretically ensured the doom of himself and his kind. Like many others, he has just visited Edinburgh to see the King, but unlike most of them, he has found his interest there less captured by the monarch than by a group of Edinburgh personages — the *literati*. "But yon's a pleasant place, yon toun of Embro'; and the literawty are just real curiosities, and a' philosophers, the whole tot of them."[106] It soon becomes clear that the political economists in particular have taken his fancy — old-fashioned followers of Adam Smith, that is to say; he has no time for more recent Malthusian innovations. (The same should not, of course, be assumed of Galt himself.) His interest is doubly quickened. On the one hand, the political economists give, or almost give, him a vocabulary and framework of ideas by which he can excuse to his own satisfaction the increasing penury suffered by himself and his hereditary land-owning brethren. On the other, the fact that the Edinburgh philosophers are *literati*, that they earn an income by writing books and articles, suggests a way in which he may escape his creditors. He too will write a book. The story of his life and opinions will be as profitable as have been those of Mr Balwhidder and Provost Pawkie, recently published.

The book which the Laird intends to write is thus itself a product of the late Scottish Enlightenment, a history, intended to demonstrate the course and necessary outcome of the conspiracy to make men of family *defuncti officii*, "cutting them off by sic legalities as writers to the signet, and advocates, and critics, frae the power of begetting a posterity".[107] This is to invert Malthusian theory. The progress of history, at least for the laird and his class, is not the unbridled growth of population, which they would prefer, but the increase of sterility. The concept recurs in the novel, especially in relation to the marriage of convenience arranged by Mrs Soorocks and the narrator between the Laird and the older of the two sisters of Barenbraes; included in it is the failure not only to beget children, but also to pass on heritable property to one's blood relations. The Laird, who has no descendent, "nor even an heir within the fifth degree of cousinship",[108] is on both counts a failure. He is deeply in debt to the wealthy representative of the new dispensation, Mr Rupees, the Nabob, whose name is as meaningful as the Laird's, and who has used the cash-emoluments of his service with the East India Company to erect in the neighbourhood a mansion, Nawaubpore, which in every way is the opposite of the derelict Auldbiggings. The novel turns on the conflict between those representatives of different stages of social evolution.

The Laird's *magnum opus* is in effect an incoherent history of money, taxation and economic life generally in Scotland. It begins with the happy pre-Union days of the pound-Scots with its useful minor sub-divisons — bodle (2d), plack (4d), bawbie (6d), and merk (13/4d). Long before the Union, it should be recollected, the pound-Scots had sunk in value to one twelfth of the English pound-sterling ($£1$ Scots = 1/8d sterling); in English terms, that is to say, a bawbie was worth a half-penny. The financial resources of an estate, however, seemed more extensive under the old system than under the one which replaced it. The 1707 Union brought with it the pound-sterling and the English National Debt, soon to be supplemented by the Sinking Fund, intended to counteract the latter, and instituted by Walpole in 1717. The basic gold coin, in Scotland after the Union, as earlier in England, became the guinea, first struck in England in 1663 with the nominal value of 20s., but from 1717 until its disappearance in 1813 circulating as legal tender at the rate of 21s.. In 1772 the Ayr Bank broke with losses for its creditors of considerably more than half a million pounds sterling, and at much the same time turnips were introduced as a staple crop. In 1799, the younger Pitt imposed an income tax, the maximum rate of which was 10%, and which was not abolished until after Waterloo. In 1817, the sovereign was introduced to replace the old guinea, and circulated, to the distress of the Laird and others, at 20s., not at the guinea rate of 21s..

This analysis, giving form not only to the Laird's grievances, but to his conspiracy theory, finds most coherent expression in an early exchange with the narrator, who does not yet realise how precarious the financial situation has become:—

> "'But in what manner, Laird, have you shown the existence of this alleged conspiracy between the government and the people, to overthrow the ancient gentry of his Majesty's hereditary kingdom?'
>
> 'Is na there changes in the value of money? I can assure you that I have well considered this portion of the bullion question.'
>
> 'I should like,' said I, with all possible gravity, 'to hear your opinion on the bullion question — of course, you examine the causes that affect the circulating medium and originate the agricultural distress?'
>
> 'The circulating curse — it's as clear a tax of five per cent of our income, as the five and ten deevelry of the war.'
>
> 'But, no doubt, you have exposed it properly, and in its true colours — will you have the goodness to read what you have said upon the subject? — for it is a subject which comes home to the business and bosoms of us all. Five per cent! really, Laird, you surprise me — I never imagined it was so much.'
>
> 'No man can maintain that it's one farthing less — for, since the coming out of the sovereign, and the crying down of the old honest coin of the realm, both in the price of horse and horn-cattle, a mulct of a full shilling in the pound has been inflicted on the whole agricultural interest.'
>
> 'And where does that shilling go to, Laird?'
>
> 'Where? but to the bottomless pit, the pouch o' government that they call the sinking fund; and is that no a depreciation?'

'Not to interrupt you, Laird,' said I, 'but how does the change in the money affect your income?'

'How! I'll show you how — is na small coin the evidence of cheap labour; and when labour is cheap, has not a man of rental the mair to hain for lying money? But the sight o' a farthing now-a-days is good for sair een; it's no to be met wi', but now and then in the shape of a blot in a town grocer's 'count, made out by his prentice in the first quarter of the school-laddie's time. It was a black day for Scotland that saw the Union signed, for on that day the pound sterling came in among our natural coin, and, like Moses' rod, swallow't up at ae gawpe, plack, bodle, merk, and bawbie, by the which mony a blithe ranting roaring rental of langsyne has dwinet and dwinlet into the hungry residue of a wadset.'"[109]

Moses' rod comes from *Exodus* 8.8.ff.:—

"And the Lord spake unto Moses and unto Aaron, saying, When Pharaoh shall speak unto you, saying, Shew a miracle for you: then thou shalt say unto Aaron, Take thy rod, and cast it before Pharaoh, and it shall become a serpent. And Moses and Aaron went in unto Pharaoh, and they did so as the Lord had commanded: and Aaron cast down his rod before Pharaoh, and before his servants, and it became a serpent. Then Pharaoh also called the wise men and the sorcerers: now the magicians of Egypt, they also did in like manner with their enchantments. For they cast down every man his rod, and they became serpents, but Aaron's rod swallowed up their rods."

Much of the Laird is revealed in this reference. He is well acquainted with scripture, the phrases of which he applies more or less aptly to his own situation; financial transactions are, for him, a species of magic; the Scots are the Egyptians, despoiled by the enchantments of the pound-sterling. Elsewhere, he occasionally implies that he is himself in some degree responsible for the loss of his fortune. "My book I canna write — to work I'm no able," he cries in chapter XXXI,[110] implying a parallel between himself and the Unjust Steward of *Luke* 16.4., "I cannot dig; to beg I am ashamed". Here, however, there is nothing immediately parallel. He sees his money, all money, as in fact disappearing into the wilderness:—

> "'But consider,' cried Mrs Soorocks, 'There's Mr Caption —'
>
> 'Whare?' cried the Laird, starting and looking round.
>
> 'And Mr Angle,' resumed the lady, 'demanding, as I am told, twenty golden guineas for his curiosity.'
>
> 'He may thank the government,' replied the Laird, 'that it's an impossibility to get them; was na the guineas put doon and hidden frae the light o' day, and the sight and reach o' man, in the bottomless dungeons o' the Bank o' England, like prisoners doomed to everlasting captivity, a' to let the King raise money by a stamp act on bank notes, by the which—'
>
> Here the old man was getting on his hobby when Mrs Soorocks interfered with —
>
> 'Hoot, toot, Laird, we dinna want to hear o' your standard unit the noo when we're speaking o' marriage — so ye'll just come to your tea and meet your bloomin bride and leave a' the lave o' the trouble to folk that understand thae matters better than yoursel.'"[111]

The theoretical exposition is completed in chapter XXXV, after the Laird's marriage, and in the course of negotiations for the sale of the superiority of Auldbiggings:—

> "I told him that I considered it a great Godsend but remarked that, as it was not sufficient to procure for him any effectual relief from his mortgage, it would be much better to give up the estate at once to the Nabob and buy an annuity with the money on the joint lives of himself and Mrs Mailings.
>
> 'Had we no a prospect of a family, what ye counsel would be worth hearkening to.'
>
> 'I doubt, Laird, that's but a barren prospect and, besides, you ought to consider the great wickedness of augmenting our national distress, by increasing the

population of the country already so redundant. I beseech you, Mr Mailings, to respect the admonitions of economical philosophy.'

'Hoots, Hoots — dinna talk sic Malthusian havers to me. The cause o' our national decay and agricultural distress, broken merchants, ravelled manufacturers, and brittle bankers come a'thegither frae another well e'e — Were sic calamities ever heard o' in this reawlm before the turnip farming cam into vogue? Answer me that? Weel do I mind that it was in the hairst o' that vera year, when the first park o' turnips was sawn in the shire, that the sough came through the kintra o' the Ayr bank gaun to pigs and whistles — My auntie, wha was then in the laun o' the livin and has since been sleeping in Abraham's bosom wi' Sarah his wife and the rest o' the patriarchs, said, on that melancholious occasion — and she was a judicious woman — that to gar sheep and kye crunch turnips was contrary to nature, their teeth being made for garss and kailblades, and that it would be seen that the making o' turnip pastures would prove a sign o' something — Never did I forget her words o' warning, though I was then but a bairn, a very babe and suckling, in a sense, and I hae noted, year by year, that her prophecy has been mair and mair coming to pass for, with the ingrowth o' turnip farming, there has aye been a corresponding smasherie amang the looms and sugar hoggits. Last year, I was in a terror for what was to happen when I saw sae mony braw parks that used to be ploughed for vittle to man, saun for fodder to beasts.'

'Your theory, Laird,' said I, 'well deserves the attention of his Majesty's Ministers, for some of them, in my opinion, have been finding similar effects, as legitimately descended from causes equally proximate. But if turnip fields were sown with corn, would the distress be abated?'

'How can ye misdoot it? — and the redundant population would be abated too — for, as they baith came in wi' the turnips, would na they gang out wi' them? Is na that a truth o' political economy?'"[112]

N

The truth of the book as a whole is a truth of political economy, or at least a satirical and comic caricature of one. The Laird was quoted earlier as comparing himself to the Unjust Steward, who saved his skin by making for himself friends of the Mammon of unrighteousness. In his own extremity, he follows the same course, with the part of Mammon taken, firstly by Miss Shoosie Minnigaff, usurper of the entail of the house of Barenbraes, whom he marries, secondly by the feudal superiority, the *dominium directum*, of Auldbiggings, which carried with it voting rights for the old corrupt unreformed House of Commons, and which in law had an existence completely separate from *dominium utile*, actual possession of the lands of Auldbigging. This *dominium directum* he and his women folk auction, with superb success, to the highest bidder, not, as might have been expected, Mr Rupees, whose store of ready cash seems likely to be much diminished by the miraculous restoration of the orphan, Charles Bayfield, but Mr Loopy, "of the respectable house of Loopy and Hypothec, writers in Glasgow", who has ambitions for himself or his client to become a "parchment baron" by purchasing the superiority. Political economy remains in the forefront throughout the negotiations, from the Laird's observation that Mr Loopy's hypothetical client is "a capitalist and kens hoo to mak his outlay productive", and his "Three hunder poun, Mr Loopy! I wud na tak three thousan: the superiority o' Auldbiggings is 720 pun scots, auld valuation, and it wud na be kittle to mak a piecing, as ye weel ken hoo, that wud gie ye the poore and capacity o' twa votes instead o' yin"; from this, by way of the later remark that "there's a standard o' value by which the price of every thing may be measured and all we want to know is what this natural standard is?", to the final triumphant "Twa thoosan sax hun'er and fifty pounds sterling — Mak it guineas, Mr Loopy, and bargain's yours."[113] The Laird has even turned back the course of time to restore his much-loved guineas.

Political economy is thus the dominant, though not of course the only, shaping force in *The Last of the Lairds*. I have already noted how scriptural references, such as those to Malachi, Moses, Abraham and the Unjust Steward, are worked into the pattern. They are numerous, especially in the latter part of the novel, and often provide an implied satiric commentary on the economic theme. Original sin, the ultimate source of all economic activity, enters by way of Adam and Eve whom the Laird in chapter XXXI blames for his downfall, and to whom Mrs Soorocks in chapter XXXV, when everything seems lost, compares the newly-wed couple:— "Here's likewise the Nawbob in a' his glory, comin nae doot to drive you and the Laird, like Adam and Eve, out o' this pleasant paradise and garden o' Eden, that it might be, for the sma' cost o' a little reparation".[114] The passage emphasises the Laird's cash deficiencies and includes a submerged reference to the hostile description of Solomon in the Sermon on the Mount (Matthew, 6.28-29).[115]

Again in chapter XXXI the Laird compares Mr Rupees, "that golden image of Nebuchadnedzor", to the false idol, the image of gold, which Nebuchadnezzar commanded his people to worship in the plain of Dura (Daniel, 3.1-6). His proposed marriage at this point he regards as equivalent to the sale of Joseph to the Ismaelites for twenty pieces of silver (Genesis, 37.28), and threatens to abandon both Old and New Testaments:—"D——l tak baith law and gospel, I'll no marry her yet—"[116] an attitude which absolutely contradicts Mrs Soorocks' opinion that the marriage is a work of mercy.

When Mrs Soorocks and the narrator emerge from Nawaub-pore, under the mistaken belief that they have rescued the Laird from his immediate difficulties, they "bade adieu to the Nabob at the Fakeir gate, or, as Mrs Soorocks called it, 'The Beautiful Gate'".[117] The reference here is to the apostolic act of charity carried out at the gate of the Temple in Jerusalem (Acts, 3,1-8:—

> "Now Peter and John went up together into the temple at the hour of prayer, being the ninth hour. And a certain man lame from his mother's womb was carried, whom they laid daily at the gate of the temple which is called Beautiful, to ask alms of them that entered into the temple; who seeing Peter and John about to go into the temple asked an alms. And Peter, fastening his eyes upon him with John, said, Look on us. And he gave heed unto them, expecting to receive something of them. Then Peter said, Silver and gold have I none; but such as I have give I thee: In the name of Jesus Christ of Nazareth rise up and walk. And he took him by the right hand, and lifted him up: and

immediately his feet and ancle bones received strength. And he leaping up stood, and walked, and entered with them into the temple, walking, and leaping, and praising God."

Mrs Soorocks remark is primarily sentimental and flattering — a part of her campaign of man-management aimed at Mr Rupees. Her momentary and accidental emphasis on the importance to a fallen world of non-economic factors is not noticed by her or echoed elsewhere. The parable of the Unjust Steward, as puzzling as anything in the New Testament, receives, as has been seen, very literal interpretation. The only other to be given some kind of prominence is that of the Prodigal Son, horribly misread by the newly-married Mrs Mailings:— "'Hold your tongue, Auldbiggings,' exclaimed Mrs Mailings, 'and dinna mak yoursel a prodigal son; an ye wad pairt wi' your patrimony in that gate, ye wud weel deserve to eat draff wi' the swine; na, na, a thousan pounds is ower little!'".[118] The world of *The Last of the Lairds*, dominated by the economic factor, is very far from the primitive church or the Gospel.

Galt intended *The Last of the Lairds*, in the form restored to us by Professor Gordon, to complete and round off the series of Scottish novels and studies which, five years earlier, had begun with *The Ayrshire Legatees*. By way of the Laird's theories, as well as his reminiscences of his father and other characters of an earlier generation, it offers an analysis of the movement of history during the eighteenth century and in the first quarter of the nineteenth. It embraces the old as well as the new economics, and hints at the political developments which were so soon to follow its publication. All this it does in a rural setting by way of characters whose intellectual capacity is limited or blinkered. In narrative technique, it plays a brilliant series of variations on the first-person point-of-view generally adopted by Galt — the Laird's, the narrator's, Mrs Soorocks', Jock's — but with a virtuosity unparalleled elsewhere. In some ways it goes beyond anything he had already attempted. Unusually for Galt or any other respectable nineteenth century author, the sexual urge, as given historical expression, for instance, in the life-style adopted by Burns, is allocated something of its full importance, socially and personally. The book is at once human, comic, bawdy, satirical and bitter — not perhaps Galt's most powerful achievement, but one, nevertheless, in which he gave expression to the full range of his remarkable intellect and imagination.

NOTES

Ian A. Gordon has done more than anyone else in recent years to promote Galt's reputation, both by his biography, *John Galt. The Life of a Writer* (Edinburgh, 1972), and by his various editions: *The Entail* (London, 1970); *The Provost* (London, 1973); *The Member* (ASLS, Edinburgh and London, 1975); *The Last of the Lairds* (Edinburgh and London, 1976); *Selected Short Stories* (ASLS, Edinburgh 1978). To these last may be added: J. Kinsley (ed.), *Annals of the Parish* (London, 1967); E. Waterston (ed.), *Bogle Corbet* (Toronto, 1977 — an edition limited to the Canadian third volume of the novel); Patricia J. Wilson (ed.), *Ringan Gilhaize* (ASLS, Edinburgh, 1984). An earlier biography than Gordon's is Jennie W. Aberdein, *John Galt* (London, 1936), and there are critical studies: Erik Frykman, *John Galt's Scottish Stories 1820-1823* (Uppsala, 1959), and Henri Gibault's expert and wide-ranging *John Galt. Romancier écossais* (Grenoble, 1979). This last, like Gordon's biography, contains a useful bibliography. Christopher A. Whatley (ed.), *John Galt 1779-1979* (Edinburgh, 1979) is a bicentennial volume of studies by several hands.

A notably large proportion of the studies listed above are the work of scholars living furth of the British Isles.

Where possible, quotations are taken from the editions listed above; elsewhere, they are from first or early printings.

1. John Galt, *Letters from the Levant* (London, 1813), Letter XIV, p.113.
2. Letter XI, pp.74-5.
3. Letter XVI, pp.130-1; Letter XVII, p.132.
4. Letter XVI, p.129.
5. Letter XVII, p.135.
6. Letter XIV, p.116.
7. Letter XVII, p.134.
8. Letter XVII, p.135.
9. Book I, viii, p.11.
10 *Annals of the Parish*, "Introduction". Kinsley, *ed. cit.*, p.1.
11. Kinsley, p.4.
12. *Institutes of the Christian Religion* 1.16.2.4.. Quoted in Francois Wendel, *Calvin*, trs. Philip Mairet (London, 1963), p.180.
13. *The Literary Life and Miscellanies of John Galt* (3 vols., London, 1834), I., pp.287-8.
14. *Scottish Literature and the Scottish People 1680-1830*, p.158.
15. (London, 1926: Penguin ed., Harmondsworth, 1938, often reprinted). References are to the latter.
16. Kinsley, p.31.
17. Kinsley, p.41.
18. Gordon, *ed. cit.*, p.86.
19. Kinsley, pp.41-2.

20 Kinsley, p.41.
21. Kinsley, pp.33-4.
22. Kinsley, p.37.
23. Kinsley, pp.136-7.
24. Kinsley, pp.137-8.
25. Kinsley. p.19.
26. Kinsley, p.132.
27. Kinsley, p.18.
28. Kinsley, pp.38-9.
29. Tawney, *op.cit.*, pp.225-6.
30. Chapter 14 (II., chapter 3).
31. Wilson, *ed. cit.*, p.1. The approach to the novel proposed by Douglas Mack ("'The Rage of Fanaticism in Former Days': James Hogg's *Confessions of a Justified Sinner* and the Controversy over *Old Mortality*" in Ian Campbell (ed.), *Nineteenth Century Scottish Fiction*, pp. 39-50) underestimates the subtlety of Galt's treatment, although it does set the novel in the immediately appropriate historical *milieu*.
32. Wilson, p.147.
33. Wilson, pp.275-6.
34. Wilson, p.282.
35. This was written before the appearance in 1984 of Patricia J. Wilson's edition. See also her article "*Ringan Gilhaize* — A Neglected Masterpiece?" in Christopher A. Whatley (ed.), *John Galt 1779-1979*, pp.120-50.
36. Wilson, p.321.
37. See the edition by James Kirk (Edinburgh, 1980).
38. Wilson, p.272.
39. Wilson, p.140.
40. Wilson, p.201.
41. Wilson, p.222.
42. Wilson, p.305.
43. Wilson, p.141.
44. Wilson, p.64.
45. Wilson, p.233.
46. Wilson, p.191.
47. Gordon, *ed. cit.*, p.6.
48. Gordon, p.58.
49. Gordon, pp.146-7.
50. Gordon, pp.62-3.
51. Gordon, p.349.
52. Book VII.i., p.247.
53. Book I.vii., p.10.
54. *Progress and Poetry.*, pp.140ff..
55. Gordon, p.5.
56. I.xxxiii.; Gordon, p.109.
57. Gordon, pp.210-11.
58. Gordon, p.222.
59. Gordon, p.245.
60. Duncan Forbes (ed.), *An Essay on the History of Civil Society* (Edinburgh, 1966), p.8.

61. *Progress and Poetry*, pp.59, 61ff..
62. Gordon, p.5.
63. For the failure of the Ayr Bank, cf. also above, pp.64, 181-2.
64. Gordon, p.44.
65. Gordon, pp.46-7.
66. Gordon, pp.231-2.
67. pp.102-3.
68. Gordon, p.125.
69. Chapter VIII, "The Queen's Trial", Letter XXVII.
70. Chapter IX, "The Marriage", Letter XXXII.
71. Chapter 47 (III., chapter 1).
72. John Galt, *The Life of Lord Byron* (London, 1830), "Introduction", p.4.
73. p.175.
74. Gordon, *ed. cit.*, chapter XXXII, p.105.
75. *The Steamboat* (Edinburgh and London, 1822), chapter X, "The Coronation", p.207.
76. *The Ayrshire Legatees or The Pringle Family . . . the second edition, to which is added The Gathering of the West* (Edinburgh and London, 1823), pp.342-3.
77. J. Logie Robertson (ed.), *The Poetical Works of Sir Walter Scott*, p.747.
78. J. Kinsley (ed.), *The Poems and Songs of Robert Burns*, II., pp.524-5. Kinsley's text is taken from volume 3 of James Johnson's *The Scots Musical Museum* (Edinburgh, 1790).
79. Burns Martin and J.W. Oliver (eds.), *The Works of Allan Ramsay II* (STS, Edinburgh and London, 1953), p.230.
80. Above, p.3.
81. *The Ayrshire Legatees etc.*, pp.366-8.
82. Chapter XXVII, Vol. I., pp.237, 240-1.
83. Basil C. Skinner, "Scott as Pageant-Master", *Scott Bicentenary Essays*, pp.228-37.
84. Chapter IV, Letter IX, p.64.
85. Chapter X, pp.74-5.
86. Kinsley, *ed. cit.*, pp.143-4.
87. William Ferguson, *Scotland 1689 to the Present* (Edinburgh, 1968: paperback ed., 1978), p.284.
88. *The Ayrshire Legatees etc.*, pp.291-2.
89. *The Ayrshire Legatees etc.*, pp.293-302.
90. Gordon, *ed. cit.*, chapter XXXV, pp.115-8.
91. Gordon, chapter XXXVI, p.119.
92. Gordon, chapter XXXVI, p.120.
93. *Ibid.*
94. Gordon, *ed. cit.*, chapter XXIII.pp.73-4.
95. Kinsley, *ed. cit.*, pp.117-8.
96. Kinsley, Chapter XXXV, "Year 1794", p.147.
97. *The Radical. An Autobiography* (London, 1832), chapter V, p.40.
98. Chapter VIII, p.62.
99. Chapter XV, p.116.
100. Chapter XXV, p.196.
101. Chapter XIV, pp.105-6.
102. Chapter IX, pp.63-6.

103. Chapter XXI, pp.162-3.

104. Chapter XI, pp.84-6.

105. *An Inquiry into the Nature and Causes of the Wealth of Nations* (London, 1776), I.xi., "Of the Rent of Land".

106. Gordon, *ed. cit.*, chapter II, p.6.

107. Chapter II, p.7.

108. Chapter VI, p.25.

109. Chapter II, pp.8-9.

110. p.133.

111. Chapter XXXI, p.135.

112. pp.152-3.

113. Chapter XXXIV, pp.146, 147-8, 151: chapter XXXVI, p.159.

114. p.155.

115. Compare (above p.141) Maudge Dobbie's use of the same passage in *The Entail*.

116. p.135.

117. Chapter XXIII, p.95.

118. Chapter XXXIV, p.149.

CHAPTER IV

JAMES HOGG

In Book I of *An Essay Concerning Human Understanding*, first published in 1689, two years later than the first book of Newton's *Principia*, John Locke (1632-1704) dismisses the possibility that innate principles can play any part in the activities of the mind. The argument of Book 2 begins with a celebrated and influential statement of the proposition that all ideas come from sensation or reflection:—

> "Let us then suppose the mind to be as we say, white paper, void of all characters, without any ideas; how comes it to be furnished? Whence comes it by that store which the busy and boundless fancy of man has painted on it with an almost endless variety? Whence has it all the materials of reason and knowledge? To this I answer, in one word, from *experience*. In that all our knowledge is founded, and from that it ultimately derives itself. Our observation employed either about external sensile objects, or about the internal operations of our minds perceived and reflected on by ourselves, is that which supplies our understandings with all the materials of thinking. These two are the fountains of knowledge, from whence all the ideas we have, or can naturally have, do spring".[1]

Locke, like most of his contemporaries and immediate successors, appears not to have noticed or cared about the contradiction implicit in the idea of the mind being "white paper, void of all characters", yet at the same time possessing unexplained "internal operations", upon which it is possible for something else — a separate mind, presumably — to reflect. The infinite regression thus involved might, they felt, safely be ignored, because Locke's philosophical approach otherwise harmonized so exactly with the inductive methods of natural philosophy, which had attained their self-evident triumph in the work of Newton. The terms "Mind" or "Understanding", as Locke had attempted to define them, virtually replaced "Soul" or "Spirit" (with all the overtones of possible supernatural origins and experience which these words contained) in philosophical discourse. The inner world self-evidently had to be dominated by the external regularities of the physical world of bodies in motion. From this assumption stems the hostility to thought with any kind of metaphysical content, already noticed as a characteristic of the Enlightenment.

Most of this Scott and Galt accepted as a series of almost unconscious presuppositions. The feelings of indignation and contempt occasionally expressed, in particular by Scott, for the manner and some of the incidents in the prose writings of James Hogg (1770-1835) stem from the realization that the philosophic assumptions — or rather, as Scott would have seen it, the superstitions — of his friend and *protegé* were substantially different from his own, and those of his contemporaries who had received the full benefits of education.[2] Yet Hogg was not the unthinking mouthpiece of his own inherited beliefs. His thinking is expressed most clearly in the introductory paragraphs to the story, with its appropriately metaphysical title, "On the Separate Existence of the Soul", which first appeared in the December 1831 number of *Fraser's Magazine* (Blackwood, it should be noted, was afraid to offer it space in *Maga*).[3] Hogg's words combine much of himself with some philosophy, and with elements, one might think, derivative from Adam Ferguson, and prophetic, even, of the much later studies of Sir James Frazer (1854-1941), author of *The Golden Bough*, concerning the perils of the disembodied soul:—

> "So natural is the knowledge and belief of the soul's existence and immortality, that we find traces of it in all ages, and among nations even the most barbarous. This must have originated in the soul's conscious feelings of her own existence, — a sort of crude conception of her own being and qualities. Men saw that her powers continued paramount amidst the successive changes of our material frame, and thence drew inferences of immortal existence. But, strange, as

it may appear, as men have advanced in science, they
have retrograded in certainty regarding the nature and
qualities of the soul, and its primitive substance. The
Epicureans considered it to be a subtile air, composed
of atoms or primitive corpuscles. The Cartesians made
thinking the essence of the soul, and thus deduced its
immateriality and immortality. But Spinosa, who
maintains that nothing exists beside matter, asserts the
soul to be of the same substance with the body.

Now, I have sometimes tried to side with this sage,
on the ground of the obvious certainty that the soul
grows and expands with the body's growth and
strengthens with her strength — dwindling away again
in drivelling and palsied age to a mere withered stem of
the once glorious mental flower. But I found that this
theory would never do — at least that it would never
do for me; as it destroyed all the fine fairy visions
which I had so long entertained of the soul's separate
existence: not after death, for that I never presumed to
call in question; but in deep sleep, in trances, and all the
other standings-still of the corporeal functions, it is well
known that I have always maintained that the soul
roams at large, and by that means views scenes and
draws conclusions predictive of future events. Indeed,
the soul in human nature seems to be all in all. Its
various states of changeful feelings direct all the body's
motions and affections. It is the soul that makes the
body what it is; and in a future state of existence the
same soul will still make the same individual being, of
whatever component parts its body may be
composed."[4]

Hogg obviously includes Mind as part of the more general
concept of Soul; what he offers in his first paragraph is, in effect,
a brief and highly selective history of doctrines concerning the
nature of mental phenomena from the ancient Epicureans to the
comparatively recent Spinoza (1632-1677). The history is not
entirely accurate; it is unfair, for instance, to say that in Spinoza's
philosophy "nothing exists beside matter". Hogg may be confus-
ing matter with ultimate Substance, which latter Spinoza equates
with God. Body and Soul for Spinoza are modes respectively of

the more general Extension and Thought, both of which, in turn, are attributes, the sole ones open to human experience, of Substance or God. The slight preference apparently expressed ("*But* Spinosa") for the ideas of Descartes (1596-1650) probably results from the celebrated Cartesian dualism. The expresssion given to this by at least one sentence from the *Discourse on Method* (1622) comes very close to Hogg's own opinion, as expressed in the passage just quoted:—

> "And although I may, or rather, as I will shortly say, although I certainly do possess a body with which I am very closely conjoined; nevertheless, because, on the one hand, I have a clear and distinct idea of myself, in as far as I am only a thinking and unextended thing, and as, on the other hand, I possess a distinct idea of body, in as far as it is only an extended and unthinking thing, it is certain that I (that is, my mind, by which I am what I am) is entirely and truly distinct from my body, and may exist without it."[5]

Compare with this last a few words from the introduction to another of Hogg's stories, "George Dobson's Expedition to Hell", which appeared in the May 1827 number of *Blackwood's Magazine*:—

> "Dreams themselves . . . prove to the unlettered and contemplative mind, in a very forcible manner, a distinct existence of the soul, and its lively and rapid intelligence with external nature, as well as with a world of spirits with which it has no acquaintance, when the body is lying dormant, and the same to it as if sleeping in death."[6]

Descartes would no doubt have rejected much which Hogg accepts, but the ideas of the two men overlap in content and expression to a considerable degree. Hogg was aware of the difference between his own countrified opinions and those of his brother authors in Edinburgh, with their fine educations and distinguished social backgrounds, and was always eager to make use of any intellectual help which might enable him to maintain some kind of equality with them.

The doctrines of Spinoza and Descartes alike are essentially metaphysical, and so offensive to the central sensibilities of the Enlightenment. Whatever their absolute importance, they stand well apart from the norm of eighteenth-century thought. In *Progress and Poetry* I quoted a passage from Herschel Baker which is especially relevant to this point:—

> "Broadly speaking, the seminal minds of the seventeenth century evolved two strategies for the pursuit of natural knowledge, the rationalistic and the empirical. The great continental rationalists best represented by Galileo, Descartes, and Spinoza generally conceived of reality in terms of mathematical relationships subsuming the fluctuations and deceptions of sensory appearance — relationships that could, under proper conditions, be intuited directly by the mind of man and then for purposes of description and explanation applied mathematically to the data of sensation. Their methodology, in short, was essentially deductive and essentially Platonic, for they hypostatized a fundamentally rational structure in the universe which the human mind, by rigorous and systematic intellection, could isolate and comprehend. On the other hand, such English empiricists as Bacon, Hobbes, and Locke sought not to transcend sense by a process of pure deduction and intuition, but by purifying and correcting the processes of sensation to find in the systematic observation of natural processes ('bodies in motion') the key to the understanding and thus to the control of nature. Their method, then, was essentially inductive."[7]

The latter method became the basis of Enlightenment thought; Descartes and particularly Spinoza consequently became objects of dislike and even derision. I quote as a typical example Hume's ironic use of Spinoza's absurdities as he saw them, to mock *any* doctrine of the immateriality of the soul:—

> "The fundamental principle of the atheism of *Spinoza* is the doctrine of the simplicity of the universe, and the unity of that substance, in which he supposes both thought and matter to inhere. There is only one

substance, says he, in the world; and that substance is perfectly simple and indivisible, and exists everywhere, without any local presence. Whatever we discover externally by sensation; whatever we feel internally by reflection; all these are nothing but modifications of that one, simple, and necessarily existent being, and are not possesst of any separate or distinct existence. Every passion of the soul; every configuration of matter, however different and various, inhere in the same substance, and preserve in themselves their characters of distinction, without communicating them to that subject, in which they inhere. The same *substratum*, if I may so speak, supports the most different modifications, without any difference in itself; and varies them, without any variation. Neither time, nor place, nor all the diversity of nature are able to produce any composition or change in its perfect simplicity and identity.

I believe this brief exposition of the principles of that famous atheist will be sufficient for the present purpose, and that without entering farther into these gloomy and obscure regions, I shall be able to shew, that this hideous hypothesis is almost the same with that of the immateriality of the soul, which has become so popular."[8]

So much for the philosopher whom Novalis described as drunk with God! So much, at least by implication, for Hogg's excursus on the history of philosophy, and his concept of the separate existence of the soul!

I believe it was in full consciousness of the conflict between his own system and the received wisdom of the Enlightenment that Hogg chose to give such prominence to Descartes and Spinoza. *The Wars of Truth*, the title which Herschel Baker gave to his book, refers to the seventeenth century conflict between the advocates of the two approaches to the nature of the physical world, a conflict which ended with the Enlightenment in the apparent triumph of the empiricists. Hogg, in his way, is resuming the battle. That is not to imply that he had himself undertaken any process of rigorous and systematic intellection, or that he conceived of reality in terms of mathematical relationships. It means simply that he reacted against the inadequacies of an empiricism based on the exploitation of nature, and found himself drawn to a form of thought which others would have regarded as obscurantist. Yet at the same time a substantial proportion of his writing keeps within the parameters which we have gradually been establishing for the historical novel.

Within these parameters, Hogg uses the concept of the separate existence of the soul, not so much for itself, as to attack the concepts and procedures of philosophers, political economists and Improvers, concepts and procedures which had dominated so many of the practical achievements of the Enlightenment. In "On the Separate Existence of the Soul", the nearest approach to a villain is a young laird, who is also a most profound political economist, eager to discuss circulating mediums, monopolies, stocks and natural productions, and capable of quoting in his own interest Adam Smith, Ricardo, even the somewhat anticlimactic figure of Dr Coventry. When he succeeds to Gillian Brae, his father's estate, his first concern is to improve it by the application of the most modern scientific methods. These necessarily involve the consolidation of his land, the dismissal of small tenant farmers, and the introduction of new work-patterns which conflict painfully with practices long customary. The laird's position resembles that of the Shetland landlord sympathetically described by Scott in the journal of his voyage quoted above. His innovations are seen, however, not from the point of view of another landlord, but from that of an employee, who finds his traditional form of belief despised, and whose way of life the innovations change for what he feels to be the worse.

These innovations are repudiated in the course of the story. The laird dies on the same night as Robin Robson, the employee referred to, an old Calvinist shepherd, and the two disembodied souls meet at the scene of their former disagreements. A seraph informs them that neither is yet ready for eternal reward or punishment, and begins their training for the next world by compelling the laird's soul to enter the body of Robin, and Robin's that of the laird. The transmigration gives Robin the opportunity to cancel all the improvements which the laird had begun:—

> "But the astonishment that reigned at Gillian Brae
> was now beyond description, and all the people blessed

> God for their master's temporary death. All the extra-
> vagant speculations in improvement were laid aside at
> once, save a few which it was absolutely necessary to
> finish. One hundred and forty workmen were paid off
> in one day, mostly artificers, drainers, and hedgers. The
> old farmers were all restored to their farms, and things
> went on exactly as they had done in the days of the
> former laird."[9]

Seven years later, the laird's soul is finally released from the
body of his old servant; his original body, however, continues to
serve its new occupant for many years:—

> "When the laird was on his deathbed, he told the
> clergyman who attended him, that he had then existed
> in this life and in this same world for a hundred and
> forty-three years; that he had experienced the extremes
> of poverty and riches; and that, after all, he found the
> poor and virtuous man's life the happiest."[10]

Hogg characteristically adds: "I feel much disposed to dispute
the truth of this assertion, although I cordially agree with
another sentiment which he was heard often to express; which
was, that no tongue could describe the advantage of an old and
experienced soul getting possession of a young and healthy
frame."

It is not difficult to see why Blackwood was afraid to offer this
story to the Edinburgh readers of the 1830's, when the play of
mind, characteristic of the Enlightenment, had lost popular
appeal, and only half-a-dozen years before the accession of
Victoria. It seems to belong to another and, on the whole, a later
age. Of the parallels which most immediately suggest themselves, the less striking, Frederick Anstey's *Vice Versa*, was not
published until 1882, while the American Robert Heinlein's *I
Will Fear No Evil* made its first appearance as a magazine serial in
1970. Both later novels are in some sense science-fiction, and
much the same, I suppose, might be said of Hogg's story,
putting, as it does, a startling series of events into an apparently
scientific and philosophical context, which is also psychologically
convincing. Like much science fiction, it has roots in the *conte
philosophique*, although in purpose it differs greatly from the
norm of the Enlightenment.

Hogg gains his effect of verisimilitude partly by applying this technique to historical subjects. The suspense of disbelief necessary for "On the Separate Existence of the Soul" is achieved, not least because the clash between improving landlord and resentful shepherd is historically convincing. Hogg uses a similar technique in his verse-narratives, as well as in short stories and the full-length novel. The first may be illustrated by "Kilmeny" from *The Queen's Wake* (1813); the second by many of the short stories, which appeared in *Blackwood's* and *Fraser's Magazine*; the third by some aspects of *The Three Perils of Man* (1822), and in particular by *The Private Memoirs and Confessions of a Justified Sinner* (1824). All share something of the metaphysical emphasis found in "On the Separate Existence of the Soul", and each is historical in the sense that it links Hogg's present with an aspect of the more or less remote past.

The immediate setting of "Kilmeny"[11] is the middle sixteenth century; the poem is presented as sung by the thirteenth of seventeen bards in a competition held before the young Queen Mary (1542-1567) on her return to Scotland from France. Kilmeny herself belongs to a period still earlier, and the poem is linked to Hogg's own days, and given its scientific and philosophic justification, by three from a series of several visions granted to her during her initial residence in the Land of Thought, to which she has been miraculously transported. The first foretells the struggle between monarchy and Protestantism during the Reformation, a struggle which led to the exile and death of Queen Mary; the second, events in the seventeenth century, in particular the execution of Charles I, the campaign of the Covenanters, and the Glorious Revolution; the third, the Napoleonic Wars as far as the Battle of Leipzig (1813). Galt, who like Hogg here and in his prose fiction generally, more or less ignores the '45, would probably have accepted Hogg's brief list as representing the really significant political events of the previous two hundred and fifty years; so also, given that single addition, would Scott.[12]

The three visions, however, differ from anything in Scott or Galt. In the first place, they are prophecies rather than transcripts of reality, and the figures which appear — lion, maiden, gruff grim carle, eagle — are symbolic, rather than representative of individuals. Only Mary is shown in something like her own form. Again, as has been indicated, the three visions which have some kind of historical significance form only part of the series; the others are "an endless whirl of glory and light", which may represent the world, or possibly Scotland, in the redeemed or the pre-lapsarian state; a geographical overview of an idealized, but undoubtedly Scottish, landscape, and finally, a vision of the end of the present world:—

> But she saw till the sorrows of man were bye,
> And all was love and harmony;
> Till the stars of heaven fell calmly away,
> Like the flakes of snaw on a winter day.
>
> (260-264)

Again, the visions are seen, not from an earthly viewpoint, but from "the lowermost vales of the storied heaven", the Land of Thought, to which Kilmeny has been bodily assumed. She is to bring word of it back to earth as a guide and warning to others:—

> To tell of the place where she had been,
> And the glories that lay in the land unseen;
> To warn the living maidens fair,
> The loved of Heaven, the spirits' care,
> That all whose minds unmeled remain
> Shall bloom in beauty when time is gane.
>
> (266-271)

The total effect is metaphysical, other-worldly, unlike anything in Scott or Galt, but closer in a way to the more attractive side of Thomas Boston, mentioned in *Progress and Poetry*.[13] The Ettrick Shepherd, however, is less evangelistic and dogmatic, more Platonic, one might almost say, than the former minister of his parish. His independence of accepted doctrinal formulations, whether scriptural or philosophic, makes him in a real sense more intellectual than his better-educated predecessors and contemporaries. The contrast with Boston is plain. Much Enlightenment thought is characterized by acceptance of this as the best of all possible worlds; Hogg is as far from this as he is from the doctrinal rigidity of Boston:—

> It wasna her hame, and she couldna remain;
> She left this world of sorrow and pain,
> And returned to the land of thought again.
>
> (328-330)

"Kilmeny" forms only one episode in *The Queen's Wake* , the emotional tone of which is to a substantial degree governed by the tragedy of Mary's eventual fate, foreshadowed as it is by one incident of the vision. In the same way, several of Hogg's short stories and personal reminiscences form part of the larger pattern which he called "The Shepherd's Calendar", and which appeared in *Blackwood's* at intervals between 1819 and 1828. Here his intention was to link the life of the shepherd to the general passage of time by the narration of events which were of particular importance for his view of the world — events such as the great blizzards of the period from 1620 to 1795, the last of which Hogg had himself experienced. Other notable occurrences, for instance, "Deaths, Judgments, and Providences", "Dreams and Apparitions", "Fairies, Brownies and Witches", were also included.

The history with which Hogg is best acquainted is what nowadays would be called oral, based on tradition passed on by work of mouth. Its most notable events are often ignored by the political record. "Storms" opens with a passage which puts the shepherd's life into a context where the precision of the Gregorian calendar does not matter, and where many past happenings, of importance to others, have no great significance, but which nevertheless extends over centuries. Even matters of intense personal concern, like agricultural improvements, lose some of their significance in the face of remembered natural calamity:—

> "These" (storms, that is to say) "constitute the various aeras of the pastoral life. They are the red lines in the shepherd's manual — the remembrancers of years and ages that are past — the tablets of memory by which the ages of his children the times of his ancestors and the rise and downfall of families are invariably ascertained. Even the progress of improvement in Scots farming can be traced traditionally from these, and the rent of a farm or estate given with precision, before and after such and such a storm, though the narrator be uncertain in what century the said notable storm happened. 'Mar's year' and 'that year the heelanders raide' are but secondary mementos to *the year Nine* and *the year Forty* — these stand in

bloody capitals in the annals of pastoral life as well as many more that shall hereafter be mentioned."[14]

"Mar's year " is that of the first Jacobite rising (1715) under the Earl of Mar, while "that year the heelanders raide" is 1745. Years of merely political unrest seem insignificant in comparison with the abnormal cold spells of 1709 and 1740, on which J.M. Stratton comments:—

> "**1709** This was another bad year with a very backward spring and general scarcity. A severe period of frost began on January 7th, lasting over 50 days, during which the Thames froze. Intense frost occurred from January 9th onwards, with heavy snowstorms and much mortality among cattle, sheep and wild birds."
>
> "**1740** The severe spell which started on December 24th, 1739, lasted for at least nine weeks, and cold weather continued till late in the spring. A Frost Fair was held on the frozen Thames from Christmas 1739, till February 17th, 1740. Souvenirs were printed on printing-presses set up on the ice, and also on the ice of the Ouse at York.
>
> 'Many hens and ducks, even the cattle in the stalls, died of cold; the trees split asunder. Not only beer, but wine in cellars, froze. Deeply sunken wells were covered with impenetrable ice. Crows and other birds fell to the ground, frozen in their flight. No bread was eatable, for it was as cold and hard as a stone' (from Brocke's *Contentment in God*). On the coldest night the temperature fell to 2°F."[15]

These extracts refer to conditions in England. In Scotland things were, if anything, worse. It is not surprising that eras were marked by such years, rather than by events in 1715 and 1745 which left the life of the Border shepherd virtually untouched.

The worst storm mentioned by Hogg is also the earliest, *The Thirteen drifty days* of 1620, almost exactly two centuries before he published his essay. By using a different form of tradition (Class IX. Fairies, Brownies and Witches), he is able to extend his chronology by another century to the period before the Reformation of 1560 (the period of Kilmeny, that is to say). "In this class of my pastoral legends", he comments in the introductory paragraph to "Mary Burnet", first published in 1828, "I must take a date, in some instances, a century earlier than the generality of those of the other classes, and describe a state of manners more primitive and visionary than any I have witnessed, simple and romantic as these have been; and I must likewise relate scenes so far out of the way of usual events, that the sophisticated gloss and polish thrown over the modern philosophic mind, may feel tainted by such antiquated breathings of superstition."[16] Later he identifies the period more closely in terms of the figure of a lady who makes a spectacular entrance to Moffat fair in Annandale: "The word instantly circulated in the market, that this was the Lady Elizabeth Douglas, eldest daughter of the Earl of Morton, who then sojourned at Auchincastle, in the vicinity of Moffat, and which lady at that time was celebrated as a great beauty all over Scotland. She was afterwards Lady Keith; and the mention of this name in the tale, as it were by mere accident, fixes the era of it in the reign of James the Fourth, at the very time that fairies, brownies, and witches, were at the rifest in Scotland."[17]

James IV reigned from 1488 to 1513. Lady Elizabeth Douglas was the daughter of John, 2nd Earl of Morton, and married Robert, Lord Keith, who was killed with James at Flodden in 1513. The lady of the story, it should be noted, is not in fact Elizabeth Douglas, but an Otherworld figure, perhaps the translated Mary Burnet of the title, who has returned to ensure that young John Allanson should pay the penalty appropriate to his earlier bad behaviour.

The classification of the material, and the attempt at dating the action by an incidental mention of a historically identifiable person, may seem to be in the full tradition of scientific Enlightenment scholarship. The final phrase — "at the very time that fairies, brownies, and witches, were at the rifest in Scotland" — shatters the illusion. Hogg may be writing ironically, but, if so, the irony is directed at Enlightenment scholarship, not at the concept of supernatural beings. Compare the earlier phrase, "the sophisticated gloss and polish thrown over the modern philosophic mind". Nowadays the word "sophisticated" has in general usage lost the pejorative overtones it formerly possessed; "sophisticated" once implied "corrupt", a sense which in Hogg's usage it certainly retains. The phrase expresses the same regret and condemnation which in "On the Separate Existence of the Soul" Hogg extends to modern scientific doubts about the nature and qualities of the soul, and its primitive substance. Hogg, in other words, takes moderate pains with the details preserved in written history, but does not see them as in any way necessarily a dominating influence.

Notably, almost all the pieces contain an element of the supernatural. Even "Storms", the most factual and autobiographical, concludes with an account of the belief, known by Hogg to be erroneous, that the blizzard of 1794-95 had been caused by a group of young men, his friends, who had called up the Devil in a remote shieling which had been the epicentre of the storm:—

"The storm was altogether an unusual convulsion of nature. Nothing like it had ever been seen, or heard of in Britain before; and it was enough of itself to arouse every spark of superstition that lingered among these mountains — It did so — It was universally viewed as a judgement sent by God for the punishment of some heineous offence, but what that offence was, could not for a while be ascertained: but when it came out, that so many men had been assembled, in a lone unfrequented place, and busily engaged in some mysterious work at the very instant that the blast came on, no doubts were entertained that all had not been right there, and that some horrible rite, or correspondence with the powers of darkness had been going on. It so happened too, that this shieling of Entertrony was situated in the very vortex of the storm; the devastations made by it extended all around that, to a certain extent; and no farther on any one quarter than another. This was easily and soon remarked, and upon the whole the first view of the matter had rather an equivocal appearance to those around who had suffered so severely by it. But still as the rumour grew the certainty of the event gained ground — new corroberative circumstances were every day divulged, till the whole district was in an uproar, and several of the members began to meditate a speedy retreat from the country; some of them I know would have fled, if it had not been for the advice of the late worthy and judicious Mr. Bryden of Crosslee."[18]

Hogg knew that the young men were no more than members of a literary and debating club, who had chosen to meet in a remote spot to avoid interruption; he had himself planned to attend until he was turned back by intimations of the approaching storm. For the most part he defended the good name of his friends. Yet even he was shaken by a report that one of their number had been offered in sacrifice to the devil so that the others should escape:—

> "Lord how every hair of my head, and every inch of my frame crept at hearing this sentence; for I had a dearly loved brother who was one of the number, several full cousins, and intimate acquaintances; indeed I looked on the whole fraternity as my brethern, and considered myself involved in all their transactions. I could say no more in defence of the society's proceedings, for to tell the truth, though I am ashamed to acknowledge it, I suspected that the allegation might be too true."[19]

The last few words may well imply a good deal. In the popular mind, at least, a close connection existed between diabolism and radical politics. To a substantial extent, this resulted from the connection believed to exist between the radicals and the freemasons. At home as on the continent, radicals tended to be freemasons, whose assumed connection with the devil Burns, himself a brother of the craft, had already made ironically clear:—

> When Masons' mystic *word* an' *grip*,
> In storms an' tempests raise you up,
> Some cock, or cat, your rage maun stop,
> Or, strange to tell!
> The *youngest brother* ye wad whip
> Aff straught to *H–ll*.[20]
>
> ("Address to the Deil", 79-84)

In the Scotland of 1794, a more or less secret meeting of young agricultural labourers probably included several freemasons in its number; equally probably, the agenda included the forbidden subject of radical politics and the need for reform, if not revolution. Hogg had himself prepared "a flaming bombastical essay" for the meeting, and had his "tongue trained to many wise and profound remarks".[21] The phrases are vague, but in 1819 (the year of Peterloo) when the article was first published, it was probably wiser to be no more specific. Slight indications of the true state of affairs are perhaps to be found in the account of the meeting which Hogg's worried mother wormed out of the servant-girl Mary, who was present during the entire meeting. The level of mutual incomprehension revealed in the dialogue almost deserves a place in Galt's *The Radical*:—

> "'But dear Mary, my woman, what were the chiels a met about that night?'
> 'Oo they were just gaun through their papers an' arguing.'
> 'Arguing? What were they arguing about?'
> 'I have often thought about it sin' syne, but really I canna tell preceesely what they were arguing about.'
> 'Were you wi' them a' the time?'
> 'Yes a' the time but the wee while I was milkin' the cow.'
> 'An' did they never bid ye gang out?'
> 'Oo, no; they never heedit whether I gaed out or in.'
> 'It's queer that ye canna mind ought ava. Can ye no tell me ae word that ye heard them say?'
> 'I heard them sayin' something about the fitness o' things.'
> 'Aye, that was a braw subject for them!'"[22]

The influence of Clarke's metaphysical *A Discourse concerning the Being and Attributes of God* (1706) and of Hartley's *Observations on Man* (1749) is perhaps just visible in the reference to "the fitness of things". Hogg's mother was concerned about traffic with the devil; there is a touch of irony in the fact that her questioning leads at worst to political and metaphysical beliefs, the significance of which she does not herself understand.

Radicalism occasionally makes an appearance elsewhere in Hogg's writings — once at least in the context of diabolism. I mention the possibility here chiefly to show the extent to which

belief in the supernatural, in an evil as well as a good metaphysical order, dominated his mind in the course of ordinary daily
existence. When the events described took place, he was not yet
twenty five years old. His reactions should, not, however, be put
down simply to youth, the effect of a rural upbringing, and his
comparative lack of education. "On the Separate Existence of the
Soul" appeared almost forty years later, when he had read
extensively and become well acquainted with the scepticism of
polite and educated society, yet one of the most convincing
features of the story is the reaction, not only of Robin, but also
of the supposedly enlightened laird, to the seraph's announce-
ment that they are both unfit for heaven, and doomed to a very
different destination. Both misunderstand, and assume that the
only alternative is Hell:—

> "'Oh, I am sorry for it, honest spirit!' cried Robin,
> vehemently; but he could get no further for utter
> vexation; and both spirits again set up a howl of despair
> louder than ever, until the bright messenger was
> obliged to lay a hand on each of their mouths, and
> compel silence."[23]

Robin, it should be noted, reveals traces of the antinomian
temperament; he is vexed rather than overwhelmed to discover,
as he thinks, that he has not in fact attained the justified state,
which he had previously assumed to be his portion. The reaction
of the laird is the simpler — a recognition that he is at last about
to receive the deserts which the other had always prophesied,
and which he himself suspected to be fully deserved.

"Kilmeny" and "On the Separate Existence of the Soul" both
lay their final emphasis on metaphysical blessedness. The coun-
terbalance to this, the diabolic and the possibility of damnation,
no more than hinted at in the second of these stories, makes a
rather prolonged appearance elsewhere; sometimes, as in
"Storms", only to be dismissed; sometimes, as in *The Brownie of
Bodsbeck* (1817), to be rationalized away; but usually with a
subtlety of presentation which demands a considered response
from the reader. The subject of "George Dobson's Expedition to
Hell" is a dream, unrecognised as such by the dreamer, which
apparently is directly and terrifyingly related to subsequent
reality. The time assumed in relation to the date of publication is

the not very distant past — George Dobson "was part proprietor and driver of a hackney coach in Edinburgh, when such vehicles were scarce"[24] — probably, that is to say, during the later years of the eighteenth century. Hackney coaches are not mentioned in Fergusson's *Auld Reikie* (1773). By contrast, on 19th September, 1774, James Boswell records that he and his uncle, Dr Boswell, returned from Colinton to Edinburgh "in a hackney-coach which my wife sent for us". The Dr Wood who is mentioned in Hogg's story is Alexander Wood, an Edinburgh surgeon of some distinction who lived from 1725 to 1807. He was acquainted with Boswell, who interestingly in terms of the story, records a conversation with him on the nature of the soul:—

> "Wood got into a disagreeable kind of sceptical conversation about the soul being material, from all that we could observe. It is hard that our most valuable articles of belief are rather the effects of sentiment than of demonstration. I disliked Wood because he revived doubts in my mind which I could not at once dispel. Yet he had no bad meaning, but was honestly and in confidence expressing his own uneasiness. He said that the fear of death sometimes distressed him in the night. He seemed to have formed no principles on the subject, but just had ideas, sometimes of one kind, sometimes of another, floating in his mind. He had a notion, which I have heard the Reverend Mr. Wyvill support, that only some souls were designed for immortality. What a blessing it is to have steady religious sentiments."[25]

The immediate occasion of the discussion is the approaching execution of Boswell's client, John Reid, for sheep stealing, and the plans which were being made for the resuscitation of the corpse after it had been cut down from the gallows, plans in which Dr Wood had reluctantly agreed to take part. His counter-argument, that Reid had got over the bitterness of death, and that he might curse Boswell for bringing him back, saying that he had kept him from heaven, was of great weight in the eventual decision to abandon the attempt.[26] Obviously the Doctor combined professional reputation with considerable force of personality. Hogg's portrayal, in particular of his way of speech, is notably idiosyncratic, perhaps based on first or second-hand acquaintance with the man himself, and the action of the story is clearly related both to his individual character and opinions, as revealed by Boswell, and also to something in the general climate of thought at that time. Chirsty Halliday, George Dobson's wife, has gone to summon the Doctor and tells him of the dream in which, he believes, he has made a solemn engagement to meet Mr R** of L***y (in the dream his passenger of the previous day) in Hell at twelve o'clock precisely:—

> "'He maunna keep it, dearie. He maunna keep that engagement at no rate.' said Dr Wood. 'Set back the clock an hour or two, to drive him past the time, and I'll ca' in the course of my round. Are ye sure he hasna been drinking hard?' She assured him he had not. 'Weel, weel, ye maun tell him that he maunna keep that engagement at no rate. Set back the clock and I'll come and see him. It is a frenzy that maunna be trifled with. Ye maunna laugh at it, dearie, — maunna laugh at it. Maybe a nervish fever, wha kens.'
>
> The Doctor and Chirsty left the house together, and as their road lay the same way for a space, she fell a-telling him of the two young lawyers whom George saw standing at the gate of hell, and whom the porter had described as two of the last comers. When the Doctor heard this, he staid his hurried stooping pace in one moment, turned full round on the woman, and fixing his eyes on her that gleamed with a deep unstable lustre, he said, 'What's that ye were saying, dearie? What's that ye were saying? Repeat it again to me every word.' She did so. On which the Doctor held up his hands, as if palsied with astonishment, and uttered some fervent ejaculations. 'I'll go with you straight,' said he, 'before I visit another patient. This is wonderfu'! It is terrible! The young gentlemen are both at rest — both lying corpses at this time! — fine young men — I attended them both — died of the same exterminating disease. — Oh this is wonderful; this is wonderful!'"[27]

The dream itself is convincing. The journey is to an unnamed place somewhere in the vicinity of Edinburgh, and although

George claims never to have heard of it, his passenger retorts that no man in Scotland knows the way better than he. "'Very well, sir,' says George, 'I'll drive you to hell if you have a mind, only you are to direct me on the road.'"[28] The route is smooth and downhill all the way, and darkness gradually overtakes them as they go. On their arrival, George is dismissed without his fare, but on condition that he returns next day at twelve o'clock precisely. He is given a ticket to enable him to pass the toll-gate, which is always open for arrivals, but closed against anyone wishing to leave. It is guarded by an austere toll-man, accompanied by the two young lawyers, whom George recognises, because "he had of late driven them to Roslin on a Sunday, along with two ladies, who, he supposed, were their sisters, from their familiarity, when not another coachman in town would engage with them." George jocularly asks the keeper why he has such men for assistants:—

> "'Because they are among the last comers,' replied the ruffian, churlishly. 'You will be an assistant here tomorrow.'
> 'The devil I will, sir?'
> 'Yes, the devil you will, sir.'
> 'I'll be d— if I do then — that I will.'
> 'Yes, you'll be d— if you do, that you will.'
> 'Let my horses go in the meantime then, sir, that I may proceed on my journey.'
> 'Nay.'
> 'Nay? — Dare you say nay to me, sir? My name is George Dobson, of the Pleasance, Edinburgh, coach driver, and coach proprietor too: and I'll see the face of the man d— who will say *nay* to me, as long as I can pay my way. I have his Majesty's licence, and I'll go and come as I choose — that I will. Let go my horses there, and say what is your demand.'
> 'Well, then, I'll let your horses go,' said the keeper; 'but I'll keep you for a pledge.'"[29]

The horses dash off with the coach, but it is only after a long struggle with the toll-man, and after signing the ticket to guarantee his return on the next day, that George is allowed to pursue them. The violence of their flight has overturned the coach, killing one of the horses and breaking two legs of the other. George is lamenting over them when his wife wakens him. All apparently is a mere dream. Despite the attentions of Dr Wood and a clergyman of famed abilities, George dies in paroxysms at the appointed time. On the day of his funeral, news arrives that Mr R★★ of L★★★y and his son had been drowned on the very night of the dream.

Throughout the episode, George's language indicates both the kind of life he has led in the past, and his present immediate apparent suitability for damnation. The evidence that he *is* finally damned appears overwhelming. In one point only the dream appears not to correspond with reality; George's niggardly patron, Mr R★★ of L★★★y, is not accompanied by the son, who was drowned together with him. This however may mean only that the eternal destination of the son differed from that of the father.

The introduction to the story, the passage on dreams already quoted,[30] puts any such conclusion into doubt. Hogg claims not to understand dreams, "nor have I any desire to do so." He does say that dreams "prove to the unlettered and contemplative mind, in a very forcible manner, a distinct existence of the soul, and its lively and rapid intelligence with external nature, as well as with a world of spirits with which it has no acquaintance, when the body is lying dormant, and the same to it as if sleeping in death." Here nothing more than the existence of a world of spirits is assumed: the development of the plot might be taken to indicate a belief that in relation to the natural world they possessed a measure of prophetic power. Hogg goes on to say that he accounts nothing "of any dream that relates to the actions of the day"; in these there is no real division between matter and mind, "but they are mingled together in a sort of chaos — what a farmer would call compost — fermenting and disturbing one another."[31] The dreams which emerge from such a compost relate entirely to the natural world, and he gives examples of their usefulness from his own experience and that of his friends — dreams which make use of the symbols of the dreamer's business or profession, in general an outdoor one, and in particular those which use these symbols to provide a kind of weather forecast. These he calls professional dreams, and it is to this class that he assigns the vision of George Dobson, which he describes as well-known, even at some distance from Edinburgh in the cot of the shepherd. It was in such surroundings, he implies, that he first heard it, and it is for this reason that it it included in *The Shepherd's Calendar.*

The professional dreams which he lists tend towards the ludicrous, as Hogg himself seems to recognise. "I know a keen sportsman, who pretends that his dreams never deceive him. If he dream of angling, or pursuing salmon in deep waters, he is sure of rain; but if fishing on dry ground, or in waters so low that the fish cannot get from him, it forebodes drought; hunting or shooting hares, is snow, and moorfowl, wind &c." Were one to apply this principle seriously to the story as a whole, it would mean that the only prophetic elements in George's dream concerned the time of death of a number of individuals, including himself, and that it had no validity for the afterlives of any among the deceased. At most, it would indicate the fate which George in his waking life thought most appropriate for each. Even so, a prophetic, which is to say a metaphysical, element is necessarily present. Hogg is allowing that the soul has powers denied to it by most thinkers of the Enlightenment. The energy and vividness of the story would almost lead us to accept George Dobson's own opinion, but this, I suggest, the method of presentation does not allow.

George Dobson suffers in a sense from split personality. On the one hand he is a self-confident and self-possessed coach driver, prepared to go anywhere, or do anything. At the same time, the words which he uses reveal a man in considerable need of self-justification, or reassurance, a need springing from a sense of moral unease with the life he has led. His conversation is full of the devil, Hell and damnation. It is his own subconscious fear of the last as the inevitable penalty, for himself and for many of the fares whom he has driven, which renders him so susceptible to the apparent meaning of his dream, and which may even be its cause. He shares this trait of personality with the young laird in "On the Separate Existence of the Soul", who is secretly terrified of the likely consequence of the atheistic philosophy to which he gives free expression. Each of them meets his *doppelganger*, the laird after the exchange of bodies with Robin, George in his encounter with the austere toll-man, who echoes his words with a significance the opposite of everything he had intended.

"Strange Letter of a Lunatic" (1830) carried the process a stage farther. The narrator, James Beatman, repeatedly encounters himself, quarrels with himself, eventually fights a duel with himself. These encounters are regarded by others, who never see more than one James Beatman, as drunken fantasies, which eventually cause him to be confined to a lunatic asylum. Drink is certainly prominent in the story; one encounter with himself takes place in an Edinburgh tavern, a second in the elegant saloon of a steamboat plying the Forth between Newhaven and Alloa, where Beatman swigs a mixture of ginger beer and brandy. In his own opinion, however, drink has nothing to do with his misfortunes; he traces them all to a meeting on the Castle Hill in Edinburgh with an old man, whom he comes to regard as the devil:—

"Last summer in June, I happened to be in Edinburgh, and walking very early on the Castle Hill one morning, I perceived a strange looking figure of an old man watching all my motions, as if anxious to introduce himself to me, yet still kept at the same distance. I beckoned him, on which he came waddling briskly up, and taking an elegant gold snuff-box, set with jewels, from his pocket, he offered me a pinch. I accepted of it most readily, and then without speaking a word, he took his box again, thrust it into his pocket, and went away chuckling and laughing in perfect ecstasy. He was even so over-joyed, that, in hobbling down the platform he would leap from the ground, clap his hands on his loins, and laugh immoderately.

'The devil I am sure is in that body,' said I to myself, 'What does he mean? Let me see. I wish I may be well enough! I feel very queer since I took that snuff of his.' I stood there I do not know how long, like one who had been knocked on the head, until I thought I saw the body peering at me from a shady piece in the rock. I hasted to him; but on going up, I found myself standing there. Yes, sir, myself. My own likeness in every respect. I was turned to a rigid statue at once, but the unaccountable being went down the hill convulsed with laughter."[32]

By the simple act of beckoning him over and accepting snuff, Beatman, it seems, has put himself into the power of the diabolic old man. He is confounded to discover that his *alter ego* has the same opinion, only, as it were, in reverse:—

"'Sir, I have no other character to appear in,' said I. 'I was born, christened, and educated as James Beatman, younger, of Drumloning, and that designation I will maintain against all the counterfeits on earth,'

'Well, your perversity confounds me,' replied he; 'for you must be perfectly sensible that you are acting a part that is not your own. That you are either a rank counterfeit, or, what I rather begin to suspect, the devil in my likeness.'

These words overpowered me so much, that I fell a trembling, for I thought of the vision of last night, and what the old man had told me; and the thought of having become the devil in my own likeness, was more than my heart could brook, and I dare say I looked fearfully ill.

'O ho! old Cloots, are you caught?' cried he, jeeringly; 'well, your sublime majesty will choose to keep your distance in future, as I would rather dispense with your society.'

'Sir, I'll let you know that I am *not* the devil,' cried I, in great wrath, 'and if you dare, sir, it shall be tried this moment, and on this spot, who is the counterfeit, and who is the *right* James Beatman, you or I.'"[33]

The last remark leads to the duel and to Beatman's eventual confinement in the asylum.

The effectiveness of the story rises from the isolation of the narrator, who is the prisoner, it would seem, of the motiveless but malignant sequence of events which leads to his ruin. It is not so much Beatman as the world he inhabits which is the lunatic. Hogg shatters the comfortable assurance, characteristic of the Enlightenment, that we live in the best of all possible worlds, and that every event necessarily has a material cause. Hume's self-complacent account of the philosophy of Spinoza, or his dismissive "Essay on Miracles",[34] may serve as examples of the targets attacked by Hogg. In fact, he does not stand in complete opposition to Hume, who himself demolished the philosophic respectability of causality, but he is prepared, as Hume never was, to follow his ideas to the logical conclusion. Again, one might compare later science fiction based on a similar assumption, Heinlein's story "They" (1941), for instance, or his disturbing novella, *The Unpleasant Profession of Jonathan Hoag* (1942). (Is there any connection, incidentally, between the surnames Hoag and Hogg?)

The *doppelganger* appears elsewhere in Hogg's work, most notably in *The Private Memoirs and Confessions of a Justified Sinner* (1824), which will be discussed at greater length below. One of the minor feats performed by the necromancer, Michael Scott, in his contest with Roger Bacon, as narrated in *The Three Perils of Man* (1822), is to produce duplicates of three members of the embassy sent to him by the Warden — Charlie Scott, the Deil's Tam, and the Laird of the Peatstacknowe. The effect is comic rather than serious, but the diabolic associations remain clear.

Hogg's world possesses strange powers and is capable of an active malignancy towards the beings who inhabit it. The theme receives its most substantial expression in the two novels just mentioned. In its own time, neither was successful; the first was reprinted only in a savagely abbreviated and bowdlerised form until 1924; the second, Hogg, or some other, drastically revised and shortened for re-publication after his death as *The Siege of Roxburgh* (1837); the original had to wait until 1972 for reissue. Even in 1969, John Carey could describe it as a "potboiler historical romance".[35] Both books take the form of historical novels; one is set in the time of Robert II (1371-1390), the other in the late seventeenth and early eighteenth century. Both claim to be based on contemporary records, *The Three Perils of Man* on "the manuscript of an old Curate, who had spent the latter part of his life in the village of Mireton, and was given to the present Editor by one of those tenants who now till the valley where stood the richest city of this realm" (i.e. Roxburgh).[36] The pretence is maintained throughout the novel. In *The Private Memoirs and Confessions of a Justified Sinner*, the machinery is more elaborate; the author purports to be merely the editor of a pamphlet, part printed, part manuscript, found in the grave of an eighteenth century suicide, the justified sinner of the title. The pamphlet had been produced in the Queen's printing house in Edinburgh, "then conducted by a Mr James Watson"[37] (James Watson, Queen's printer in Edinburgh from 1711 to 1722, best remembered today for the three volumes of his *Choice Collection*, 1706-1711, an influential anthology of earlier Scottish verse).[38] Included is an account of how the pamphlet itself came to be printed, and how all the other copies were destroyed. A page of the manuscript section is reproduced in facsimile.[39] The editor's narrative, which precedes the reprint, is based partly on history, but chiefly on local tradition. The account of the discovery of the suicide's body is very circumstantial, including as it does corroborative references to Scott,[40] Lockhart, Laidlaw, even one to Hogg himself, who is clearly distinguished from the editor. This last, the book suggests, hails from the Whig and Covenanting west — Glasgow or its immediate neighbourhood, of which he speaks with great familiarity.

Hogg's technique of receding planes of authorship at once distances and focuses his material in a way already familiar from the work of his contemporaries. His quality as a historical novelist, however, stems from his ultimate trust in oral tradition as opposed to written report; it is here, he seems to claim, that metaphysical, as opposed to literal, historical truth is to be found. The very extravagances and impossibilities of the oral record, if properly presented, are proof of its essential truth. I have already mentioned that the Enlightenment in Scotland tended in its account of the human mind to emphasize the limitations of intellect and the importance of the non-rational passions and emotions. In this, Hogg is at one with his period. The diabolism and black magic to be found in his stories are extreme examples of the tendency, elsewhere found in Galt's analyses of obsession, and Scott's concern with "curious anomalous facts in the history of mind." At a first glance, they do not seem to form part of the Enlightenment; to a degree this is true, but a more detailed analysis will show that in some respects at least there is no conflict.

In terms of any written record, Dr Gifford has shown what scarcely needs to be demonstrated, that *The Three Perils of Man* is wildly unhistorical. The events in the novel turn on a siege of Roxburgh castle, undertaken, and brought eventually to a successful conclusion, by James, Earl of Douglas and Mar, during the reign of Robert II:—

> "The major discrepancy between history and Hogg's version of it relates to the taking of Roxburgh castle. Contrary to Hogg's statement that it had been 'five times taken by the English, and three times by the Scots, in less than seventeen months', in the entire fourteenth century the Scots took the castle only twice:

in 1313 Sir James Douglas took it for Robert I, in 1342
Sir Alexander Ramsay recaptured it from the English,
but it was lost after the battle of Durham in 1346, and
thenceforth not retaken till the siege of 1460 that was
fatal to James II. Roxburgh town and district was often
the scene of violent and bloody action in the reign of
Robert II, but even at the height of Douglas success in
recovering Teviotdale and most of its castles in 1384
Roxburgh stood out as the exception. James, second
Earl of Douglas, did try, with French help, to recapture
it, but abandoned the siege after eight days.

One important event in Hogg's romance demonstrates exactly his treatment of real events. In the closing
stages of the tale he has Douglas sore beset by diver-
sionary English troops from Northumberland and the
garrison at Berwick, under Sir Thomas Musgrave, who
is described by Hogg as governor of Berwick. In the
battle that ensues Douglas is aided by a Sir John
Gordon, who captures Musgrave. Hogg is in fact
conflating two separate events. In 1372 Sir John Gordon captured Musgrave when he was on his way to
help Percy of Northumberland, one of the English
wardens of the Marches. In 1378, William, first Earl of
Douglas, captured Musgrave on his way to Melrose
with an advance party from Northumberland. Neither
occasion falls within the period of James, second Earl of
Douglas (1384-1388), nor was Musgrave governor of
Berwick within that period, although he was governor
from 1373-1378."[41]

There is incidentally some difficulty in seeing how Roxburgh
could possibly have been taken five times by the English and
three time by the Scots in seventeen months or any other period
— at least, if the action involved no party other than the Scots
and English. Dr Gifford mentions in passing the most striking
anachronism of all, the prominent position taken by Michael
Scott (c.1160-1235) and Roger Bacon (1214-1292), whose true
period preceded that of the action by something like a century
and a half.[42] Hogg, no doubt, had some idea of their dates, but
because both figured in traditional lore as magicians, he was
prepared to overlook such merely documentary detail. In *The*

Lay of the Last Minstrel, Walter Scott had been even more cavalier in his treatment of Michael Scott and his period, and as *The Three Perils of Man* is in some respects a companion-piece to that poem, Hogg might well have adduced it in his own defence. Michael Scott and Roger Bacon accordingly both find a place in Hogg's alternative system of history. He was not concerned with precise temporal relationships between events in the remoter period of his lore. The remoter, the more uncertain in factual detail, and the greater the probability of a supernatural presence — that was his basic philosophy of history, as revealed, for example, in the passage already quoted from "Mary Burnet".[43] In the times of James IV, Scotland was rife with fairies, brownies, and witches; how much the more so in the even earlier reign of Robert II. "How these traditions have originated, I leave to the professors of moral philosophy, in their definitions of pneumatology, to determine."[44] By "pneumatology" he presumably intends the older definition, "the science, doctrine, or theory of spirits or spiritual beings; considered as comprehending the doctrine of God as known by natural reason, of angels and demons, and of the human soul", although he may also have included the later development by which the term became synonymous with the modern "psychology".[45]

Much the greater part of *The Three Perils of Man* is taken up with events at Aikwood, home of Michael Scott. The book ends, not with the capture of Roxburgh castle and the restoration to her parents and lover of the princess Margaret, but with Michael's death in elemental conflict with Satan, in which, although he loses his life, he retains possession of his magic book, which is buried with him in Melrose Abbey, only once afterwards to be discovered by Walter Scott's William of Deloraine.

As may be shown by the long passage which introduces chapter XXIV, the life of Michael Scott marks an epoch in Hogg's alternative history:—

> "Few were the nightly journies on the banks of the Ettrick in those days, and few the midnight noises that occurred, save from the wild beasts of the forest. There were no wooer lads straying at that still and silent hour, to call up their sweethearts for an hour's kind conversation. Save when English marauders were abroad, all

was quietness by hamlet and steading. The land was the abode of the genii of the woods, the rocks, and the rivers; and of this the inhabitants were well aware, and kept within locked doors, whose lintels were made of the mountain ash, and nightly sprinkled with holy water. Cradle and bed were also fenced with cross, book, and bead; for the inmates knew that in no other way could they be safe, or rest in peace. They knew that their green and solitary glens were the nightly haunts of the fairies, and that they held their sports and amorous revels in the retiring dells by the light of the moon. The mermaid sung her sweet and alluring strains by the shores of the mountain lake, and the kelpie sat moping and dripping by his frightsome pool, or the boiling caldron at the foot of the cataract. The fleeting wraiths hovered round the dwellings of those who were soon to die, and the stalking ghost perambulated the walks of him that was lately living, or took up his nightly stand over the bones of the unhouseholded or murdered dead. In such a country, and among such sojourners, who durst walk by night?

But these were the natural residenters in the wilds of the woodland, the aboriginal inhabitants of the country; and however inimical their ways might be to the ways of men, the latter laid their account with them. There were defences to be had against them from holy church, which was a great comfort. But ever since Master Michael Scott came from the colleges abroad to reside at the castle of Aikwood, the nature of demonology in the forest glades was altogether changed, and a full torrent of necromancy, or, as Charlie Scott better expressed it, of *witchcraft*, deluged the country all over, — an art of the most malignant and appalling kind, against which no fence yet discovered could prevail. How different, indeed, became the situation of the lonely hind. Formerly he only heard at a distance on moonlight eves the bridle bells of the fairy troopers, which haply caused him to haste homewards. But when the door was barred and fenced, he sat safe in the middle of his family circle as they closed round the hearth, and talked of the pranks of *the gude neyboris*.

When the speats descended, and floods roared and
foamed from bank to brae, then would they perceive
the malevolent kelpie rolling and tumbling down the
torrent like a drowning cow, or mountain stag, to
allure the hungry peasant into certain destruction. But,
aware of the danger, he only kept the farther aloof,
quaking at the tremendous experiment made by the
spirit of the waters. It was in vain that the mermaid
sung the sweetest strains that ever breathed over the
evening lake, or sunk and rose again, spreading her
hands for assistance, like a drowning maiden, at the
bottom of the abrupt cliff washed by the waves, — he
would not be allured to her embraces.

But what could he do now? His daughters were
turned into roes and hares, to be hunted down for sport
to the Master. The old wives of the hamlet were
saddled and bridled by night, and urged with whip and
spur over whole realms. The cows were deprived of
their milk, — the hinds cast their young, and no
domestic cat in the whole district could be kept alive
for one year. That infernal system of witchcraft then
began, which the stake and the gibbet could scarcely
eradicate in a whole century. It had at this time begun
to spread all around Aikwood; but of these things our
Border troopers were not altogether aware. They
dreaded the spirits of the old school, the devil in
particular; but of the new prevailing system of meta-
morphoses they had no comprehension."[46]

The passage is not mere whimsy. I have myself heard in the
same terms a passionate defence of the truth of supernatural
events in ballads and folktales uttered by a modern traveller,
himself an accomplished traditional singer and story-teller.
Witches are now too far off to demand special explanation, but
his argument concerned the supernatural in general, and ran
thus: Things are not so now, but long ago — in the Catholic
times, say — they were different. There is no reason to suppose
that the boundaries of nature remain immutable through the
centuries. With this qualification, Hogg's own general approach
to the supernatural is not unlike that of Robert Kirk, the
scientific analyst of fairy-lore, whose work was discussed in

Progress and Poetry[47], but closer analogues, perhaps, are to be found in the famous song by Richard Corbet (1582-1635), "Fairies Farewell", posthumously published in 1647,[48] and in Kipling's "Dymchurch Flit", last story but one in *Puck of Pook's Hill* (1906). Corbet may have written with tongue in cheek, and Kipling's story is intended for children. This should not be allowed to obscure the fact that all three writers deliberately go against two major postulates of seventeenth and eighteenth century inductive science and Enlightenment thought, summarized by Newton in his "Rules of Reasoning and Philosophy". In *Progress and Poetry*[49] I quoted Thomas Reid's version of the first; here are both together, rendered by Sir James Jeans (1877-1946), an important populariser of the physics which during the twentieth century replaced Newton's:—

> RULE I. We are to admit no more causes of natural things than such as are both true and sufficient to explain their appearance.
>
> To this purpose the philosophers say that Nature does nothing in vain, and more is in vain when less will serve; for Nature is pleased with simplicity, and affects not the pomp of superfluous causes.
>
> RULE II. Therefore to the same natural effects we must, as far as possible, assign the same causes.
>
> As to respiration in a man and in a beast; the descent of stones in Europe and America; the light of our culinary fire and of the sun; the reflection of light in the earth and in the planets.[50]

Newton does not directly say so, but implicit in his words is the idea that identical laws of causality apply to past and to present, a point of view central to the historical work of his followers during the Enlightenment and afterwards. Hogg, like some others (William Blake, for instance) disagrees; he is prepared more or less to grant that an event in the present or recent past will follow Newtonian Law, but holds that in the more distant past this was not necessarily so; that other factors might then have predominated. To limit oneself to a single example, a modern drowning is the result of carelessness or mere chance or direct interference by another human; in pre-Reformation Scotland, the cause might have been the supernatural temptation offered by a mermaid, or the equally supernatural assault of a water-kelpie. The story of "Mary Burnet", already mentioned, introduces even wider possibilities.

As the subtitle indicates, during the fourteenth century the Three Perils of Man were War, Women, and Witchcraft, arranged thus in ascending scale of importance. The initial pair survived into the nineteenth century and beyond, but by that time the third and most powerful had been extirpated. In the novel, the first is represented primarily by events immediately connected with the siege of Roxburgh; the second by the escapades of the joint causes of the siege; the English Lady Jane Howard and the Scottish Princess Margaret. As the events of the siege all stem, directly or ultimately, from these two, they represent a peril even greater than war. But primacy unmistakeably attaches to the third peril, the only one, significantly, with a metaphysical dimension. Witchcraft nowadays is generally associated with women, and so might have been regarded as an extension of the second peril, but in the novel it has a male representative, Michael Scott, championed, as he is for the greater part of the action, by a male Devil accompanied by several of his male entourage. Women here are secondary and subordinate.

It is worth noting that Hogg is well aware that witchcraft belongs, not to the early, but to the late Middle Ages and the Reformation period. He would certainly have scorned the idea that its rites were in any sense survivals of a pre-Christian religious system, although he might have allowed that certain other countryside beliefs had such an origin. The devil, of course, has pre-Christian origins, but the influence which he exerts in the novel is something new.

Even witchcraft has its antidote. Master Michael is opposed, even outclassed, by the gospel friar, who is never given his full name, but whom the reader is encouraged to identify with the celebrated Roger Bacon. The competition between the two, narrated in chapter xv, together with the tales told by the individual members of the embassy during their captivity on the necromancer's tower, is the allegorical heart of the work, in relation to which the full significance of the remainder is to be assessed.

Bacon's three competitive feats depend on knowledge of what in the Scottish universities is still called natural philosophy, and in particular on optics and chemistry. Two turn on the properties of lenses — he gives a magic-lantern show, and inserts a distorting pane of glass in a window of Aikwood to produce the illusion that the neighbouring peak of Cope-Law has been divided in three. The third depends on chemistry — the friar has in his possession a supply of gunpowder, manufactured by himself, with which he blows up the evil seneschal, Gourlay.

By contrast, Michael relies entirely on the metaphysical aid of his three familiars, Prig, Prim, and Pricker, for his response to the first two. It is they who produce doubles of Charlie Scott, the Deil's Tam and the Laird of the Peatstacknowe, and who leave the Master helpless when at his instruction they go off to divide in three the peak of Eildon, which until that time had been single. The destruction of Gourlay takes place during their absence, and the Master does not even attempt a reply. It is only by the intervention of Bacon that he is saved from the clutches of a demon sent to drag him to Hell.

All this might suggest that the Friar is superior because he is himself a precursor of the Enlightenment, a practical and experimental scientist born out of his due time, and by the superiority to his period which he demonstrates, inevitably incurring persecution, exile, and the enmity of such charlatans as Michael Scott. Hogg thinks otherwise. The feats of the friar are in effect nothing. Michael Scott operates by spiritual rather than natural means. The creation of the doubles, still more that of three peaks on Eildon, is prodigious to a degree greater than anything performed during the competition by Bacon.

Even earlier than this, however, Bacon has demonstrated that his real power, like that of Michael, is spiritual, dependent on metaphysical influences, and that it is capable of vanquishing even the familiars who later divide the peak. He is himself the first of the embassy to enter Aikwood, and when Gourlay descends to the courtyard, the state of affairs there astonishes him:—

> "When he came nigh to the scene of action, he looked as if he expected the friar to have been dead, and was rather astonished when he saw him raise his head, and utter a solemn anathema against the pages, who fled back as if awed and overcome."[51]

As it first appears, the contrast between the friar and Michael is absolute — light against darkness, good against evil — but it remains in touch with the life of ordinary human beings, partly because it is seen in Christian terms, partly because the friar is accompanied by the other, unmistakeably human, members of the embassy. The extent of his power is revealed, not so much by its relationship to the necromancer and his associates, as by comparison with the strengths of one particular individual among his own companions, who may be said to represent the limits for the novel of merely human physical capacity, muckle Charlie Scott of Yardbire. Of the three perils, war scarcely affects him — his closest associates are his horse, Corby, and his gigantic sword, the Eskdale souple; his natural haunt is the battlefield. With women he is less at ease, although Lady Jane Howard is destined, finally and surprisingly, to be the wifely ornament of his board and bed. Against witchcraft, he is generally completely helpless. In this field, his one great exploit is to overcome the physical strength of Gourlay, but he flees from the mere words of Michael's witch-housekeeper, after which Prim, Prig, and Pricker overthrow him in an instant, truss him hand and foot, and offer him to the wizard for sacrifice. It is the friar who overcomes the housekeeper, and afterwards miraculously discovers the desperate plight of Charlie when even he is forced to seek metaphysical aid:—

> "With that he whispered a prayer to the Son of the Virgin, that He would save a warrior from a death like this.
>
> Charlie's prayer was heard, short as it was; for at that very moment, while yet the syllables hung on his lips, entered the gruff figure of the friar, with the keys of the castle over his arm, and followed by his associates.
>
> 'What seek you here, you dogs?' cried the Master, turning about with the great knife in his hand: 'Am I thus to have my privacy disturbed, and my abode ravaged by a pack of carrion hounds from the hills? Brave pages mine, bind them all, and cut me them in a thousand pieces.'
>
> Scarcely was the order given ere they had the poet on the floor, and bound with strong cords. The rest prepared to escape; but the great enchanter placed his back to the door, brandished his great knife, and dared them to approach him. The mettledness of these pages

cannot be conceived, far less described; they seemed but
to will a thing and it was done. Ere one of the intruders
had time to rally his thoughts, or almost to think at all,
three of them and the boy were all lying bound in
fetters. But when the imps came to seize the friar, they
could not. They skipped about and about him, but they
had not power even to touch his frock. The virgin
stood behind him trembling; and on their feeling their
want of power over the friar, they turned to lay hold
on her. But the moment they touched her robe, they
retired back in dismay.

Michael looked as if he dreaded there was something
about these two that boded him no good; but he wist
not what it was, for he had never seen the prowess of
his bond spirits counteracted before; therefore he
awaited the event for a space, when he perceived them
vanquished.

The friar had time to rally his thoughts, and remembered that the maid had the blessed gospel concealed in
her bosom; and judging that these were perhaps fiends
with whom they had to do, who durst not stand
against the word of truth, he drew his cross from
below his frock, — that cross which had been consecrated at the shrine of Saint Peter, bathed in holy water,
and blessed with many blessings from the mouths of
ancient martyrs — had done wondrous miracles in the
hands of saints of former days, — and lifting that
reverendly up on high, he pronounced the words from
holy writ against which no demon or false spirit's
power could prevail. In one moment all the three imps
fled yelling from the apartment. The countenance of
the enchanter fell, and he quaked where he stood; but
the eye of the friar was kindled up with exultation and
joy.

'There worketh the hand of my master!' exclaimed
he: 'There have I trusted, and I am not, like thee,
ashamed of my trust. I have a strong-hold of hope, and
it is founded on a rock, but thy habitation trembleth
beneath thee; and dost thou know, or hast thou
considered, what is underneath?'

The friar then went up and loosed the bonds of his

friend Charlie, and of all the rest, one by one, exulting in his creed, and pouring forth such sentences of sublime adoration as are not suited for an idle tale.

The master at length took courage and rebuked him, saying, 'It is vain for thee, foolish dupe of a foolish creed, to multiply such great swelling words of vanity. What though thy might hath, for once, prevailed above my might, and thy spell proved more powerful than mine? I will engage, nevertheless, that in nine times out of ten, mine, on fair trial, shall prevail over thine. And at all events I can at this time call in the arm of flesh to my assistance, and do with you whatever seemeth to me good.'

'Ay, gude faith, and that's very true, Master Michael Scott,' said Charlie: 'and that we saw wi' our ain een. It is great nonsense to quarrel with the lord of a castle aneath his ain roof, although, I confess, I was the first to do it mysel'. But there's an auld saying, wha wad sit i' Rome and strive wi' the pope? or misca' a Macdonald in the raws o' Lochaber? We came wi' nae sic intent, but in fair friendship, and on courteous errand. And now when we are a' rather on equal footing again, let me beg o' you, great and powerful Master, to be a reasonable man for aince. Answer the warden's request, and let us gae; for really, great Sir, our master canna well want us; and mair nor that, I'm feared yon chaps at the mill dinna gie Corby ony water.'"[52]

To a degree, Hogg is writing mock-heroic, parodying elements of Gothic romance. Elsewhere he had already shown himself a master parodist,[53] and in *The Three Perils of Man* he uses a range of styles for persons and incidents, so as almost to rival in technique the James Joyce of *Ulysses*. The effect, as far as the Master is concerned, is deflatory: despite his fustian he is unable to deal with the friar, and his claim that he will use the arm of flesh, although it is accepted by Charlie, is based solely on the three hundred rats whom he had transformed to act as a household retinue for the now-captive Gourlay. His only other attendant is the housekeeper, also now a prisoner. On no previous occasion had he required anything more in the way of service by mere humans. It is a sad decline for him to threaten physical violence. His change of attitude shows the extent of the friar's victory.

The passage as a whole is kept in touch with reality by the honesty and strong proverbial content of Charlie's colloquial Scots interjection. He is the human norm, who keeps his generosity through defeat, and never loses his concern for the Warden and for Corby. Unlike the Master, he has no pretences. But the friar is the only person in the room who has not been defeated, a fact which no parody can disguise. Behind this parody, moreover, are to be discovered reminiscences of the genuinely Christian medieval romance which is one source of Hogg's inspiration. The appearance of the friar in answer to Charlie's prayer is like the appearance of Bercilak's castle in response to the prayer of Gawain for harbourage on Christmas Eve in *Sir Gawain and the Green Knight*.[54] The power of the cross against evil spirits is paralleled by the yelling flight of the succubus in *Queste del Sangreal*, when Perceval, by a providential accident, glances at the cross inlaid in the hilt of his sword.[55] It is curious that Hogg's sympathies, normally so much for the Protestant Reformation and the Covenanters, should extend in this way to the Catholic Middle Ages, but he certainly did not mean his parody to blunt his intention in this part of his narrative.

When on a technicality of protocol the friar and Delany are finally expelled from Aikwood, the remainder of the party are wholly at the mercy of Michael and the Devil who has taken the form of the abbot of Melrose. The Laird of the Peatstacknowe has already been selected, much against his will, to succeed Gourlay as Michael's seneschal. Tam Craik signs away his soul. The others are humiliated by witches, and finally transformed into wild cattle before they are released. But at least they bring with them the message which the warden desires, and it is the friar who eventually restores them to their proper form.

The action thus moves within a Christian spiritual framework, of which most of the actors are seldom more than half-conscious. Even Charlie fears that the book which the friar urges on Delany — in fact, the New Testament — is some kind of collection of spells. This is the book which protects her against the Master's pages. Throughout, good and evil maintain a counterpoint, in which evil, at least initially, sometimes seems on the point of victory. All the significant events of the story occur in a period delimited by festivals in the calendar of the Christian year, from the feast of St Leonard on 6th November, through that of the Conception of the Blessed Virgin on 8th December, to the festivities of Christmas Eve, Christmas Day and Twelfth Night: most in fact belong to the period between 6th November and 8th December. In Roxburgh as well as at Aikwood, evil takes its most concentrated form during this period, opening, as it does, with the cruel and unnecessary public hanging of the five English soldiers who accompanied Lady Jane to Scotland, and the retaliatory execution of the Scottish fisherman, Sandy Yellow-lees, who had intercepted the supplies intended for the besieged English garrison. It closes with the preparations for the execution of Sir Richard Musgrave and the public violation of Lady Jane, which are disrupted by the suicide of Lord Musgrave, brother of Sir Richard and affianced to Lady Jane, who for many months has maintained the defence of Roxburgh Castle. The interim is occupied with the executions of the innocent substitutes for Sir Richard and Princess Margaret, and with the embassy sent by Sir Ringan Redhough to his kinsman, Master Michael Scott, the members of which suffer the afflictions of black magic and diabolic intervention.

Events in the two main localities are carefully synchronised. In particular, the storm which occurs when Prim, Prig, and Pricker are dividing Eildon gives the garrison of Roxburgh their opportunity to break out and attempt the rescue of Lady Jane and Sir Richard. The attempt is a failure, but one of the captives taken during it is the disguised Princess Margaret. Douglas believes that she is subsequently hanged. Later complications are mainly the result of this belief on his part.

The ambassadors escape from Aikwood just before 8th December, and the oracle which they bring from Michael finally enables Sir Ringan to capture Roxburgh. The Christmas period is as a consequence reasonably festal. The arrival of the King and Queen on Christmas Eve is followed by the restoration of Princess Margaret on Christmas Day, and her subsequent marriage to Douglas. Even during this period, however, the narrative refers again and again to the experiences of the embassy in Aikwood, and, as has been mentioned, the book ends with the account given by the Laird of the Peatstacknowe of Michael's death in an encounter with the Devil.

The ending is surprising not merely in that it sets Devil and necromancer at odds, but that, in a sense, the necromancer has the better of the conflict. He dies because he has overcome his adversary; he does not surrender his mighty book, but still clasps it to his bosom when he is buried in the consecrated precincts of Melrose Abbey. One might almost say that he dies a Christian, although one of a decidedly peculiar kind.

For most of the characters involved, the course of the book is a pilgrim's progress towards self-knowledge. The sole exception is the friar. His name is never given, and that, paradoxically, signifies that he has already reached such knowledge. The events of the siege cure the self-conceit and self-centredness of Douglas, Lady Jane and the Princess. But it is the Aikwood party which is most affected. The competition between the friar and Michael is succeeded by another, this time in story-telling, where the penalty for the loser is to be eaten by his companions, trapped and starving as they are on the battlements. It is, in other words, a matter of life and death for the contestants, whose stories appear to concentrate on their own lives, but for the most part turn out to be revelations concerning the lives of the others. The friar's tale reveals the identity of the virgin Delany, intended to be a sacrificial offering to Michael (one, ironically, in whom he has no real interest). The subject of the tale told by the Laird of the Peatstacknowe turns out to be Tam Craik, the Deil's Tam; the tale shows how the nickname is justified. Charlie Scott's tale reveals the origins of the bard or minstrel, Colley Carol. Tam Craik's own tale confirms the appropriateness of his nickname, and shows that he is victim as well as villain; that he is pre-ordained to misfortune and perhaps damnation. The poet Colley Carol's tale, told after the Devil in person has scared away would-be rescuers, is the only one with no direct relevance for any single prisoner; in form it is a consolatory saint's legend, dealing with the triumph of Christian weakness over pagan strengths. That, of course, is relevant both to the prisoners' immediate plight, and to the action of the novel as a whole.

The release of the captives from the tower is delayed, as I have said, by the arrival of the Devil, to whom Prig, Prim, and Pricker, sing a hymn,[56] the revolutionary and radical, almost Shelleyan, overtones of which deserve some notice:—

Speed thee, speed thee!
Liberty lead thee!
Many this night shall hearken and heed thee.
Far abroad.
Demigod!
What shall appal thee?
Javel, or Devil, or how shall we call thee?
Thine the night voices of joy and of weeping,
The whisper awake, and the vision when sleeping:
The bloated kings of the earth shall brood
On princedoms and provinces bought with blood,
Shall slubber,[57] and snore, and tomorrow's breath
Shall order the muster and march of death:
The trumpets shall sound, and the gonfalons flee,
And thousands of souls step home to thee . . .

Hail, patriot spirit! thy labours be blest!
For of all great reformers thyself were the first;
Thou wert the first, with discernment strong,
To perceive that all rights divine were wrong;
And long hast thou spent thy sovereign breath,
In heaven above and in earth beneath,
And roared it from thy burning throne,
The glory of independence alone;
Proclaiming to all, with fervor and irony,
That kingly dominion's all humbug and tyranny;
And whoso listeth may be free,
For freedom, full freedom's the word with thee!

This is relevant, of course, not only to the immediate situation, but to the general course of Hogg's thought, as illustrated by the earlier piece, "Storms", discussed above. It is counterbalanced, a few pages later, by the "Hymn to the Redeemer",[58] which appears in the Poet's tale, the saint's legend already mentioned, which occupies chapter XXII. The emphasis here is on salvation, and the reconciliation of apparent opposites. The contrast between the two summarises the central conflict of the book.

Michael Scott shares in the progress towards self-knowledge. For some considerable time he is able to maintain a level with the friar. The story makes it obvious, however, that by ordering his

familiars to divide Eildon, he has overreached himself. Not
without cause, he becomes apprehensive for his own safety. A
demon is in the very act of dragging him off, when the friar
appears to the rescue. Michael is humbled, but not fully
repentant, and when he sees that the Eildons have in fact been
divided, he seems to go back to his old allegiance. The apparent
reconciliation ends when Michael musters the powers of air and
water against the Devil's earth and fire. His fatal success in the
final encounter shows that the friar's sermon has not been
entirely wasted. Unlike Tam Craik, Michael, it would seem, is
not predestined to damnation. During the conflict, the Devil
takes the form of a dragon. One should not forget an earlier
conflict which involved both a dragon and a Michael.

That *The Three Perils of Man* is faulty in some of its details, no
one would deny. The escape from hanging of Sir Richard
Musgrave and the Princess Margaret in unconvincing, as well as
cruel. One member of the embassy, the boy Elias, is given
apparent prominence at the beginning, but plays no part in the
subsequent action. As a whole, nevertheless, the book is carefully, even brilliantly, constructed. Hogg's metaphor of himself
as no more than a waggoner performing a difficult and tedious
task is to be taken with a pinch of salt. The prominence given to
the embassy, almost totally removed in Hogg's later version, has
now, I hope, been fully justified.

On more than one occasion, Hogg hints that the book is
substantially an allegory. The word itself he allows the friar to
use in the Poet's tale; "Peradventure it may be an ancient
allegory of our nation, in which manner of instruction the
fathers of Christianity amongst us took great delight".[59] Hogg
does not himself use it of the book as a whole, but very
noticeably, in the final chapter xxxii, the Laird of the Peatstacknowe and the abbot of Melrose (the genuine one, this time)
combine to give an allegorical interpretation of the latest
episodes in the life of Michael Scott. Among much else, this
returns to the theme of radicalism, once before proposed in the
"Hymn to the Devil". The Devil and Michael have separated
with mutual threats and insults:—

> "Thus parted these two once-bound associates, but
> now jealous and inexorable foes, — a good lesson to all
> those who form combinations inimical to the laws or

authority of the land in which they reside. Like those master-spirits, such are likewise conspirators against rightful sovereignty, although on a smaller scale; and like those whom they imitate, and by whom they are moved, their counsels will always be turned either to foolishness or against themselves."[60]

It may or may not be important that these words are uttered by the insignificant and prosy figure of Gibbie Jordan.

There might be difficulties in defending an allegorical interpretation of every petty detail; but once the general principle is accepted, most of the apparent structural difficulties in the work disappear.

The suggestion is also convincing in another way. In England and Scotland alike, one stage in the development of the novel as a literary form is represented by prose allegory. Examples which come to mind include such differing works as Bunyan's *The Pilgrim's Progress* and Arbuthnott's *The History of John Bull*, the latter of which was briefly discussed above.[61] The titles — *Pride and Prejudice, Sense and Sensibility, Persuasion* - of several among the novels of Jane Austen demonstrates the continuity of the tradition in nineteenth century England, and it may also, as I have attempted to show, be illustrated from Scott. There is nothing therefore surprising in the fact that Hogg adapted the technique to his own purposes. In such a context, the recurrent figure of the *doppelganger* has an obvious potential, exploited to its most powerful effect in *The Private Memoirs and Confessions of a Justified Sinner*.

Through the *persona* of the editor, Hogg himself hints at the presence of allegory in the *Justified Sinner*. The comments are directed to the "Memoir", supposedly written by the Sinner himself, which forms the second part of the book:—

> "What can this work be? Sure, you will say, it must be an allegory; or (as the writer calls it) a religious PARABLE, showing the dreadful danger of self-righteousness? I cannot tell."[62]

The editor is commenting on the method used by the Sinner to persuade the Queen's Printer to bring out the pamphlet which constitutes the "Memoir". He told him that "it was a religious parable, such as the *Pilgrim's Progress*". Mr Watson's reaction was "that religious pamphlets, especially if they had a shade of allegory in them, were the very rage of the day".[63] The precise meaning attached to the term by Hogg is open to dispute, but there can be little doubt that some kind of allegory played a part in his scheme from the beginning.

The theme of the *doppelganger*, prominent in the novel to a degree extraordinary even for Hogg, offers possibilities already seized upon by some of his contemporaries. Notably, it is recurrent in Shelley, where it receives its most elaborate development in *Prometheus Unbound* (1820). The most direct statement is to be found in the words which the Earth addresses to the Titan, her son:—

> Ere Babylon was dust,
> The Magus Zoroaster, my dead child,
> Met his own image walking in the garden.
> That apparition, sole of men, he saw.
> For know there are two worlds of life and death:
> One that which thou beholdest; but the other
> Is underneath the grave, where do inhabit
> The shadows of all forms that think and live
> Till death unite them and they part no more;
> Dreams and the light imaginings of men,
> And all that faith creates or love desires,
> Terrible, strange, sublime and beauteous shapes.
> There thou art, and dost hang, a writhing shade,
> Mid whirlwind-peopled mountains; all the gods
> Are there, and all the powers of nameless worlds,
> Vast sceptred phantoms; heroes, men, and beasts;
> And Demogorgon, a tremendous gloom;
> And he, the supreme Tyrant, on his throne
> Of burning gold.
>   (Act 1, 192-210)

The idea has its origin in the Platonic concept that the immediately perceptible world of the senses does no more than reflect the world of Forms, to which, as a reflection, it necessarily corresponds, in however limited a degree. It will be seen that here already the figure of the *doppelganger* is at least potentially present. A figure in this present world reflects an original in the world of Forms. When to our eyes the reflection vanishes with the onset of death, it is reabsorbed in that original. Given the concept of reincarnation, the reabsorption may be temporary or permanent, liberatory, blissful, purgatorial or finally condemnatory, depending on the state which the reflection has reached during its term of mortal existence. The relationship between reflection and original is necessarily intimate. The original is in fact the guardian spirit of the reflection, or, in later Christian terms, the guardian angel whose influence may be for good or evil.

This concept the Neoplatonists developed partly as an interpretation of the vision of Er, narrated in the tenth book of Plato's *Republic*. After his supposed death, Er, it will be recollected, travelled to a strange meadow, above which were two openings in the heaven, to which corresponded two on the earth below. One of each was for ascent, the other for descent. After judgement had been passed on the dead who had arrived, they departed according to their sentence, either upwards or downwards; likewise, the souls who had completed their reward or punishment for a past existence, returned from heaven or hell to accept their lot, and make their choice of life for the next incarnation. Some few were refused a return from the lower regions; even fewer, it must be assumed, remained permanently in the heavenly. For most, however, there was a free choice of incarnate existences in an order determined by lot, and even for the last among them a wide range of lives remained possible.

The *doppelganger* makes no appearance here, but an approximation to him is to be found in a parallel passage in the *Phaedo*. When once again Socrates is discussing the fate of the soul after death, a "guardian spirit" — the *doppelganger*, that is to say — and two "guides" appear in his discourse:—

> "When any man dies, his own guardian spirit, which was given charge over him in his life, tries to bring him to a certain place where all must assemble, and from which, after submitting their several cases to judgement, they must set out for the next world, under the guidance of one who has the office of escorting souls from this world to the other. When they have there undergone the necessary experiences and remained as long as is required, another guide brings them back again after many vast periods of time."[64]

The words in the *Republic* which come closest to this are the ones which precede the act of individual choice, spoken by a certain prophet, who is the official voice of Lachesis, one of the three Fates. "No divinity shall cast lots for you, but you shall choose your own deity."[65]

The word here translated as "divinity" and "deity", δαίμων, is the same as the one rendered "guardian spirit" in the previous passage. One should note that the *Republic* does not question the existence of such guardians, but rather insists on a specially close relationship between them and the liberty somewhat paradoxically possessed by each individual soul at the beginning of an incarnation, a relationship interpreted by the Neoplatonists as in effect a choice by the soul of the original in the world of Forms which it will reflect during a particular cycle of existence. Among much else, this liberty carries with it the possibility of final damnation, illustrated in the *Republic* by the story of the tyrant, Ardiaeus the Great, who when he attempted to return from the underworld to the meadow of judgement and incarnation was seized by "savage men of fiery aspect" and eventually hurled into Tartarus, there, one assumes, to remain permanently. Ardiaeus, like the winner of the first lot, who sprang to seize the greatest tyranny, but overlooked the fact that it involved the fate of eating his own children, is a Hellenic Justified Sinner.

The identity at one level of soul and guardian spirit is most clearly brought out by Plotinus (c. AD 203-262) in the fourth treatise of the third *Ennead*, the subject of which is "Our Allotted Guardian Spirit".[66] The treatise offers itself as an analysis and interpretation of the Platonic myths already referred to. Plotinus as much as Plato believed that the soul possessed at least a measure of liberty. The proper place of the guardian spirit is on a plane higher than the human, but from a slightly different point of view it may also be regarded as an extension of the incarnate soul; it represents the possibilities which lie open to it as a result of the choice made before birth. The guardian is, as it were, the full realization of the soul in terms of its original choice. The soul, however, has individual peculiarities, which may affect the extent to which it realises its own potential. The realization nevertheless is generally in terms of good, but Plotinus does not exclude the possibility of evil as choice or outcome:—

> "Does the spirit, then, always and in every way accomplish its task successfully? Not altogether, since the soul is of such a disposition that it is of a particular

kind in particular circumstances and so has a life and a purpose corresponding to its kind and circumstances. Now this spirit of whom we are speaking is said, when it has led the soul to Hades, no longer to remain the same, unless the soul chooses again the same type of life. But what happens before the choice of lives? The leading to judgement means that the spirit comes to the same form after the soul's departure from this life as it had before the soul's birth; as if from a different starting-point, it is present to the souls which are being punished during the time which intervenes before their next birth — this is not a life for them, but an expiation. But what about the souls which enter into the bodies of brutes? Is their guardian something less than a spirit? It *is* a spirit, a wicked or stupid one."[67]

The relevance of this to Hogg is clearest in the account of young Wringhim's first meeting with his double, Gil-Martin, on the day when he was first assured that he was one of the Elect. The term "guardian angel" is actually applied to the strange figure whom he encounters. The highly formal English of the description conveys the supernatural aura proper to the occasion:—

"That stranger youth and I approached each other in silence, and slowly, with our eyes fixed on each other's eyes. We approached till not more than a yard intervened between us, and then stood still and gazed, measuring each other from head to foot. What was my astonishment on perceiving that he was the same being as myself? The clothes were the same to the smallest item. The form was the same; the apparent age; the colour of the hair; the eyes; and, as far as recollection could serve me from viewing my own features in a glass, the features too were the very same. I conceived at first, that I saw a vision, and that my guardian angel had appeared to me at this important era of my life."[68]

Earlier in the book, although later in terms of time in the novel, Mrs Logan makes a curious remark, characterised by a certain Empsonian ambiguity: it is difficult to tell whether she is talking about Wringhim or his murdered half-brother. In either case, however, it is the relationship between human and *doppelganger* that she has in mind:—

> "'The likeness to my late hapless young master is so striking, that I can hardly believe it to be a chance model; and I think he imitates him in every thing, for some purpose, or some effect on his sinful associate. Do you know that he is so like in every lineament, look, and gesture, that, against the clearest light of reason, I cannot in my mind separate the one from the other, and have a certain indefinable impression on my mind, that they are one and the same being, or that the one was a prototype of the other.'"[69]

It is in a sense true to say that George Colwan was himself a *doppelganger* for Wringhim; one brother counterbalances the other, almost as Dr Jekyll counterbalances Mr Hyde. In this sense it is true to say that Gil-Martin is the prototype for both brothers. George represents the potential which was lost in his brother, who therefore kills him. Towards the end of the novel Wringhim, like Mrs Logan, comes to see Gil-Martin in George's form, and it is at this point, significantly, that he becomes convinced that the powers of the other are indeed demonic. "I was also certain, that he was possessed of some supernatural power, of the source of which I was wholly ignorant."[70] For the first time he applies to him the word "necromancer", which Hogg had already applied to Michael Scott. It is more appropriate here, however, where the evil spirit seems actually to animate the body of someone deceased. A murderer too is traditionally haunted by the phantom of his victim. Wringhim fulfilled his highest potential for evil when he killed his brother, who exemplified everything he lacked in himself; his guardian demon therefore adopted the form of the victim through whom he had reached that potential.

The Justified Sinner is one who has made the wrong choice before birth. The narrative makes it plain that even in childhood his inclination had been towards the malicious. Gil-Martin appears in order to lead him through death to the judgement which will result in their perpetual union in Tartarus. The Sinner's fate nevertheless has been chosen by himself. The form given to the concept by Hogg is only incidentally Calvinist; in essence it is universal. For Wringhim as for the souls in the Platonic meadow, "You shall choose your own deity".

In terms of the passage quoted from *Prometheus Unbound*, Zoroaster is one who made the choice in terms of good. The appearance to him of his *doppelganger* portended that their reunion after death would be heavenly. The appearance of the Phantasm of Jupiter has the reverse significance. Jupiter, like Ardiaeus the Great, is a cruel tyrant; when he falls, it is to a consummation in Tartarus. The appearance in this world of the *doppelganger* proclaims the approach of death, but what happens after death has been decided long before. Not surprisingly, when the Phantasm appears in answer to the summons of Prometheus, its duty is to repeat the curse imposed on Jupiter by Prometheus when he was first chained to Mount Caucasus, the curse which is now approaching fulfilment. Admittedly, the downfall of Jupiter is directly brought about, not by the Phantasm, but by another figure from the Otherworld, Demogorgon, the personification of Eternity. The *doppelganger*, or "fetch", as he is called in other traditions, is the harbinger rather than the cause of death. The instrument, Demogorgon, is roused by Asia and Panthea, the latter of whom had been with Prometheus during the appearance of the Phantasm. The spiritual messengers who in Act II lead the pair to Demogorgon in the Otherworld appear in consequence of the summons uttered by Prometheus to the Phantasm.

The choice made by Jupiter in the remote past has in effect predestined his eventual fall, a point realised by Prometheus when he pronounces his curse. In isolation, the curse did not involve any fixed term to Jupiter's rule; that became a reality only when the Phantasm, Jupiter's *doppelganger*, appeared from the Otherworld to repeat the actual words in which the curse had been expressed. When Demogorgon finally appears, Jupiter has no power of resistance; he is the plaything of the fate which he has inflicted on himself, a fate which he realises, is infinitely more rigorous than anything his enemy, Prometheus would have inflicted on him:—

> Oh,
> That thou wouldst make mine enemy my judge,
> Even where he hangs, seared by my long
>   revenge,
> On Caucasus! he would not doom me thus.
>
> (III.1. 65-68)

The sense of helplessness, of being trapped in a web of predestined events, forms an essential part of the theme. The same sense of tangled predestination is present in the mind of the Justified Sinner, and is given an almost comic expression in the literal web which entangles him in the weaver's house where he finds refuge of a kind on the first evening of his flight from Dalchastel. He is locked, it will be recollected, in a little room, a sort of box "among looms, treadles, pirns, and confusion without end",[71] and is eventually hung, upside down, in the coarse linen threads which form the warp of one loom. This is the web of his fate, and he is as helpless as Prometheus nailed to Mount Caucasus. Like him, he is assailed by Furies:—

> "My feet had slipped down through the double warpings of a web, and not being able to reach the ground with them, (there being a small pit below), I rode upon a number of yielding threads, and there being nothing else that I could reach, to extricate myself was impossible. I was utterly powerless; and besides, the yarn and cords hurt me very much. For all that, the destructive weaver seized a loomspoke, and began abeating me most unmercifully, while entangled as I was, I could do nothing but shout aloud for mercy, or assistance, whichever chanced to be within hearing. The latter, at length, made its appearance, in the form of the weaver's wife, in the same state of dishabille with himself, who instantly interfered, and that most strenuously, on my behalf. Before her arrival, however, I had made a desperate effort to throw myself out of the entanglement I was in; for the weaver continued repeating his blows and cursing me so, that I determined to get out of his meshes at any risk. This effort made my case worse; for my feet being wrapt among the nether threads, as I threw myself from my saddle

on the upper ones, my feet brought the others up through these, and I hung with my head down, and my feet as firm as they had been in a vice. The predicament of the web being thereby increased, the weaver's wrath was doubled in proportion, and he laid on without mercy.

At this critical juncture the wife arrived, and without hesitation rushed before her offended lord, withholding his hand from injuring me farther, although then it was uplifted along with the loomspoke in overbearing ire. 'Dear Johnny! I think ye be gaen dementit this morning. Be quiet, my dear, an' dinna begin a Boddel Brigg business in your ain house. What for ir ye persecutin' a servant o' the Lord's that gate, an' pittin' the life out o' him wi' his head down an' his heels up?'

'Had ye said a servant o' the deil's, Nans, ye wad hae been nearer the nail, for gin he binna the auld ane himsel, he's gayan sib till him. There, didna I lock him in on purpose to bring the military on him; an' in place o' that, hasna he keepit me in a sleep a' this while as deep as death? An' here do I find him abscondit like a speeder i' the mids o' my leddy's wab, an' me dreamin' a' the night that I had the deil i' my house, an' that he was clapper-clawin me ayont the loom. Have at ye, ye brunstane thief!' and, in spite of the good woman's struggles, he lent me another severe blow."[72]

Wringhim's position suggests to the woman that he is a saint undergoing martyrdom, like St Peter, upside down, in the most humiliating of postures. Her husband she identifies on the contrary with the malignants who defeated the Covenanters at Bothwell Bridge. Both interpretations Wringhim would gladly accept. To the weaver however, he is an evil spider trapped in his own web; he is either Satan or his near relative, against whom the Covenanters had so often fought. Events, even as related in the stilted English which Wringhim uses throughout his narrative, seem to support the latter, but there is at least a trace of compassion for the sufferer.

The curse, which plays so important a part in *Prometheus Unbound*, is twice paralleled in Hogg's narrative, first, so far as the reader is concerned, by the actual curse which the Rev.

Robert Wringhim calls down on George Colwan in revenge for his temporary success at law against his supposed brother, Robert. The curse is summed up by the verse from the metrical version of Psalm 109, the singing of which precedes the formal excommunication, and which, as Hogg or the Editor remarks, "it is a pity should ever have been admitted into a Christian psalmody":—

> Set thou the wicked over him,
> And upon his right hand
> Give thou his greatest enemy,
> Even Satan, leave to stand.[73]

It is this verse which seems to summon Robert's Satanic *doppelganger* to keep company with George, and eventually to bring about his death, but whose appearance also, it should be noted, gives warning of the approaching death of Robert. During the entire period of the visitation, Robert was confined to his chamber, suffering from the delusion that he was two persons:—

> "When I lay in bed, I deemed there were two of us in it; when I sat up, I always beheld another person, and always in the same position from the place where I sat or stood, which was about three paces off me towards my left side. It mattered not how many or how few were present; this my second self was sure to be present in his place, and this occasioned a confusion in all my words and ideas that utterly astounded my friends, who all declared that, instead of being deranged in my intellect, they had never heard my conversation manifest so much energy or sublimity of conception; but, for all that, over the singular delusion that I was two persons my reasoning faculties had no power. The most perverse part of it was that I rarely conceived *myself* to be any of the two persons. I thought for the most part that my companion was one of them, and my brother the other."[74]

Robert, it will be noted, sees the other person on his left hand. George meantime is haunted by the constant appearance of his brother on his right — the very position demanded by the verse from Psalm 109.

In terms of assumed time in the novel, all this is preceded by the *doppelganger*'s first appearance, narrated by Robert in his "Memoir". Apparently this results from a blessing rather than a curse — the revelation to the Rev. Robert Wringhim that his namesake and ward has been admitted to the company of the just made perfect, and that, as a consequence, he will "set his face against sin, and sinful men, and resist even to blood, as many of the faithful of this land have done, and your reward shall be double".[75] (There is a fine ambiguity in the last word.) An exaltation of the spirit overtakes young Robert, and prepares him for the meeting with Gil-Martin, the great sovereign, who is also his twin. When he returns home, he is again blessed by his putative father. The terms used, however, are more meaningful if the Lord is identified, not with God, but with Gilmartin, whom young Wringhim always treats as an exalted person:—

> "'I give him unto Thee only, to Thee wholly, and to Thee for ever. I dedicate him unto Thee, soul, body and spirit. Not as the wicked of this world, or the hirelings of a Church profanely called by Thy name, do I dedicate this Thy servant to Thee; Not in words or form, learned by rote, and dictated by the limbs of Antichrist, but, Lord, I give him into Thy hand, as a captain putteth a sword into the hand of his sovereign, wherewith to lay waste his enemies. May he be a two-edged weapon in Thy hand and a spear coming out of Thy mouth, to destroy, and overcome, and pass over; and may the enemies of Thy Church fall down before him, and be as dung to fat the land!'"[76]

Mr Wringhim does not name the power to which he is dedicating young Robert, and again there is ambiguity in the phrase "a two-edged weapon".

As the end makes clear, the appearance of Gil-Martin is Hogg's ironic comment on these blessings, a point almost grasped by the Sinner himself when in the course of his last despairing flight he realises that he is still being pursued by his enemy:—

> "It was long before I durst look over my shoulder, but, when I did so, I perceived this ruined and debased potentate coming slowly on the same path, and I

prayed that the Lord would hide me in the bowels of the earth or depths of the sea. When I crossed the Tweed, I perceived him still a little behind me; and, my despair being then at its height, I cursed the time I first met with such a tormentor: though on a little recollection it occurred that it was at that blessed time when I was solemnly dedicated to the Lord, and assured of my final election, and confirmation, by an eternal decree never to be annulled. This being my sole and only comfort, I recalled my curse upon the time, and repented me of my rashness."[77]

It is a mark of the sinner's pride and wilful self-deceit that he regards his companion as the disguised Russian Czar, Peter the Great, who somewhat earlier had made his *incognito* visit to the British Isles. For the reader, the image of the ruined and debased Potentate has other and more sinister associations.

Prometheus Unbound has a political and ecclesiastic bias which the mature Hogg would have found unacceptable. Nor could two men have been more different than Hogg and Shelley in education or social background. They possess in common, however, a series of concepts and beliefs. These they derive from very different, but ultimately related, sources — Shelley from his reading of Plato and the Neoplatonists, the Caballa, alchemical literature and Gothic romance; Hogg primarily from the traditions of his own countryside. The two overlap, but naturally there are also cultural differences, not least, that Shelley's poetry was aimed at the Established and comfortable Church of England and the mode of government with which it was associated, Hogg's prose at some features of the no less established, but much less comfortable, Calvinist Kirk of Scotland and the loss of national independence, caused, Hogg seems to have felt, in some degree by the adherents to its doctrines. Shelley uses classical myth and Aeschylean drama; Hogg the more recently discovered form of the historical novel. The comparison between the two helps to bring out that the Calvinistic doctrine which governs the action of the *Confessions* is no more than a particular instance of a general human belief, equally exemplified in Plato, Plotinus and Shelley.

Hogg's attitude to fine historical detail remains cavalier, although not quite to the extent found in *The Three Perils of*

Man. To the casual reader, indeed, events may seem to be dated with unusual precision; thus we are told that the older George Colwan succeeded to the lands of Dalchastel and Balgrennan in 1687; young Robert Wringhim was welcomed into the community of the just upon earth on 25th March 1704; George Colwan was murdered on 18th February, 1705, and the suicide of Robert was on 18th February, 1712. Apart from the first, which is provided by the Editor in his preliminary "Narrative", all these dates are to be found in the second part, Robert Wringhim's autobiography, discovered when his grave was opened in 1823. Beneath this surface precision, a more careful reading reveals a host of inconsistencies. The marriage, for instance, of Miss Orde to the elder George Colwan clearly takes place after the latter had succeeded to his estates in 1687. Robert Wringhim is the second child of the marriage, and cannot have been born before, say, 1689. Yet he subsequently states that on 15th March 1704, he had just entered the eighteenth year of his age.

Again, it is fairly clear from the Editor's "Narrative" that Mrs Logan made the acquaintance of Arabella Calvert some eighteen months after the murder of George Colwan in 1705, that is to say, in the autumn or early winter of 1706. The immediately subsequent actions of these two cause the final flight of Robert from Dalchastel. Robert's diary, however, puts the events of the flight some six years later, in the year 1712, a date confirmed by his reference to James Watson as Queen's Printer, an appointment taken up by him in 1711, although he had then been in the printing trade for some time.

Hogg may have intended no more than to pepper his narrative with individual, unconnected references to a particularly significant period. The latest date to be mentioned in "Introduction" or "Memoir" is 1715; The Honourable Thomas Drummond, falsely accused of George Colwan's murder, "became a distinguished officer in the Austrian service, and died in the memorable year for Scotland, 1715",[78] the year, that is to say, of the first Jacobite rising in favour of the Old Pretender, the son of James VII. We are perhaps meant to understand that (unlike his counterpart in the historical record) Drummond played some role in the rising, and was killed in action.

The political ambience of the novel is thus clear. The earliest date mentioned is 1687, one year before the accession of William of Orange, whose replacement of James VII created the Jacobite movement. A document discovered after the death of the elder George Colwan, granting him the lands of Kipplerig and Easter Knockward in return for the losses and hardship which Colwan had undergone "on behalf of his Majesty's rights and titles", was registered in the name of King James on 26th September, 1687.[79] The family estate is situated somewhere near Glasgow, in distinctively Whig and covenanting territory, likely to favour the Union. Just as clearly, both Georges are Tories — Cavaliers, as they were styled — opposed in politics and religion to the majority of their neighbours. The feud between the two brothers which leads to the murder of the elder takes place in Edinburgh in 1705, as an incident during the acrimonious last Scottish Parliament (1703-1707) which initiated and brought to eventual completion the Union of 1707, thus leading in due course to the Hanoverian (Whig) succession in Scotland as well as in England. Politically the brothers belong to opposing sides; George and his father are adherents of the Earl of Tullibardine, later Duke of Athol, a leading Jacobite, who had been induced to accept office by the Earl of Seafield's assurance that if he did so (in 1703 he became Lord Privy Seal), recognized Queen Anne, and supported the Government against the Country Party, he and his friends "would be tolerated as Episcopalians and allowed to have a share in the conduct of affairs". An indemnity was issued for all acts of treason since the Revolution. The Cavaliers were hostile to the Union in the form which it eventually took.

By contrast, Robert and his putative father, Wringhim, are Old or Revolution Whigs, who had consistently supported William of Orange, and who now favoured Union. Their leader was the Duke of Argyll, who in 1705 succeeded Queensberry as Commissioner representing the Monarch. The character of the party was well analysed by the Tory Earl of Cromarty, writing in 1703 to Queen Anne:—

> "Whig in Scotland hath a very different signification from what it hath in England; for by Whig I understand a party who principaly oun a design for parity in church Government by presbytry and are enimys to what is opposite to that, for, tho they be not against monarchy absolutely, yet it hath but the second place in their esteem. In this party are two classes, the one

who think presbytery of a divine right, and with those
it is a principal head of their religion, and all concerns
must cede to it: others of them, tho they esteem it
much, yet they will not readily either fight or suffer for
it: those are less enimys to monarchy than the first,
which is truely inconsistent with monarchy or any
government which wil not be subjected to their mode
of heirarchie or common-welth of pop's."[80]

[The Rev. Robert Wringhim is a Whig of the first kind,
"blowing the coal of revolutionary principles with all his
might".[81] The matter is not overemphasised, but Hogg insinu-
ates that the sins of the younger Robert are compounded by his
political allegiance,[82] and the constitutional developments to
which it led. George's death, in a sense, is the death of the old
Scotland; the succession of Robert is the establishment of the
new order, with consequences visible to all.

The recurrent amnesia which forms part of Robert's affliction
is powerfully represented, and may contribute to the overall
effect of temporal uncertainty. Increasingly he becomes aware of
gaps in his own perception of events. Something of the kind is
already implicit in the narrative of the illness suffered by him,
while his double was engaged in the persecution of George, but
it is after his succession to the estates of Dalchastel that they
become most prominent. The first example is his encounter with
Mrs Keeler, a woman of the neighbourhood, who claims that he
has seduced her daughter, a claim denied by him on the grounds,
chiefly, of the short time he has been in residence:—

>   "'And how long does your Christian reverence
> suppose you have remained in this place since the late
> laird's death?' said she.
>   'That is too well known to need recapitulation,' said
> I. 'Only a very few days, though I cannot at present
> specify the exact number; perhaps from thirty to forty,
> or so. But in all that time, certes, I have never seen
> either of your two daughters that you talk of. You
> must be quite sensible of that.'
>   My friend shook his head three times during this
> short sentence, while the woman held up her hands in
> amazement and disgust, exclaiming, 'There goes the
> selfrighteous one! There goes the consecrated youth,

who cannot err! You, sir, know, and the world shall
know, of the faith that is in this most just, devout, and
religious miscreant! Can you deny that you have
already been in this place four months and seven days?
Or that in that time you have been forbid my house
twenty times? Or that you have persevered in your
endeavours to effect the basest and most ungenerous of
purposes? Or that you *have* attained them?'"[83]

Mrs Keeler's explanation of his amnesia — that all the time he
has been drunk — closely parallels the excuse produced by
another Justified Sinner, Holy Willie, for his fornications, and is
not wholly denied by Robert, though it much offends his
sensibilities. His perplexities are increased by the appearance of
Linkum, the lawyer, with whom he had been doing more
underhand business of which he now has no recollection. A
subsequent bout of drinking leads to a longer gap in his
recollection, lasting for more than six months, in the course of
which he has apparently made away with his mistress, Mrs
Keeler's daughter, as well as his mother, for whom he has begun
to feel a passionate dislike. It is here that he attains the clearest
perception of his own divided personality, and receives a
significant response from his diabolic companion:—

> "'If this that you tell me be true,' said I, 'then is it as
> true that I have two souls, the one being all unconsci-
> ous of what the other performs; for as sure as I have at
> this moment a spirit within me, fashioned and destined
> to eternal felicity, as sure am I utterly ignorant of the
> crimes you now lay to my charge.'
> 'Your supposition may be true in effect,' said he.
> 'We are all subjected to two distinct natures in the same
> person. I myself have suffered grievously in that way.
> The spirit that now directs my energies is not that with
> which I was endowed at my creation. It is changed
> within me, and so is my whole nature. My former days
> were those of grandeur and felicity. But would you
> believe it? *I was not then a Christian.* Now I am. I have
> been converted to its truths by passing through the fire,
> and, since my final conversion, my misery has been
> extreme.'"[84]

R

Robert first realised his own duality when his double was engaged in the persecution of George. Here it is suggested that Gil-Martin is also responsible for the later crimes attributed to Robert. The reader is left to judge Gil-Martin's more metaphysical and more universal generalization.

It is impossible, however, to find in these bouts of amnesia any explanation of the dates which the Sinner gives for events in the latter stages of his life. Their effect is always to make him think that time has come to a halt, whereas the dates given for events are late rather than early. Time, in other words, has accelerated.

There remains one supplementary possibility. Hogg, like Scott and Galt, is concerned with the methods by which his story of the past has been transmitted to the present. Partly, the editor claims, it is based on documents — charters, justiciary records, and the "Memoir" which was preserved in the grave until its rediscovery in September, 1823. The chronology set out in these sources may be regarded as reliable. For the rest the Editor depends on local tradition, the shortcomings of which are most immediately presented in the third part of the book, the account of how he came into possession of the "Memoir". In this Hogg for once consents to caricature himself as the uncouth Ettrick Shepherd of *Noctes Ambrosianae*, present tenant of Eltrive, the Ault-Righ where the Sinner spent the last weeks of his life. The Editor is moved to action by a letter from Hogg, published in the August, 1823, number of *Blackwood's Magazine*, which gives an account, later proved unreliable, of popular traditions concerning the Sinner's suicide. In this letter, Hogg makes some attempt to put a date to events:—

> "A nephew of that Mr Anderson's who was with the hapless youth that day he died says that, as far as he can gather from the relations of friends that he remembers, and of that same uncle in particular, it was one hundred and five years next month (that is September 1823) since that event happened; and I think it likely that this gentleman's information is correct. But sundry other people, much older than he, whom I have consulted, pretend that it is six or seven years more. They say that they have heard that Mr James Anderson was then a boy of ten years of age; that he lived to an old age, upwards of fourscore, and it is two and forty years

since he died. Whichever way it may be, it was about that period some way: of that there is no doubt."[85]

Hogg's estimate, based on tradition, is that the Sinner died in September 1717, five years later than the date given by the "Memoir". The clumsiness and *naivete* of the writing emphasises the fact subsequently established by the Editor that the Shepherd is floundering in depths well beyond his historical skill. At the same time, it shows the difficulty, pointed out elsewhere by Hogg himself, of establishing a correlation between tradition and precise historical fact. If we classify *The Private Memoirs and Confessions of a Justified Sinner*, not as a historical novel, but as a novel of oral history, one of its most convincing features is the chronological distortion.

The possibility, of course, remains that Hogg ignored, or was incapable of controlling, fine chronological detail. The total effect of the novel, however, is one of control. The other historical details given are accurate within oral limits. Hogg seems himself to be aware of the difficulties.

One additional effect of the episode is certainly to make a distinction between the adherent of tradition, James Hogg, and the adherents of scientific method, the Editor and his friends, a distinction which helps to control the reader's total assessment of the novel, and which does not wholly favour the scientists. Their labours have only a limited success in clarifying the sequence of events. Their motives are mixed; they are impelled no more than partly by the scientific and psychological aspects of the quest; a ghoulish element of prying curiosity is also present, as is a mere thirst for souvenirs. To a degree they are caricatures of the less pleasant aspects of the Enlightenment; in Wordsworthian phrase, they are of the kind which would "peep and botanize upon his mother's grave". Laidlaw comes closest to Hogg (the author, that is to say as opposed to the Ettrick Shepherd who figures in the market scene of the action) in the metaphysical excitement which he displays at the discovery of the pamphlet:—

"'Grave, man!' exclaimed Laidlaw, who speaks excellent strong broad Scots: 'My truly, but ye grave weel! I wad esteem the contents o' that spleuchan as the most precious treasure. I'll tell you what it is, sir: I hae often wondered how it was that this man's corpse has been miraculously preserved frae decay, a hunder times langer than ony other body's, or than even a tanner's. But now I could wager a guinea, it has been for the preservation o' that little book. And Lord kens what may be in't! It will maybe reveal some mystery that mankind disna ken naething about yet.'"[86]

It is notable that Laidlaw (1780-1845), a former sheep-farmer and a close friend of Hogg, speaks Scots (in Hogg, always a validating signal) and is alone among the investigators in adopting a metaphysical point of view, which also, incidentally, brings out one of the scientifically interesting aspects of the situation, the reasons for the long preservation of the corpse, a matter ignored by the others. He is well laughed at for his pains by Walter Scott's son-in-law and future biographer, J. G. Lockhart, whose approach represents some limited aspects of the Enlightenment tradition. Lockhart has occasionally been credited with a hand in the composition of *The Private Memoirs and Confessions of a Justified Sinner*. There are many reasons for doubting this; an additional one is perhaps the fact that on this occasion Hogg's auctorial sympathies are so clearly with Laidlaw.

The novel, nevertheless, is so constructed as to make it possible for the reader to adopt a rationalistic approach; to interpret it, not so much as a record of fact, but rather as an account of the subjective experiences of an unbalanced criminal mind. Even if we admit that the account provided by Mrs Logan and Arabella Calvert derives from legal records rather than oral tradition, it might well still be regarded as suspect on the grounds that both are women of dubious character with marked hysterical tendencies. When Mrs Calvert witnessed, or thought she witnessed, the murder of young Colwan, her judgement was likely to be clouded:—

> "'You shall hear. I had been abandoned in York, by an artful and consummate fiend; found guilty of being art and part concerned in the most heinous atrocities, and, in his place, suffered what I yet shudder to think of. I was banished the country — begged my way with my poor outcast child up to Edinburgh, and was there obliged, for the second time in my life, to betake

myself to the most degrading of all means to support two wretched lives. I hired a dress, and betook me, shivering, to the High Street, too well aware that my form and appearance would soon draw me suitors enow at the throng and intemperate time of the parliament. On my very first stepping out to the street, a party of young gentlemen was passing. I heard by the noise they made, and the tenor of their speech, that they were more than mellow, and so I resolved to keep near them, in order, if possible, to make some of them my prey. But just as one of them began to eye me, I was rudely thrust into a narrow close by one of the guardsmen. I had heard to what house the party was bound, for the men were talking exceedingly loud, and making no secret of it: so I hasted down the close, and round below to the one where their rendezvous was to be; but I was too late, they were all housed and the door bolted. I resolved to wait, thinking they could not all stay long; but I was perishing with famine and like to fall down.'"[87]

At York she had been publicly flogged and branded before her expulsion from the city; in Edinburgh, her prostitute's dress made her the target of attention by the City Guard. She was starving. She had just completed a humiliating act of intercourse with the man she picked up on the street when she saw, or claimed to see, the murder of young Colwan by Wringhim and another who had taken on the appearance of the Honourable Thomas Drummond. The incident was visible only by the light of the moon and from the third-floor window of a shabby little tavern some distance away from the scene. Her claim, finally, to be an Englishwoman of quality fallen on evil times is thrown in some doubt by the Scots words and phrases with which her speech is larded — in the passage quoted, "art and part" and "throng" (Scots "thrang") are examples. In any court of law her evidence would be regarded with some suspicion. Yet it is at once accepted by Mrs Logan.

"'The dark suspicions of my late benefactor have been just, and his last prediction is fulfilled,' cried she. 'The murderer of the accomplished George Colwan

has been his own brother, set on, there is little doubt,
by her who bare them both, and her directing angel,
the self-justified bigot. Aye, and yonder they sit,
enjoying the luxuries so dearly purchased, with perfect
impunity! If the Almighty do not hurl them down,
blasted with shame and confusion, there is no hope of
retribution in this life. And, by his might, I will be the
agent to accomplish it!'"[88]

An element of self-interest forms an obvious part of the
conviction thus expressed. Mrs Logan herself has been the
mistress of the elder George Colwan, and after his death had
retained possession of some of his property in a way that the
Wringhims at least regarded as criminal. She seems anxious to
obtain more. She is animated by a vindictive spirit, in particular
towards the Sinner's mother, whose place she had taken in the
Colwan household. She regards the elder Wringhim as the evil
angel of the group. All in all, she might easily be presented as a
being more or less on a parallel with Bell Calvert.

The tendency, finally, of both women to a contagious kind of
hysteria is shown by their behaviour at Dalchastel, when they
first catch sight of young Wringhim and his sinister companion.
Mrs Logan recovers from the fainting fits induced by the
encounter:—

> "'O, Mrs Calvert, hold me, else I shall fall into
> hysterics again! Who is he? Who is he? Tell me who
> you suppose he is, for I cannot say my own thought.'
>
> 'On my life, I cannot remember.'
>
> 'Did you note the appearance of the young gentle-
> man you saw slain that night? Do you recollect aught
> of the appearance of my young master, George
> Colwan?'
>
> Mrs Calvert sat silent, and stared the other mildly in
> the face. Their looks encountered, and there was an
> unearthly amazement that gleamed from each, which,
> meeting together, caught real fire, and returned the
> flame to their heated imaginations, till the two associ-
> ates became like two statues, with their hands spread,
> their eyes fixed, and their chops fallen down upon their
> bosoms. An old woman who kept the lodging-house,

having been called in before when Mrs Logan was fainting, chanced to enter at this crisis with some cordial; and seeing the state of her lodgers, she caught the infection, and fell into the same rigid and statue-like appearance. No scene more striking was ever exhibited; if Mrs Calvert had not resumed strength of mind to speak, and break the spell, it is impossible to say how long it might have continued. 'It is he, I believe,' said she, uttering the words as it were inwardly. 'It can be none other than he. But, no, it is impossible! I saw him stabbed through and through the heart; I saw him roll backward in the green in his own blood, utter his last words, and groan away his soul. Yet, if it is not he, who can it be?'

'It *is* he!' cried Mrs Logan, hysterically.

'Yes, yes, it *is* he!' cried the landlady, in unison.

'It is who?' said Mrs Calvert; 'whom do you mean, mistress?'

'Oh, I don't know! I don't know! I was affrighted.'

'Hold your peace then till you recover your senses, and tell me, if you can, who that young gentleman is, who keeps company with the new Laird of Dalcastle?'

'Oh, it is he! it is he!' screamed Mrs Logan, wringing her hands.

'Oh, it is he! it is he!' cried the landlady, wringing hers.

Mrs Calvert turned the latter gently and civilly out of the apartment, observing that there seemed to be some infection in the air of the room, and she would be wise for herself to keep out of it."[89]

The evidence that the second young gentleman had the appearance of George Colwan is thoroughly unsatisfactory — it would be laughed out of any court. Bell Calvert seems to have had no idea of a resemblance until she was touched by Mrs Logan's contagious hysteria, which also infects the landlady. The metaphorical language used to describe the emotional transfer is better than Freudian, an astonishing piece of psychological insight for an author of the early nineteenth century. The effect, however, is to cast doubts on the conclusion which both women come to accept as gospel truth.

Unfortunately for the reader's peace of mind, Hogg does not allow the matter to rest there. Independent evidence goes some way to confirm that the women's testimony is, at least to a degree, trustworthy. In most aspects, Wringhim's account of George Colwan's death contradicts Bell Calvert's by making his own part in the affair seem at once more active and more creditable. This is more or less what one might expect; but the words which follow put the matter in a different light, and at the same time establish the presence of at least one external, probably male, witness to the murder, who can only be the man whom Bell had picked up from the street, and whose accusations of unfair play she had herself claimed to hear. Wringhim is the speaker:—

> "I will not deny, that my own immediate impressions of this affair in some degree differed from this statement. But this is precisely as my illustrious friend described it to me afterwards, and I can rely implicitly on his information, as he was at that time a looker-on, and my senses all in a state of agitation, and he could have no motive for saying what was not the positive truth.
>
> Never till my brother was down did we perceive that there had been witnesses to the whole business. Our ears were then astounded by rude challenges of unfair play, which were quite appalling to me; but my friend laughed at them, and conducted me off in perfect safety."[90]

If a male by-stander were present, and capable of seeing what was happening, it seems reasonable to conclude that Bell also was there, and that her narrative of events is at least approximately correct. Indeed, Wringhim himself later confirms her presence, if in somewhat dubious terms:—

> "It seems, that about this time, I was haunted by some spies connected with my late father and brother, of whom the mistress of the former was one. My brother's death had been witnessed by two individuals; indeed, I had always an impression that it was witnessed by more than one, having some faint recollec-

tion of hearing voices and challenges close beside me; and this woman had searched about until she found these people; but, as I shrewdly suspect, not without the assistance of the only person in my secret, — my own warm and devoted friend. I say this, because I found that he had them concealed in the neighbourhood, and then took me again and again where I was fully exposed to their view, without being aware."[91]

Wringhim retains some doubts — one notices the introductory "It seems", qualifying the entire subsequent narrative. Characteristically, he is prepared to interpret the actions even of his "friend" in the most sinister light. The possibility remains that his "friend" may have influenced his recollections in this as in other matters. To a certain extent, nevertheless, his words further confirm Bell's narrative. Indeed, the sordid background admitted by both women — Mrs Logan, herself a kept woman, first discovers Bell as a prisoner in jail, under threat of death by hanging as a common thief, then later, when she has rescued her by perjury on the part of her maid-servant, hears the tale of her doings in Edinburgh — is itself a backhanded kind of guarantee of the authenticity of their evidence. Had either intended to deceive, she would have invented a story which reflected greater credit on herself. Equally, the tendency of the oral process is to glamourise events which fall within its ken. Neither form of activity seems illustrated by the narrative.

Wringhim himself also confirms that Gil-Martin's latter appearance is in George's form. When after six months of amnesia, he goes out walking, he meets someone whom at first he does not recognise:—

"At the extremity of the Colwan wood, I perceived a figure approaching me with slow and dignified motion. The moment that I beheld it, my whole frame received a shock as if the ground on which I walked had sunk suddenly below me. Yet, at that moment, I knew not who it was; it was the air and motion of someone that I dreaded, and from whom I would gladly have escaped; but this I even had no power to attempt. It came slowly onwards, and I advanced as slowly to meet it; yet when we came within speech, I still knew not who it was. It bore the figure, air, and features of my late brother, I thought, exactly; yet in all these there were traits so forbidding, so mixed with an appearance of misery, chagrin, and despair, that I still shrunk from the view, not knowing on whose face I looked. But when the being spoke, both my mental and bodily frame received another shock more terrible than the first, for it was the voice of the great personage I had so long denominated my friend, of whom I had deemed myself for ever freed, and whose presence and counsels I now dreaded more than hell. It was his voice, but so altered — I shall never forget it till my dying day. Nay, I can scarcely conceive it possible that any earthly sounds could be so discordant, so repulsive to every feeling of a human soul, as the tones of the voice that grated on my ear at that moment. They were the sounds of the pit, wheezed through a grated cranny, or seemed so to my distempered imagination."[92]

The sequence of events mirrors the first meeting of the two. Gil-Martin's initial words then, it will be recollected, were: "You think I am your brother".[93] At the time, Wringhim had not ever seen in the flesh the brother whose murderer he has now become, when Gil-Martin appears in the form of the murdered man. Voice alone reveals his earlier identity, the voice, which in terms of all that has gone before must be an echo of Wringhim's own, the voice too by which all his actions have been governed. Two factors are combined. The first is the visual; the horror felt by Wringhim results from encountering the likeness of the brother whom he had murdered. This primary effect is partly disguised by the words used — Wringhim does not want to admit to the fear that he is encountering a vengeful ghost, a situation familiar from ballads and folk-tales, but quite inappropriate in any context of the just man made perfect. The second is auditory, the shock of hearing a distorted version of the speech of his "friend" coming from the lips of the revenant. The distortion reflects his own distorted mind — it foreshadows the glimpse which he later receives of the ruined and debased potentate who limped behind him across the Tweed — but the power of the passage comes from the combined yet contradictory assault on Wringhim's sensibilities by the two primary human faculties, sight and hearing. Almost incidentally, the passage confirms Mrs Logan's belief that Wringhim is accompanied by someone in the likeness of his dead brother.

In his introduction to the influential 1947 reissue of the *Justified Sinner*, André Gide comments on the skill with which Hogg keeps open both possible interpretations of Gil-Martin; one that he is, in fact, Satan; the other, that he is nothing more than a projection of Wringhim's disordered mind.[94] In a measure, this is true. Throughout the book, both possibilities appear to remain valid. In interpreting this, it is tempting to remember Hogg's own dismissive classification of "George Dobson's Expedition to Hell" as a professional rather than a prophetic dream; it certainly indicates the nature of the approach to the supernatural generally adopted by him in the later stages of his career as a writer. "George Dobson" first appeared in 1827, three years after the failure of the *Justified Sinner*, five years after that of *The Three Perils of Man*. Personally, however, I am inclined to think that the lack of critical recognition for these two books, into which he had put the best of his intellect and imagination, had an inhibiting effect on Hogg, that after 1824 he was less willing to commit himself to the metaphysical positions he had previously sustained, more inclined to present them in a disguised and qualified way.[95] "Strange Letter of a Lunatic" lacks the subtle checks and balances present in the *Justified Sinner*; only in "On the Separate Existence of the Soul" with its defiant metaphysical introduction, does be return to his earlier stance. That story, it will be recollected, was published in London rather than Edinburgh. In the *Justified Sinner*, Hogg's final intention was, I think, to persuade the reader of the independent external existence of Gil-Martin as a supernatural agent.

Metaphysician though he may have been, Hogg was not a predestinarian in either the Calvinist or the Platonic sense. The Sinner allows himself to act as the pawn of Gil-Martin, but sometimes comes close to breaking the grip in which he is held. More than once, he makes a serious resolve to escape, most notably in the course of his abortive attempt to kill his brother by throwing him down from Arthur's Seat. George sets out first for the hilltop, and on his way there through the morning mist, experiences the almost supernatural sight of the "bright halo in the cloud of haze, that rose in a semi-circle over his head like a

pale rainbow",[96] by means of which he afterwards sees
Wringhim's distorted shadow as he prepares to ambush him. In
the same morning mist, Wringhim receives the clearest indication of his own moral predicament and his freedom to escape
from it, presented in terms which are allegorical, almost in the
fashion of the Morality play, and which are rendered doubly
effective by the very brevity of their presentation:—

> "In this desponding state, I sat myself down on a
> stone, and bethought me of the rashness of my underta-
> king. I tried to ascertain, to my own satisfaction,
> whether or not I really had been commissioned of God
> to perpetrate these crimes in his behalf, for in the eyes,
> and by the laws of men, they were great and crying
> transgressions. While I sat pondering on these things, I
> was involved in a veil of white misty vapour, and
> looking up to heaven, I was just about to ask direction
> from above, when I heard as it were a still small voice
> close by me, which uttered some words of derision and
> chiding. I looked intensely in the direction whence it
> seemed to come, and perceived a lady, robed in white,
> who hasted toward me. She regarded me with a
> severity of look and gesture that appalled me so much,
> I could not address her; but she waited not for that, but
> coming close to my side, said, without stopping,
> 'Preposterous wretch! how dare you lift your eyes to
> heaven with such purposes in your heart? Escape
> homeward, and save your soul, or farewell for ever!'
> These were all the words that she uttered, as far as I
> could ever recollect, but my spirits were kept in such a
> tumult that morning, that something might have
> escaped me. I followed her eagerly with my eyes, but
> in a moment she glided over the rocks above the holy
> well, and vanished. I persuaded myself that I had seen a
> vision, and that the radiant being that had addressed me
> was one of the good angels, or guardian spirits,
> commissioned by the Almighty to watch over the steps
> of the just. My first impulse was to follow her advice,
> and make my escape home; for I thought to myself,
> 'How is this interested and mysterious foreigner, a
> proper judge of the actions of a free Christian?'

> The thought was hardly framed, nor had I removed
> in a retrograde direction six steps, when I saw my
> illustrious friend and great adviser descending the ridge
> towards me with hasty and impassioned strides. My
> heart fainted within me; and when he came up and
> addressed me, I looked as one caught in a trespass."[97]

Even without the apparition of the lady in white, the Old
Testament phrase "a still small voice" is enough to indicate that
Wringhim still has an alternative course of action open to him, a
course of action which he might have followed, despite the
immediate intervention of his evil angel. The power and
significance of the voice of Gil-Martin has already been emphasised, but in this as in other episodes, it is neither still nor
small. In the Old Testament, the figure who corresponds to the
Sinner on Arthur's Seat, is the prophet Elijah, who has retreated
to Mount Horeb with motives for his action very similar to
those imposed on Wringhim by Gil-Martin and earlier by his
putative father. "I have been very jealous for the Lord God of
hosts: because the children of Israel have forsaken thy covenant,
thrown down thine altars, and slain thy prophets with the
sword; and I, even I only, am left; and they seek my life to take
it away."[98] In Scotland after 1690 this text was frequently in the
mouths of the faithful remnant, the Cameronians, of whose
extreme Calvinist wing Wringhim and his immediate family
were ardent representatives. The Sinner justified his actions in
terms of that text. Initially, Elijah holds the same egoistic point
of view: the honour of God depends on him alone. He is
corrected, first by the sensual contrast between nature in its more
spectacular manifestations — the great and strong wind, the
earthquake, the fire — which do not contain God, and the still
small voice which does; secondly, by the revelation that God
possesses resources of which he knew nothing. There is no need
to be jealous for God. For the Sinner, the best course of action is
simply to go home, as he has begun to do when he allows Gil-
Martin to prevent him.

The passage contains other verbal indications of the true state
of affairs — in particular, the Lady is angry with him because he
is about to pray, not for help to express penitence, but for advice
on whether or not he should commit what he himself calls a
crime. The phrase used, "whether or not I had been commis-

sioned of God to perpetrate these crimes in his behalf", carries its own self-evident answer, and, as the Lady points out, Wringhim's inability to see that, reveals the peril in which his soul stands, although, as she also indicates, salvation is still possible. The Lady, incidentally, unlike Gil-Martin, is in no sense Wringhim's *doppelganger*: she is a genuinely external figure.

Hogg is less entangled than Wringhim in questions of predestination, and at one point, speaking through the mouth of the latter's manservant, Penpunt, a staunch, but ignorant, Cameronian, allows himself to comment on the doctrine and its adherents, using as his vehicle the story of the famous town of Auchtermuchty. Penpunt purports to be recounting the words of Lucky Shaw, one of the witch-wife inhabitants of Dalchastel clachan, who describes how the people of Auchtermuchty had become so devout as to cause consternation among the devils of Hell. The countermeasure was to send one of their number to preach a sermon on an appropriate text:—

> "The eyes of all the congregation were riveted on the sublime stranger, who was clothed in a robe of black sackcloth, that flowed all around him, and trailed far behind, and they weened him an angel, come to exhort them, in disguise. He read out his text from the Prophecies of Ezekiel, which consisted of these singular words: 'I will overturn, overturn, overturn it; and it shall be no more, until he come, whose right it is, and I will give it him'."[99]

The sermon produced a delighted conviction of damnation on the part of all the inhabitants. "Nothing in the world delights a truly religious people so much, as consigning them to eternal damnation"[100] — a fate which the people of Auchtermuchty avoided only by the intervention of Robin Ruthven, who "just took haud o' the side an' wide gown, an' in sight o' a' present, held it aside as high as the preacher's knee, and, behold, there was a pair o' cloven feet!"

> "The auld thief was fairly catched in the very height o' his proud conquest, an' put down by an auld carle. He could feign nae mair, but gnashing on Robin wi' his teeth, he dartit into the air like a fiery dragon, an'

keust a reid rainbow our the taps o' the Lowmonds."[101]

The ostensible purpose of the fable is to demonstrate that someone who looks and sounds fair (like Gil-Martin in his first appearance) may none the less be Satan in disguise. The immediate moral is "Look for the cloven foot". But there is more to the tale. The method used by Satan to bring about his purposes is as important as his eventual exposure. He successfully exploits the fact that his audience (like Wringhim) holds to the doctrine of predestination — whether to destruction or salvation makes little difference. In addition, the text (Ezekiel 21.27), on which he preaches, is one he can use to flatter his congregation. In fact, it prophesies the fall of Jerusalem in 586 BC, but the preacher makes it refer, not to the Holy City, but to Auchtermuchty, and in the process identifies the Chosen People with the inhabitants of that small town, an identification which they accept and extend with enthusiasm. "'He is a prophet of the Lord,' said one, 'sent to warn us, as Jonah was sent to the Ninevites.' 'O, he is an angel sent from heaven, to instruct this great city,' said another, 'for no man ever uttered truths so sublime before.'"[102] (Nineveh, according to the book of Jonah, contained "more than sixscore thousand persons that cannot discern between their right hand and their left hand; and also much cattle."[103] Auchtermuchty is built on a smaller scale.) The failure, in other words, of the people of Auchtermuchty is not so much that they have failed to penetrate the preacher's disguise; rather, it is an over-assessment of their own importance; the failure, already discussed, of Elijah and Wringhim to recognise, when they heard it, the meaning of the still small voice, with implications well brought out by Lucky Shaw, although Penpunt, the Cameronian, wholly fails to understand them. The chief fault of the people of Auchtermuchty is spiritual pride, the sole remedy for which is the recognition of the humanity which is common to all men and women:—

> "'Now, this is a true story, my man,' quo the auld wife; 'an' whenever you are doubtfu' of a man, take auld Robin Ruthven's plan, an' look for the cloven foot, for it's a thing that winna weel hide; an' it appears whiles where ane wadna think o't. It will keek out frae

aneath the parson's gown, the lawyer's wig, and the Cameronian's blue bannet; but still there is a gouden rule whereby to detect it, an' that never, never fails.' — The auld witch didna gie me the rule, an' though I hae heard tell o't often an' often, shame fa' me an I ken what it is!"[104]

The golden rule is to be found in Matthew 7.12., "Therefore all things whatsoever ye would that men should do to you, do ye even so to them: for this is the law and the prophets". Wringhim is able to apply it to his own case, but fails in an extraordinary way to realise the implications for Gil-Martin:—

> "I then went to try my works by the Saviour's golden rule, as my servant had put it into my head to do; and, behold, not one of them would stand the test. I had shed blood on a ground on which I could not admit that any man had a right to shed mine; and I began to doubt the motives of my adviser once more, not that they were intentionally bad, but that his was some great mind led astray by enthusiasm, or some overpowering passion."[105]

Wringhim's somewhat mechanical application of the rule comes close to Hutcheson's mathematical calculation on subjects of morality mentioned in the first chapter of this book, while his refusal to apply the full rigour of Lucky Shaw's prescription to his patron approaches sentimentality, in the eighteenth century sense of the word, rather than the rational process of deduction required. When eventually he is forced to ask himself whether his friend may not in fact be the devil, his rejection of the idea is couched in terms of the grossest superstition. The theologian who had once prided himself on his acuity has sunk beneath the level of Penpunt.

> "I was even so weak, as, the next time I met with him, to look stedfastly at his foot, to see if it was not cloven into two hoofs. It was the foot of a gentleman, in every respect, so far as appearances went, but the form of his counsels was somewhat equivocal, and if not double, they were amazingly crooked."[106]

The Sinner's knowledge of metaphor has survived his power
to apply it. At this point he is forced into the flight which ends in
his despairing suicide. The Golden Rule has established a moral
norm, against which the reader must judge the extent of his
perversion, the first cause of which has been the idea of
predestined justification.

Scott and Galt both saw obsession in the individual as a
possible instrument for general human advancement. Jeannie
Deans and Claude Walkinshaw, in very different ways, are
examples. Both authors realised the *quantum* of suffering involved, and set it against the ultimate general gain which, in their
opinion, more than counterbalanced any personal loss. Hogg saw
the same society as the other two, but interpreted it with a
different and, at least in *The Private Memoirs and Confessions of a
Justified Sinner*, with a more pessimistic emotional emphasis.
Scott on occasion approaches his manner. *St Ronan's Well*, for
instance, published in the same year as Hogg's novel, is an
obsessional and destructive tragedy of fraternal strife, set in the
nineteenth century, but in overall effect much resembling
Hogg's work. Hogg remains unique, however, in the complexity of the metaphysical psychology which he brought to bear on
the development of his theme.

NOTES

Interest in the novels of James Hogg was rekindled by the London 1947
edition of *The Private Memoirs and Confessions of a Justified Sinner*, with an
Introduction by André Gide. Later editions, with more elaborate apparatus, are
those by John Carey (Oxford, 1969: paperback ed., 1981 and subsequent
reprints), and by John Wain (Penguin Books, Harmondsworth, 1983). Douglas
Gifford edited *The Three Perils of Man: War, Women and Witchcraft* (ASLS,
Edinburgh and London, 1972): Douglas S. Mack *The Brownie of Bodsbeck*
(Edinburgh and London, 1976), and *Selected Stories and Sketches* (ASLS,
Edinburgh, 1982); he had previously brought out *Memoir of the Author's Life
and Familiar Anecdotes of Sir Walter Scott* (Edinburgh and London, 1972), and
has since produced *Anecdotes of Sir Walter Scott* (Edinburgh, 1983). David
Groves edited *Tales of Love and Mystery* (Edinburgh 1985).

Douglas Mack also produced *James Hogg, Selected Poems* (Oxford, 1970).

Critical and biographical studies are Edith C. Batho, *The Ettrick Shepherd*
(Cambridge, 1927): A.L. Strout, *The Life and Letters of James Hogg* (Vol. 1,
Lubbock, 1946; the second volume did not appear, but a typescript is in NLS);
L. Simpson, *James Hogg, A Critical Study* (Edinburgh and London, 1962);

Douglas Gifford, *James Hogg* (Edinburgh, 1976): Nelson C. Smith, *James Hogg* (Boston, 1980).

Where possible, quotations are from texts listed above. Carey's edition is used for *The Private Memoirs and Confessions of a Justified Sinner*.

1. A.D. Woozley (ed.), *An Essay Concerning Human Understanding* (London and Glasgow, 1964), pp.89-90. Locke's inadequacy, as mentioned in the text, springs from a failure to attach sufficient weight to the medieval, ultimately Aristotelian, differentiation of the Active and the Passive Intellect. "Over and above therefore passive reason, which receives, combines and compares the various objects of thought, Aristotle recognises a creative reason which *makes* objects of thought, which renders the world intelligible, and bestows on the materials of knowledge those ideas or categories which make them accessible to thought" (E. Wallace, *Outlines of the Philosophy of Aristotle*, Cambridge, 1883, p. 92). "This creative power is called active intelligence (*intellectus agens*), and in opposition to it the mind or the intelligence in which the impression is produced, under the twofold influence of the corporeal beings and the *intellectus agens*, is called *intellectus possibilis* (Maurice de Wulf, *The System of Thomas Aquinas*, New York, 1959, first published as *Medieval Philosophy Illustrated from the System of Thomas Aquinas*, New York, 1922, p.25).

2. I have particularly in mind Douglas S. Mack (ed.), *Familiar Anecdotes of Sir Walter Scott* , p.108: "When The Three Perils of Man appeared he read me a long lecture on my extravagance in demonology and assured me I had ruined one of the best tales in the world". It is chiefly the metaphysical presence, I think, which explains Scott's unwillingness to allow any suggestion of ancestral relationship between the Dukes of Buccleuch and the superstitious but resourceful pivotal figure of the plot, who in the published text appears as Sir Ringan Redhough, but at the proof stage was still Sir Walter Scott of Buccleuch. Hogg later removed the supernatural machinery to produce the less effective *Siege of Roxburgh* (1832). He adds the rueful comment: "It is manifest however that the tale had made no ordinary impression on him (Scott) as he subsequently copied the whole of the main plot into his tale of Castle Dangerous". This is unfair; Scott (and Hogg also) owes his plot to a story told in *The History of the House of Douglas and Angus* by David Hume of Godscroft (c.1560-1630). It is because Scott was familiar with this version that he calls it one of the best tales in the world.

   Scott's own attitude to the supernatural, at least in his later years, is demonstrated by a sentence from *Letters on Demonology and Witchcraft* (London, 1830; reissued with introduction by H. Morley, London, 1884: facsimile of this latter, Wakefield, 1968), p.320; "Even the present fashion of the world seems to be ill suited for studies of this fantastic nature; and the most ordinary mechanic has learning sufficient to laugh at the figments which in former times were believed by persons far advanced in the deepest knowledge of the age".

3. Mack, *Selected Stories and Sketches* , p.204.

4. *op.cit.*, p.180.

5. "Meditation VI. Of the Existence of Material Things, and of the Real

Distinction between the Mind and Body of Man". I quote the translation by John Veitch (*A Discourse on Method, Etc.*, Everyman's Library, Letchworth, 1912 and reprints), pp.132-3.

6. Mack, *op.cit.*, pp.41-2.

7. pp.7-8. The quotation is from *The Wars of Truth* (Cambridge, Mass., 1952), pp.303-4.

8. *Treatise of Human Nature* I.iv.5. Selby-Biggs ed., pp.240-1.

9. Mack, *op.cit.*, p.191.

10. *op.cit.*, p.194.

11. Mack, *Selected Poems*, pp.32-43.

12. Hogg sets the second and third of *The Three Perils of Women* (1823) against the background (wildly unhistorical in detail) of the '45. He also produced two series of *The Jacobite Relics of Scotland* (1819 and 1821), but these are not limited to the '45.

13. pp.104-5.

14. Mack, *Selected Stories and Sketches*, p.1.

15. J.M. Stratton and Jack Houghton Brown, *Agricultural Records AD 220-1977* (2nd. ed., edited Ralph Whitlock, London, 1978), pp.67, 74.

16. *op.cit.*, p.71.

17. *op.cit.*, p.83.

18. *op.cit.*, pp.15-16.

19. *op.cit.*, pp.16-17.

20. Kinsley, *Burns*, I. p.171.

21. Mack, *op.cit.*, p.5.

22. *op.cit.*, p.18.

23. *op.cit.*, p.188.

24. *op.cit.*, p.42.

25. W.K. Wimsatt Jr. and Frederick A. Pottle (eds.), *Boswell for the Defence 1769-1774* (London, 1960), p.336.

26. *op.cit.*, pp.341-2.

27. Mack, *op.cit.*, p.47.

28. *op.cit.*, p.42.

29. *op.cit.*, p.44.

30. Above, p.196.

31. Mack, *op.cit.*, p.42.

32. *op.cit.*, p.158.

33. *op.cit.*, p.165.

34. L.A. Selby-Bigge (ed.), *Enquiries Concerning Human Understanding and Concerning the Principles of Morals by David Hume* (3rd ed., Oxford, 1975), pp.109-31.

35. *The Private Memoirs and Confessions of a Justified Sinner*, p.xxxii. This is perhaps the place to note that Professor Carey's gloss of the word *aumuses* on p.261 of his edition (the word itself appears on p.198 in the course of Lucky Shaw's monologue) is certainly mistaken. The word has nothing to do with *amice* or *almuce*; it is simply a variant spelling of the common word *awmous*, "alms", in the concrete sense of "food or money given in charity to the poor" and so capable of a plural form. See SND, s.v. *awmous*. John Wain (p.243) accepts the false identification with *amice*.

36. D. Gifford (ed.), *The Three Perils of Man*, p.2.

37. Carey, *op.cit.*, p.220.
38. H. Harvey Wood (ed.), *James Watson's Choice Collection of Comic and Serious Scots Poems*, Vol. 1 (STS, Edinburgh, 1977).
39. The facsimile forms the frontispiece to the 1947 edition, but regrettably is absent from the paperback editions of 1981 and 1983. It plays a significant part in Hogg's creation of the illusion of historical actuality.
40. As Walter Scott became Sir Walter in 1820, he is not likely to be Hogg's "Mr S...t" (p.247).
41. Gifford, *op.cit.*, p.467.
42. *op.cit.*, p.468.
43. Above, p.205.
44. Mack, *op.cit.*, p.71.
45. See OED.
46. Gifford, *op.cit.*, pp.325-6.
47. pp.32-4.
48. J.A.W. Bennett and H.R. Trevor-Roper (eds.), *The Poems of Richard Corbett* (Oxford, 1955), pp.49-51. See especially lines 25-32.
49. p.45.
50. Sir James Jeans, *The Mysterious Universe* (Cambridge, 1930), p.94.
51. Gifford, *op.cit.*, p.144.
52. *op.cit.*, pp.166-7.
53. See especially *The Poetic Mirror* (1816)
54.
    He rode in his prayere,
    And cryed for his mysdede,
    He sayned hym in sypes sere,
    And sayde 'Cros Kryst me spede!'

    Nade he sayned himself, segge, bot prye,
    Er he watz war in þe wod of a won in a mote —
                    [(759-64)]
55. P.M. Matarasso (trs.), *The Quest of the Holy Grail* (Harmondsworth, 1969), pp.128-9.
56. Gifford, *op.cit.*, pp.294-6.
57. The true reading, surely, must be "slumber", not "slubber"?
58. *op.cit.*, pp.303-4.
59. *op.cit.*, p.318.
60. *op.cit.*, p.458.
61. Above, p.42.
62. Carey, *op.cit.*, p.240.
63. *op.cit.*, pp.221-2.
64. 107d6-e4; Edith Hamilton and Huntington Cairns (eds.), *The Collected Dialogues of Plato* (Bollingen Series LXXI, Princeton 1961 and reprints), p.89.
65. 617e1-2: *op.cit.*, p.841.
66. *Ennead* III.4: A.H.Armstrong (ed. and trs.), *Plotinus* (7 vols., Loeb Classical Library, Cambridge, Mass. and London, 1966-), Vol.3, pp.142-61.
67. *Ennead* III.4.6.; *op.cit.*, vol. 3, pp.154-7.
68. Carey, *op.cit.*, pp.116-7.
69. *op.cit.*, p.90.

70. *op.cit.*, p.183. On p.178 Lawyer Linkum comments on the resemblance between Wringhim's "friend" and "the young laird who was murdered". Although Wringhim gives no overt hint of seeing the resemblance, he grows pale. The full recognition that Gilmartin has adopted the physical shape of his elder brother is reserved for p.188.

71. *op.cit.*, p.214.

72. *op.cit.*, pp.216-7.

73. *op.cit.*, p.32.

74. *op.cit.*, p.154.

75. *op.cit.*, p.115.

76. *op.cit.*, p.122.

77. *op.cit.*, pp.229-30.

78. *op.cit.*, p.92.

79. *op.cit.*, pp.179-80.

80. David Daiches, *Scotland and the Union* (London, 1977), p.61.

81. *op.cit.*, p.60.

82. Carey, *op.cit.*, p.20.

83. *op.cit.*, p.175.

84. *op.cit.*, pp.191-2.

85. *op.cit.*, p.243.

86. *op.cit.*, pp.252-3.

87. *op.cit.*, pp.70-1.

88. *op.cit.*, pp.78-9.

89. *op.cit.*, pp.82-4.

90. *op.cit.*, p.171.

91. *op.cit.*, pp.204-5.

92. *op.cit.*, p.188. Cf. above, footnote 70.

93. *op.cit.*, p.117.

94. pp.xv-xvi. Cf. also, Gifford, *James Hogg*, pp.158-65.

95. Cf. Gifford, *op.cit.*, pp.186-7.

96. Carey, *op.cit.*, pp.39-40.

97. *op.cit.*, pp.157-8.

98. I Kings, 19.10.

99. Carey, *op.cit.*, p.200.

100. *op.cit.*, p.201.

101. *op.cit.*, pp.202-3.

102. *op.cit.*, p.201.

103. Jonah, 4.11.

104. Carey, *op.cit.*, p.203.

105. *op.cit.*, p.204.

106. *loc.cit.*.

CHAPTER V

EPILOGUE: the End of the Enlightenment — Thomas Carlyle

Hogg, it should now be clear, belongs only partly, if still substantially, to the Enlightenment. Galt was the last major Scottish writer to feel that the achievement of the eighteenth century, however imperfect, had been the most significant in history, and the most worthy to engage his creative talents. With him, as with many of his predecessors, a recurrent theme had been to contrast the more distant and more-or-less unenlightened past with the more recent and more-or-less enlightened times which had ushered in the present. The contrast is never absolute, but over the course of years a gradual amelioration becomes visible. A similar contrast is to be found in the works of Galt's younger contemporary, Thomas Carlyle (1795-1881), but with differences of emphasis which show how completely a few years had changed the way in which the Enlightenment was regarded. Carlyle is not a novelist;[1] he is historian, publicist, moral commentator. He retains the tendency to concentrate on the seventeenth and eighteenth centuries. In terms of bulk, his three major works are *The French Revolution* (1837), *Oliver Cromwell's Letters and Speeches* (1845), and *Frederick the Great* (1857-65). Scotland and individual Scots, however, occupy relatively little space in either these, or his collected works generally, as also does, for instance, the spread of agricultural improvement. More important, the contrast of the nineteenth and enlightened eighteenth century with the past is almost always to the advantage of the latter. *Past and Present* (1843), *Latter-Day Pamphlets* (1850), are titles which speak for themselves, and these briefer works express in concentrated form the attitude which underlies his more extended productions. To a surprising extent, Carlyle is a medievalist.

The outlook of a man born in 1795, all this is to say, differed

radically from that of one born in 1779. The difference, no
doubt, is the result partly of temperament, partly of environment, but almost equally important is Carlyle's philosophical
shift from Scottish common-sense, with its French and English
antecedents, to German transcendentalism. The consequences are
substantial. Carlyle examined the same phase of society as had
Galt; he recognised the same features, but his interpretation
differed almost entirely. In the passage which follows,[2] he is
describing French society before the Revolution, but his France
recognisably shares features with the Scotland of *The Entail*. It
lacks totally, however, any sense of the benevolent force which,
for Galt, made particular evils engender general good:—

> "Remark, meanwhile, how from amid the wrecks
> and dust of this universal Decay, new Powers are
> fashioning themselves, adapted to the new time and its
> destinies. Besides the old Noblesse, originally of Figh-
> ters, there is a new recognised Noblesse of Lawyers;
> whose gala-day and proud battle-day even now is. An
> unrecognised Noblesse of Commerce; powerful
> enough, with money in its pocket. Lastly, powerfullest
> of all, least recognised of all, a Noblesse of Literature;
> without steel on their thigh, without gold in their
> purse, but with the "grand thaumaturgic faculty of
> Thought' in their head. French Philosophism has
> arisen; in which little word how much do we include!
> Here, indeed, lies properly the cardinal symptom of the
> whole widespread malady. Faith is gone out; Scepti-
> cism is come in. Evil abounds and accumulates; no man
> has Faith to withstand it, to amend it, to begin by
> amending himself; it must even go on accumulating.
> While hollow languor and vacuity is the lot of the
> Upper, and want and stagnation of the Lower, and
> universal misery is very certain, what other thing is
> certain? That a Lie cannot be believed! Philosophism
> knows only this: her other belief is mainly, that in
> spiritual supersensual matters no belief is possible.
> Unhappy! Nay, as yet the Contradiction of a Lie is
> some kind of Belief; but the Lie with its Contradiction
> once swept away, what will remain? The five unsat-
> iated Senses will remain, with sixth insatiable Sense (of

> vanity); the whole *daemonic* nature of man will remain
> — hurled forth to rage blindly without rule or rein;
> savage itself, yet with all the tools and weapons of
> civilization: a spectacle new in History."

The egalitarian Galt had been fascinated by the effects of "an ambitious, resolute, ostentatious mind" on society. Carlyle was less egalitarian: he characterised the "ambitious, resolute, ostentatious mind" as "Plugson of Undershot with his book-keeping by double entry",[3] and archaically saw society as dependent on Heroes, who in the eighteenth century, for the most part, had been corrupted or crippled, and in the nineteenth had virtually disappeared from the earth:—[4]

> "Society is founded on Hero-worship. All dignities
> of rank, on which human association rests, are what we
> may call a *Hero*archy (Government of Heroes) — or a
> Hierarchy, for it is 'sacred' enough withal. The Duke
> means *Dux*, leader; King is *Kön-ning*, *Kan-ning*, Man
> that *knows* or *cans*. Society everywhere is some represent-
> entation, not *in*supportably inaccurate, of a graduated
> Worship of Heroes; — reverence and obedience done
> to men really great and wise. Not *in*supportably
> inaccurate, I say! They are all as bank-notes, these social
> dignitaries, all representing gold; — and several of
> them, alas, always are *forged* notes. We can do with
> some forged false notes; with a good many even; but
> not with all, or the most of them forged! No: there
> have to come revolutions then; cries of Democracy,
> Liberty and Equality, and I know not what:— the
> notes being all false, and no gold to be had for *them*,
> people take to crying in their despair that there is no
> gold, that there never was any!"

The article which he called "Shooting Niagara: and After?"[5] (1867) is proof of the extent to which he came to fear a total breakdown of hierarchy in nineteenth century English society. There is a striking contrast with Galt's treatment, for instance, of the radical weavers of Cayenneville.

But it was the "gold", the sacred part of hierarchy, that held Carlyle — for social institutions, fossilized or seen in isolation, he had no more time than Galt. The proof is to be seen in his treatment of the great breakers of hierarchies — Luther, Knox, Cromwell. No one could ever call Carlyle a Tory, however much like a Tory he might on occasion behave. And his regard was not finally so much for great men, for "men really great and wise", as for their religion, the spiritual perceptions opened to them, which acted through them on society as a whole. The secularism of the Enlightenment has disappeared. *Heroes and Hero-worship* (1841) will provide a multitude of illustrative texts. "A man's religion is the chief fact with regard to him".[6] "The unseen and spiritual in them determined the outward and actual".[7] "The thing a man does practically lay to heart, and know for certain, concerning his vital relations to this mysterious Universe, and his duty and destiny there, that is in all cases the primary thing for him, and creatively determines all the rest."[8] It is by his religion, by his perception of the unseen and spiritual that a man becomes a Hero. "A Hero, as I repeat, has this first distinction which indeed we may call first and last, the Alpha and Omega of his whole Heroism, That he looks through the shows of things into *things*."[9] All through *Heroes and Hero-worship* the same note is repeated. Of Mahomet, for instance, he says, "Such light had come, as it could, to illuminate the darkness of this wild Arab soul."[10] Of Dante, "The deeper naturally would the Eternal World impress itself on him."[11] His phrase to characterize Shakespeare is "calm creative perspicacity."[12] Of Cromwell, he says, "It is very interesting, very natural, this 'conversion' as they well name it; the awakening of a great true soul from the worldly slough, to see into the awful *truth* of things; — to see that Time and its shows all rested on Eternity, and this poor Earth of ours was the threshold either of Heaven or of Hell!"[13]

"To look through the shows of things into *things*." It is at this point that the philosophy of Hero-worship overlaps the philosophy of Clothes, as set out in *Sartor Resartus*. One of Carlyle's favourite quotations is from the Earth-Spirit's speech in Goethe's *Faust*:—

> 'Tis thus at the roaring Loom of Time I ply,
> And weave for God the Garment thou see'st Him by.

Creation, that is to say, is the garment of God; symbolic because it makes God visible. All clothes are thus in some sense symbolic, or rather, all symbols are properly clothes — "all Forms whereby Spirit manifests itself to sense, whether outwardly or in the imagination, are Clothes."[14] "In the Symbol proper, what we can call a Symbol, there is ever, more or less distinctly and directly, some embodiment and revelation of the Infinite."[15] The power of the Hero is to see the meaning in the symbol, the God beneath the garment, and partly because of this power he is himself the most meaningful, the most creative of all symbols. But as clothes wear thin, so symbols woven on the Loom of Time wear out and must eventually be discarded. The underlying reality does not change, but the symbol which clothes it must be renewed. Carlyle's image is the Phoenix, self-renewing, but also self-consumed on a pyre which to the mere observer may appear entirely destructive — particularly so to one whose misfortune it is to live at a time when the pyre is burning. It was in this way that Carlyle saw his own period. In his earlier work he was able to look beyond the fire to the renewal, but as his long life moved towards its close, he was less and less able to take the long view.

All his life through, nevertheless, he was able to pinpoint the period in which the conflagration began. "'For the last three centuries'", he makes Teufelsdrockh cry,[16] "'above all for the last three quarters of a century, that same Pericardial Nervous Tissue (as we named it) of Religion, where lies the Life-essence of Society, has been smote at and perforated, needfully and needlessly till now it is quite rent into shreds; and Society, long pining diabetic, consumptive, can be regarded as defunct; for those spasmodic galvanic sprawlings are not life; neither indeed will they endure, galvanise as you may, beyond two days.'"

Society is Religion, and Religion has been dying for three centuries — since some time after 1500, that is to say, or since the era of the Reformation. I do not think that Carlyle ever consciously faced all the implications of his own statement. The son of a Calvinist household, who himself included among his heroes Luther, Knox and Cromwell, how could he? It is not likely that he would have accepted Tawney's hypothesis about Protestantism and the rise of Capitalism, a hypothesis, none the less, which squares absolutely with Carlyle's own observations. Carlyle's reaction was different. The conscious motivation of *Cromwell* and *Frederick the Great* was to show that the Puritan/Protestant element alone enabled Europe to struggle through these three centuries. One should especially consider *Frederick the Great* III,viii, the chapter headed "The Historical Meaning of the Reformation",[17] with its dramatic question, "Protestant or not Protestant? The question meant everywhere: 'Is there anything of nobleness in you, O Nation, or is there nothing? Are there, in this Nation, enough of heroic men to venture forward, and to battle for God's Truth *versus* the Devil's Falsehood, at the peril of life or more?'" In Prussia, he answered, there was; in France there was not, and the Massacre of St Bartholomew's Eve led directly to the Terror two centuries later. The two nations comically but magnificently meet in the encounters of Frederick with Voltaire, and inevitably Frederick is the winner. The conscious motivation, I repeat, is to show the positive significance of the Puritan/Protestant element in Europe — but a different significance is plainly enough written across the face of Carlyle's works as a whole, and indeed if one looks for a uniting factor, it is surely the break-down of European society with its religious basis, a break-down which began with the Reformation, and which continued through the careers of Cromwell and Frederick, the French Revolution, Chartism and the Reform Bill of 1867. As with Galt, the epic movement of three hundred years is Carlyle's theme, but he saw it as a movement from religion to capitalism (Mammonism) to destruction — a destruction from which the phoenix might, or might not, re-emerge in splendour.

This single theme unites all Carlyle's works. He set out to be a philosophic rather than a theoretical historian, one who did not confine himself to political, economic and social aspects, but tried to grasp the totality of an epoch, and to relate it, in Fichte's phrase, to the transcendental Divine Idea of the World. He was something more than a historian, that is to say, he was a Man of Letters, again as Fichte had used the term. I may perhaps quote his discussion in the lecture on "The Hero as Man of Letters":—[18]

> "Fichte the German Philosopher delivered, some forty years ago at Erlangen, a highly remarkable Course of Lectures on this subject: 'Ueber das Wesen des Gelehrten, On the Nature of the Literary Man.' Fichte, in conformity with the Transcendental Philosophy, of which he was a distinguished teacher, declares

first: That all things which we see or work with in this Earth, especially we ourselves and all persons, are as a kind of vesture or sensuous Appearance: that under all there lies, as the essence of them, what he calls the 'Divine Idea of the World'; thus is the Reality which 'lies at the bottom of all Appearance.' To the mass of men no such Divine Idea is recognisable in the world; they live merely, says Fichte, among the superficialities, practicalities and shows of the world, not dreaming that there is anything divine under them. But the Man of Letters is sent hither specially, that he may discern for himself, and make manifest to us, this same Divine Idea: in every new generation it will manifest itself in a new dialect; and he is there for the purpose of doing that."

Three points emerge clearly enough. The definition of Hero already discussed needs to be altered to admit the Man of Letters. The Man of Letters is the distinctively modern form of the Hero. Carlyle himself, on the evidence of his work as it has been discussed, is a modern heroic Man of Letters. It is perhaps necessary to add that in Carlyle's opinion only one modern Man of Letters — Goethe — had risen to his full heroic potentiality. The others whom he chose to discuss — Johnson, Rousseau, Burns — were all in some sense failures, had all been defeated by the unheroic age in which they had been fated to live. Carlyle probably regarded himself as another failure. But such hope as he had for the future lay in literature and Men of Letters — especially German Men of Letters. "The results of this last Period of German Literature are of deep significance," he wrote,[19] "the depth of which is perhaps but now becoming visible. Here too, it may be, as in other cases, the Want of the Age has first taken voice and shape in Germany; that change from Negation to Affirmation, from Destruction to Re-Construction, for which all thinkers in every country are now prepared, is perhaps already in action there. In the nobler Literature of the Germans, say some, lie the rudiments of a new spiritual era, which it is for this and for succeeding generations to work out and realise"

The history of literature, and especially of poetry, is thus for the modern world almost the most important kind of history, because it is only here that the beginnings of a new age are to be discerned, and, by and large, it is as Men of Letters that the Heroes of modern times and of the future will function. Equally the literature, the poetry, of the past is the best way to understand what manifestations the Divine Idea had taken in the past.[20]

> "A history of German, or of any national Poetry, would form, taken in its complete sense, one of the most arduous enterprises any writer could engage in. Poetry, were it the rudest, so it be sincere, is the attempt which man makes to render his existence harmonious, the utmost he can do for that end: it springs therefore from his whole feelings, opinions, activity, and takes its character from these. It may be called the music of his whole manner of being; and, historically considered, is the test how far Music, or Freedom, existed therein; how far the feeling of Love, of Beauty and Dignity, could be elicited from that peculiar situation of his, and from the views he there had of Life and Nature, of the Universe, internal and external. Hence, in any measure to understand the Poetry, to estimate its worth and historical meaning, we ask as a quite fundamental enquiry: What that situation was? Thus the History of a nation's Poetry is the essence of its History, political, economic, scientific, religious. With all these the complete Historian of a national Poetry will be familiar; the national physiognomy, in its finest traits, and through its successive states of growth, will be clear to him: he will discern the grand spiritual Tendency of each period, what was the highest Aim and Enthusiasm of mankind in each, and how one epoch naturally evolved itself from the other."

Carlyle however concerned himself not with the history of a single literature or a single nation, but in effect with the history of post-classical Europe under every aspect, a history which he saw in terms of three possible religions.[21] First was Heathenism — "plurality of gods, mere sensuous representation of this Mystery of Life, and for chief recognised element therein Physical Force." Second was Christianism — "faith in an

T

Invisible, not as real only, but as the only reality; Time, through every meanest moment of it, resting on Eternity." Third was the Scepticism which had characterised the Enlightenment — "uncertainty and inquiry whether there was an Unseen World, any Mystery of Life except a made one; — doubt as to all this, or perhaps unbelief and flat denial." Each was succeeded by the next as the dominating factor of an epoch, though each had a quality of permanence, a significance that did not disappear with the epoch which it dominated.

In some ways Carlyle's choice of literature to represent each epoch is odd — even haphazard or fortuitous; it is certainly to some extent governed by the fact that he had once intended to write a history of German literature. For all that, it is meaningful. Every work belongs to post-classical northern and western Europe. Heathenism is represented by Old Norse — in particular the Prose *Edda* of Snorri Sturlason (1178-1241), and to a lesser extent the *Heimskringla*. Carlyle would allow the thirteenth century German *Nibelungenlied* at least an ultimate origin in Heathenism, and is well aware of its connections with Scandinavian tradition. Christianism is represented primarily by Dante and Shakespeare, supported by Jocelin of Brakelond with his *Chronicle* of Bury St Edmunds (c.1200), Hugo von Trimberg, (c.1230-1313) the *Edelstein* (1349) of Boner, *Tyll Eulenspiegel* (1519) and *Reynard the Fox* (1498). Scepticism is represented primarily by Voltaire, while its effects are shown by the defeated Men of Letters, Johnson, Rousseau and Burns. The regenerative potential in modern Europe is primarily represented by Goethe.

Carlyle showed an almost Shakespearian perspicacity when in *Heroes and Hero-worship*[22] he classified the post-Reformation figure of Shakespeare with Dante as distinctively and typically medieval. "In some sense it may be said that this glorious Elizabethan Era with its Shakespeare, as the outcome and flowerage of all which had preceded it, is itself attributable to the Catholicism of the Middle Ages. The Christian Faith, which was the theme of Dante's song, had produced this Practical Life which Shakespeare was to sing. For Religion then, as it now and always is, was the soul of Practice; the primary vital fact in men's life. And remark here, as rather curious, that Middle-Age Catholicism was abolished, so far as Acts of Parliament could abolish it, before Shakespeare, the noblest product of it, made his appearance." As one might expect, the philosophic historian who composed some fragments of the epic of modern Europe was particularly impressed[23] by the fragmentary medieval epic of the *Histories*. "There are really, if we look at it, few as memorable Histories. The great salient points are admirably seized; all rounds itself off, into a kind of rhythmic coherence; it is, as Schlegel says *epic*." It is the historian of the French Revolution who speaks a few lines later about the Agincourt scenes in *Henry V* — "one of the most perfect things, in its sort, we anywhere have of Shakespeare's. The description of the two hosts: the worn-out jaded English, the dread hour, big with destiny, when the battle shall begin; and then that deathless valour: 'Ye good yeomen, whose limbs were made in England!'" In general however, and not merely in the *Histories*, Carlyle saw Shakespeare as occupying a position in relation to the life of Christianism and the Middle Ages much like the one he felt himself capable of occupying in relation to the life of modern times. The perspicacity of Shakespeare's vision was what he most emphasised, the seeing eye capable of singling out the detail significant for the over-all Christianism of the Middle Ages,[24] "Time through every meanest moment of it, resting on Eternity." Carlyle, it is true, regarded much of this as unconscious on Shakespeare's part:[25] he had "what I call an unconscious intellect; there is more virtue in it than he himself is aware of. Novalis beautifully remarks that those Dramas of his are Products of Nature too, deep as Nature herself." Nature, one must recollect, for Carlyle was the garment, the symbol, by which we become aware of God, and I am sure that here he intends us to give the word its fullest possible significance.

His assessment of Dante is no less completely integrated with his position as a philosophic historian. Shakespeare saw Time resting on Eternity; Dante saw the eternity on which Time rests.[26] "The earthly world had cast him forth to wander, wander; no living heart to love him now; for his sore miseries there was no solace here. The deeper naturally would the Eternal world impress itself on him; that awful reality over which, after all, this Time-world, with its Florences and banishments, only flutters as an unreal shadow." Or again,[27] "He is world-great not because he is world-wide, but because he is world-deep. Through all objects he pierces as it were down into the heart of being." Or again,[28] "It" (the *Comedy*) is a sublime embodiment, or sublimest, of the soul of Christianity. It expresses, as in huge world-wide architectural emblems, how the Christian Dante felt Good and Evil to be the two polar elements of this Creation, on which it all turns; that these two differ not by *preferability* of one to the other, but by incompatibility absolute and infinite; that the one is excellent and high as light and heaven, the other hideous, black as Gehenna and the Pit of Hell! Everlasting Justice, yet with Penitence, with everlasting Pity — all Christianism, as Dante and the Middle Ages had it, is emblemed here." The breadth of Carlyle's imaginative sympathy shows most clearly in his treatment of the *Purgatorio*, that part which his Calvinist ancestors would have found most impossible to tolerate doctrinally or imaginatively. Carlyle goes straight to the heart of the artistic achievement, despite the massed critical opinion of his age. The entire paragraph deserves quotation:—[29]

"I do not agree with much modern criticism, in greatly preferring the *Inferno* to the two other parts of the Divine *Commedia*. Such preference belongs, I imagine, to our general Byronism of taste, and is like to be a transient feeling. The *Purgatorio* and *Paradiso*, especially the former, one would almost say, is even more excellent than it. It is a noble thing, that *Purgatorio*, 'Mountain of Purification', an emblem of the noblest conception of that age. If Sin is so fatal, and Hell is and must be so rigorous, awful, yet in Repentance too is man purified; Repentance is the grand Christian act. It is beautiful how Dante works it out. The *tremolar dell' onde*, that 'trembling' of the ocean-waves, under the first pure gleam of morning, dawning afar on the wandering Two, is as the type of an altered mood. Hope has now dawned; never-dying Hope, if in company still with heavy sorrow. The obscure sojourn of daemons and reprobates is underfoot; a soft breathing of penitence mounts higher and higher, to the Throne of Mercy itself. 'Pray for me,' the denizens of that Mount of Pain all say to him. 'Tell my Giovanna to pray for me,' my daughter Giovanna; 'I think her mother loves me no more!' They toil painfully up by that winding steep, 'bent-down like corbels of a building,' some of them, — crushed-together so 'for the sin of pride;' yet nevertheless in years, in ages and

aeons, they shall have reached the top, which is
Heaven's gate, and by Mercy shall have been admitted
in. The joy too of all, when one has prevailed; the
whole Mountain shakes with joy, and a psalm of praise
rises, when one soul has perfected repentance and got
its sin and misery left behind! I call all this a noble
embodiment of a true noble thought."

In *Past and Present* Carlyle counterpointed the condition of
England in his own time against the achievement of the twelfth
century Abbot Samson of Bury St. Edmunds. *Past and Present*
was published in 1843, *Heroes and Hero-worship* in 1841. They
belong, that is to say, to much the same period of Carlyle's life;
indeed, to a considerable extent they are complementary — the
counterpointing of the present against the past is as obvious in
one as in the other. Abbot Samson is a lesser hero than Dante or
Shakespeare (in some ways, indeed, he comes close to being a
hero in the pattern established by Galt), but he belongs to the
same company. A transcendental eternity is always present to
him, as it never more than occasionally is even to Ringan
Gilhaize or Claud Walkinshaw.[30] "Heaven's splendour over his
head, Hell's darkness under his feet. A great Law of Duty, high
as these two Infinitudes, dwarfing all else, annihilating all else —
making royal Richard as small as peasant Samson, smaller if need
be!" The terms too of the counterpoint in *Past and Present* had
already been laid down in *Heroes and Hero-worship*, the over-all
view of the movement and relevance of history, time related or
misrelated to eternity by one of the three religions, Heathenism,
Christianism or Scepticism, with the Middle Ages as the one
period wholly dominated by Christianism, and so producing
such Men of Letters as Dante and Shakespeare, such men of
action as Abbot Samson. Carlyle did not think that his own time
should return to Christianism; some of his finest scorn, indeed, is
reserved for the Oxford Movement, which in one sense at least
was attempting just that; he did think that until a new equivalent
linked modern times to eternity as Christianism had linked the
Middle Ages, England (in which he included Scotland) would
remain in the strange ominous condition which he found around
him.[31] "With unabated bounty the land of England blooms and
grows; waving with yellow harvests; thick-studded with work-
shops, industrial implements, with fifteen millions of workers,

understood to be the strongest, and cunningest and the willingest our Earth ever had; these men are here; the work they have done, the fruit they have realised is here, abundant, exuberant on every hand of us: and behold, some baleful fiat as of Enchantment has gone forth, saying, 'Touch it not, ye workers, ye master-workers, ye master-idlers; none of you can touch it, no man of you shall be the better for it; this is enchanted fruit!'"

Little more than twenty years separates *Annals of the Parish* from *Past and Present*, but Carlyle has moved a long way from Balwhidder's faith in improvements and a benevolent Providence.

In Carlyle then, despite the apparent prominence of the seventeenth and eighteenth centuries, the real emphasis falls on the contrast between the Middle Ages and nineteenth-century England and Europe. The eighteenth-century Enlightenment is the period of intellectual corruption which produced modern degeneracy. Scotland receives little attention. One point however remains to suggest that Carlyle might have looked with profit at late medieval Scotland for material to support his hypotheses. I have already mentioned the *Edelstein* of Boner and the comic epic of *Reynard the Fox*, two works which Carlyle discussed at some length in the essay on "Early German Literature" which in 1830 appeared in the *Foreign Quarterly Review*. The *Edelstein* is a version of Aesop's fables, which appeared in 1349, and was first printed at Bamberg in 1461; the name is derived from the first fable, the tale of the Cock and the Jewel. *Reynard the Fox*, *Reinke de Vos*, was printed in a Low Saxon translation at Lübeck in 1498. With his customary accuracy, Carlyle sets these two works, together with the others already mentioned, in the context of the flourishing commercial activities of the Hanse League and the free cities generally of late medieval Germany; in the context too of the new German universities of the fourteenth and fifteenth centuries, and of the invention of the printing press. Neither the *Edelstein* nor the *Reynard*, it may be, will appear particularly important in twentieth century eyes. But Carlyle has not simply made a mistake; the fact that he has singled out genuinely representative works may be established by a comparison with the fifteenth century in Scotland, and the work of its major poet, Henryson, most of whose poems seem to have been written in the 1470's and 1480's. The relevance of Henryson's work to the present

study has already more than once been noted.[32] He knew his
Europe, and was a careful, often satirical, observer of the social,
political and religious institutions of his day. He was also a
university man, a lawyer who during the 1460's taught in the
new university of Glasgow, but whose humanist interests, it
seems probable, led him to become master of the important
grammar school at Dunfermline. Scotland in the fifteenth
century was undergoing developments which paralleled those in
Germany. The merchants and their burghs were increasing in
importance; new universities were being founded, and printed
books were coming into extensive use. In Henryson, then, we
have a remarkable man, possessed of some of the qualities which
Carlyle regarded as heroic, living at the time when the *Edelstein*
and *Reinke de Vos* first appeared in print. His most extensive
work, generally if inaccurately known as the *Morall Fabillis of
Esope the Phrygian*, is based on the same collection as the *Edelstein*,
and begins with the same story of the Cock and the Jewel — in
Henryson's version the *Cok and the Jasp*. With the Aesopic
material, Henryson combined a number of tales derived from
the beast-epic of Reynard the Fox. Three of these are united to
form a miniature epic, which in the Bannatyne manuscript is
entitled *The Tod (The Fox)*. Henryson's fox is Lawrence rather
than Reynard, but the descent can be traced with some accuracy.
Henryson finally made his collection the vehicle for a series of
penetrating comments on many aspects of the life of his day.
There is nothing to show that Carlyle had read Henryson, but
Henryson is certainly proof that the aspects of fourteenth and
fifteenth century German literature singled out by Carlyle were
of more than merely local importance. Henryson indeed is a
better proof than the works actually selected by Carlyle to prove
his point. Carlyle's reaction against the Enlightenment might
have increased its intellectual and imaginative effect, had his eyes
been more opened, as had those of his predecessors, to the
distinctively Scottish experience of the centuries.

NOTES

Quotations from Carlyle use the text of the People's Edition (18 vols., London, 1874). A good general introduction to Carlyle's life and thought is provided by Ian Campbell, *Thomas Carlyle* (London, 1974).

1. *Sartor Resartus* bears much the same relationship to the novel as Walter Pater's *Marius the Epicurean* (1885). Both are histories of general intellectual development cast in the form of fictional biography. Carlyle abandoned several attempts at the novel proper. See *Last Words of Thomas Carlyle* (1892, reprinted 1972) and Ian Campbell, "Carlyle and Sir Gideon Dunn", *English Language Notes* 9.3. (1972), pp.185-91.
2. *French Revolution* I.ii., pp.12-3.
3. *Past and Present* III.x.
4. *On Heroes, Hero-Worship and the Heroic in History* (1840), Lecture I., p.11.
5. *Critical and Miscellaneous Essays* VII (London, 1872), pp.200-241.
6. Lecture I, p.2.
7. Lecture I. p.3.
8. Lecture I, pp.2-3.
9. Lecture II, pp.50-1.
10. Lecture II, p.53.
11. Lecture III, p.83.
12. Lecture III, p.97.
13. Lecture VI, p.196.
14. III.ix., p.187.
15. III.iii., p.152.
16. III.v., p.160.
17. p.188.
18. Lecture V, p.145.
19. "Historic Survey of German Poetry", *Critical and Miscellaneous Essays* III (London, 1872), pp.228-9. See also, here and in relation to the works of early German literature discussed below, Hill Shine, *Carlyle's Unfinished History of German Literature* (Lexington, Va., 1951).
20. *op.cit.*, pp.224-5.
21. *On Heroes, Hero-Worship and the Heroic in History*, Lecture I, p.3.
22. Lecture III,p.95.
23. Lecture III,pp.101-2.
24. Lecture I, p.3.
25. Lecture III, p.100.
26. Lecture III, p.83.
27. Lecture III, p.86.
28. Lecture III, p.90.
29. Lecture III, p.89.
30. *Past and Present* II.xv., p.100.
31. *op.cit.*, p.1.
32. *Progress and Poetry*, pp.35, 118-20; above, pp.18, 21; *Progress and Poetry*, pp.19, 20, 22, 35, 40, 51, 82, 118-19, 120.

INDEX